The Idea o

The idea of the numinous is often raised in psychoanalytic and psychodynamic contexts, but it is rarely itself subjected to close scrutiny. This volume examines how the numinous has gained currency in the postmodern world, demonstrating how the numinous is no longer confined to religious discourses but is included in humanist, secular and scientific views of the world.

Questions of soul and spirit are increasingly being raised in connection with the scientific exploration of the psyche, and especially in the context of psychotherapy. The contributors to this volume are interested in exploring the numinous in the human psyche, in clinical work, world events, anthropology, sociology, philosophy and the humanities. They originate from multi-disciplinary and multi-cultural backgrounds, bringing a variety of approaches to subjects including:

- Witchcraft: the numinous power of humans.
- Jung and Derrida: the numinous, deconstruction and myth.
- Accessing the numinous: Apolline and Dionysian pathways.
- The role of the numinous in the reception of Jung.

The Idea of the Numinous will fascinate all analytical psychologists, psychoanalysts and psychotherapists interested in investigating the overlap between therapeutic and religious interests.

Ann Casement is a training analyst at the Association of Jungian Analysts, London, which she represents on the IAAP executive committee.

David Tacey is an associate professor in the School of Communication, Arts and Critical Enquiry at La Trobe University, Australia.

The Idea of the Numinous

Contemporary Jungian and
psychoanalytic perspectives

Edited by Ann Casement and David Tacey

Routledge
Taylor & Francis Group

LONDON AND NEW YORK

First published 2006
by Routledge
27 Church Road, Hove, East Sussex BN3 2FA

Simultaneously published in the USA and Canada
by Routledge
270 Madison Avenue, New York NY 10016

Transferred to digital printing 2009

Routledge is an imprint of the Taylor & Francis Group, an Informa business

Typeset in Times by Garfield Morgan, Mumbles, Swansea
Printed and bound in Great Britain by TJI Digital, Padstow, Cornwall

Paperback cover design by Anú Design

British Library Cataloguing-in-Publication Data
A catalogue record for this book is available from the British Library

Library of Congress Cataloging in Publication Data
The idea of the numinous: contemporary Jungian and psychoanalytic
perspectives/edited by Ann Casement & David Tacey.

    p. cm.
    Includes bibliographical references and index.
    ISBN 1-58391-783-7 (hbk) - ISBN 1-58391-784-5 (pbk) 1.
    Psychoanalysis and religion. 2. Jungian psychology. 3. Holy,
    The. I. Casement, Ann, 1938- II. Tacey, David.
    BF175.4.R44134 2006 150.19'54 - dc22

                         2006020886

ISBN 978-1-58391-783-1 (hbk)
ISBN 978-1-58391-784-8 (pbk)

Contents

Note on the Text

All references to Jung's texts unless otherwise stated are taken from C. G. Jung (1953–83), *Collected Works*, eds Sir H. Read, M. Fordham, G. Adler and W. McGuire, 20 vols, London: Routledge & Kegan Paul, abbreviated as *CW* in all references to individual essays and books.

Contributors

Jorge L. Ahumada, MD *trained as a psychoanalyst in Buenos Aires and is presently a training analyst. A Mary S. Sygourney Awardee for 1996, his publishing includes papers on insight and epistemology, and the book The Logics of the Mind: A Clinical View* (London, Karnac).

Paul Bishop teaches German language, German literature and comparative literature at the University of Glasgow, where he is Professor of German. He has published variously on aspects of Jung and German intellectual history, including a study of Jung's relation to Weimar classicism (forthcoming).

Ann Casement is a training analyst at the Association of Jungian Analysts, London, which she represents on the Executive Committee of the International Association for Analytical Psychology. She is a New York Licensed Psychoanalyst. Her latest book is *Who Owns Psychoanalysis?* (London, Karnac).

Lionel Corbett is a psychiatrist and Jungian analyst. He is currently Professor of Depth Psychology at Pacifica Graduate Institute in Santa Barbara, California.

John Dourley is a Jungian analyst (Zurich, 1980). He taught in the Department of Religion, Carleton University, Ottawa, Canada and now is retired as professor emeritus. He has written widely on Jung and the religious question and latterly on Jung and mysticism.

Giorgio Giaccardi is a member of the British Association for Counselling and Psychotherapy. He is completing his training as an analytical psychologist at the Association of Jungian Analysts in London, where he works in private practice. He has published in Italian national newspapers, edited books and researched on sociology, politics and economics, both in London and in Milan.

James Grotstein, MD is Clinical Professor of Psychiatry at the David Geffen School of Medicine, UCLA and training and supervising analyst at the new centre of Psychoanalysis, Los Angeles, and at The Psycho-analytic Center of California. He is past North American Vice-President of the International Psychoanalytic Association. Dr Grotstein is the author, editor and/or co-editor of eight books. Two new books of his have been accepted for publication, *And at the Same Time and on Another Level . . ., Psychoanalytic Technique in the Kleinian/Bionian Mode: A Beginning* and *The Language of Achievement: Bion's Legacy to Psychoanalysis*, both accepted by the Other Press. He is also the author of 242 published papers. He is currently in private practice of psycho-analysis in west Los Angeles.

Lucy Huskinson, Ph.D, is a Fellow of the Centre for Psychoanalytic Studies, University of Essex and a psychodynamic counsellor of adults and children. She is author of *Nietzsche and Jung: The Whole Self in the Union of Opposites* (Brunner-Routledge, 2004).

Toshio Kawai is Professor for Clinical Psychology at the Graduate School of Education, Kyoto University. He also works as a psychotherapist in a clinic and in private practice. He was educated in clinical psychology at Kyoto University and in philosophical psychology at Zurich University where he received a Ph.D in 1987. He received his diploma from the C.G. Jung Institute Zurich in 1990.

Mark Kuras, Ph.D is a clinical psychologist and Jungian analyst. He is Assistant Professor at the College of Physicians and Surgeons of Columbia University Medical School, and a supervising psychologist at New York Presbyterian Hospital, where he is also the Clinical Director of the Acute Treatment Team in the Department of Psychiatry. He is a founding member of the Jungian Psychoanalytic Association (JPA), and currently serves as director of training. He maintains a private practice in New York City.

Roderick Main, Ph.D, is Lecturer in Psychoanalytic Studies at the University of Essex. He is the author of *The Rupture of Time: Syn-chronicity and Jung's Critique of Modern Western Culture* (Brunner-Routledge, 2004) and *Revelations of Chance: Synchronicity as Spiritual Experience* (SUNY, 2007).

Susan Rowland is Reader in English and Jungian Studies, University of Greenwich, UK. She was Chair of the International Association for Jungian Studies (http://www.jungianstudies.org) 2003–6. Her publica-tions include *Jung as a Writer* (Routledge, 2005) and *Jung: A Feminist Revision* (Polity, 2002).

Sonu Shamdasani is a historian of psychology, and Philemon Reader in Jung History at the Wellcome Trust Centre for the History of Medicine at University College London. He is the author and editor of numerous works.

Murray Stein, Ph.D was President of the International Association for Analytical Psychology from 2001 to 2004, is a founding member of the Inter-Regional Society for Analysts (USA) and of the Chicago Society of Jungian Analysts. He has written several books, including *Jung's Treatment of Christianity*, *In Midlife* and *Jung's Map of the Soul*. He is the editor of *Jungian Analysis* and also works as a publisher for Chiron Publications. Presently, he lives in Switzerland and teaches at the International School of Analytical Psychology in Zurich.

David Tacey is Associate Professor in the School of Critical Enquiry, La Trobe University, Melbourne, where he teaches courses on spirituality, analytical psychology and philosophy of religion. His recent publications include *The Spirituality Revolution* (Routledge, 2004) and *How to Read Jung* (Granta, 2006).

Foreword

James Grotstein

THE CASE FOR THE NUMINOUS

In being asked to write the Foreword to this majestic book, I feel both honored and humble, yet I should be quick to add fortunate for the exposure to such a rich and profound subject. I hope the reader will allow me a momentary divagation so that I can present my qualifications, or really the lack of them, to write this piece. The book's chapters are all exceptionally written by Jungian analysts as well as by erudite individuals who are immersed in analytical psychology and who are exceedingly well-informed on the topic of the numinous in Jung's *Collected Works* as well in other sources. What I bring to this endeavor is the following: I was originally trained as a classical Freudian analyst and subsequently became involved in the works of Fairbairn and then Klein and Bion, only the last of whom developed ideas that seem to parallel those of Jung on the subject of the numinous. Consequently, I bring a long-standing ignorance of Jungian thinking to the task. Perhaps, ironically, that very ignorance may qualify me as a juror or even jurist to assess the validity of the various and collective authors' presented arguments. Have they made a case for the existence and importance (especially *clinical* importance) of the numinous? Let me proffer my verdict immediately. I found myself profoundly impressed, convinced, and moved by each of the chapters and consider myself fortunate to have been introduced – really, *re*-introduced – to this profound and meaningful subject.

What immediately struck me were the differences between how Jung and Freud – and, for that matter, Klein – conceive of the unconscious, and, in retrospect, how two-dimensional their views now seem without the numinous dimension. I shall discuss Bion's closer approach later. Several of the authors cited Nietzsche's famous lament, "God is dead!" from *Ecce Homo*. What he was alluding to was the radical change in the Enlightenment in which man began to marginalize the deity in favor of his own newfound almost god-like capabilities, an arrogant trend (Klein would call it "manic defense" against his feelings of helplessness) that continued through the logical positivism of Freud and his followers. Freud nominated the instinctual drives as prime cause for the development and mal-development of the personality and populated the unconscious with them. He spoke of myth but settled for the oedipal myth, ignoring all others. By and large, his view of the unconscious seems often to have been one of a peremptory (mindless and subjectless), seething instinctual workshop which was ever at war with its neighbor, consciousness. This battle continued in his structural theory wherein the id, ego, and superego were ever conflictually warring neighbors (Freud always envisioned *conflict* between the divisions of the personality rather than dialectical binary *opposition*, in which the different parts of the personality cooperatively oppose one another). Freud's oedipus complex was paternalistic and his views of religion were harsh. He relegated religion to man's projections of the father principle.

After reading the contributions in this present work, I have come to realize that Freud's conception of psychoanalysis falls under the rubric of Logos, his conception of the oedipus complex under the rubric of paternalism, and his conception of the unconscious under the rubric of godless positivism. Psychoanalysis can be thought of vitalistically as an organically changing entity, as a product of the continuing *Zeitgeisten* through which it passes. Since Freud, several changes have occurred which, I have now come to believe, seem to approach the Jungian concept of the numinous. First, Klein, by trying to *extend* Freud, actually wound up *radicalizing* Freud in the direction of emphasizing the infant's relationship to its *mother* – before father – and conceived of an archaic oedipal phase involving the infant's preoccupation with mother's interiority long before father comes on the scene. Thus, Klein became arguably the first to introduce the importance of the mother principle, and her concept of the archaic "combined object" (the unconscious phantasy of omnipotent mother containing the paternal penis within her) closely resembles the image of the archaic Earth Mother archetype.

Another innovation, one that emerged from diffuse sources, was the post-modern interest in subjectivity and intersubjectivity. The ego as subject is a different matter than ego as agent. Perhaps one of the most important aspects of this post-modern trend toward subjectivity and intersubjectivity was the challenge it hurled at determinism (the primacy of the instinctual drives rather than the primacy of affects). Once psychoanalysts began to discover the importance of affects, the way was cleared to consider the importance of affects in the unconscious. Affects begin to approximate the numinous because they are, originally, infinite in nature – and numinosity does seem to constitute an expression of affect, all be it, an affect of a very particular and ineffably distinctive nature. Even more than that, however, the very idea of subjectivity paved the way for exploring the numinous mystery of "I"-ness, of which the self can only be the derivative shadow and allowed exploration of subjective "I" as the locale of the immanent deity (Bion's idea of the godhead, borrowed from Meister Eckhart).

It is to Bion we now must turn. Although there have been many psychoanalysts of late who have attempted to integrate religious experience with psychoanalytic theory, Bion seems to stand out. In fact, after one reads his later works, one cannot help regarding him as a "closet Jungian." The parallels between their ideas are uncanny. After conceiving of the importance of maternal reverie and mother's capacity as "container" to contain and process her infant's emotional distress (again, like Klein, emphasis on mother, not father), he then plunged into the dark heartland of the infant's subjectivity to discover "O." By "O" Bion means the Absolute Truth about an Ultimate Reality that is infinite, indifferent, and impersonal in nature, always evolves and envelops the individual between its two arms, i.e., emotional experience and the activation of noumena. One of the synonyms which Bion ascribes to "O" is *godhead*."

As the human subject allows him or herself to absorb the experience of emotional experience (with his or her alpha-function and capacity to contain emotions), not only does the Absolute Truth about Ultimate Reality become transformed from the infinite impersonal to the finite and personally meaningful. The subject him or herself likewise undergoes a personal transformation in accordance with the new experience. Now the following is the key part: As the subject allows him or herself to experience "O," his or her inherent pre-conceptions (Plato's Ideal Forms, Kant's noumena – Bion terms them "memoirs of the future"), which *anticipate* phenomenal experience, become activated by experiencing "O" so that an inherent *pre*-conception, upon becoming realized by its mating with the real object (phenomenon) to which it corresponds, becomes a realized, incarnated conception. In other words, "O," also known as "godhead," is Bion's idiosyncratic version of numinosity. Parenthetically, are not archetypes but another way of referring to Plato's Ideal Forms? I think that Jung is correct in assigning biology and spirituality to the archetypes. Furthermore, Bion's concept of the "messiah" may come close to Jung's conception of a corresponding numinous archetype.

When I was in analysis with Bion, he often mentioned that he was surprised that Freud ignored the religious passions (instincts) of man. He went on to say that he believed that the religious instinct was as important as if not more important than the libidinal. I now recall that, while analyzing Samuel Beckett, he had actually joined the latter in attending a lecture by Jung at the Tavistock Clinic. Jung happened to have alluded to a patient whose resistance was due to his refusal to be born. That very interpretation seemed also to apply to Beckett, who thereby overcame his writer's block and thereupon went on to become "Samuel Beckett," the Nobelist playwright. It remains a mystery why Bion, who obviously appreciated Jung's thinking, never really acknowledged Jung.

Jung's concept of synchronicity now comes to mind in regard to Bion's invocation of Kant's concept of the "noumen," the "thing-in-itself." "Noumen" or especially "noumena" sounds like "numinous" but they have different genetic roots. Yet one wonders in the synchronicity of things whether or not they might not be mystically related.

I was impressed that Jung saw through the camouflage of the paternalistic God to see the residues of the Great Earth Goddess. It makes sense to think of God, first as a woman and then as a man. I also was appreciative of and in full agreement with the mystical notion of the *immanence* of God within the unconscious. I truly believe that the unconscious is as close to godliness as any human can hope to get. Having stated that, however, I should like to approach this issue of the gender and hegemony of the godhead from another angle – from the angle of birth myths. *I* read *Genesis* as follows: God, the Infant, upon opening His eyes, believes, as do all newborn infants, that He created everything and everyone His eyes opened up to, including Himself and His parents, Adam and Eve. Upon gradually feeling more helpless and dependent on His mother, Eve, and upon noticing that, in between nursing Him and on weekend breaks, she left Him for Adam (father), God thought of mother as a treacherous "snake in the grass," forbade her to leave Him for Adam-father, and, when that failed, cursed the parental intercourse, thereby separating Adam and Eve, forever. To this very day, the Judeao-Christian God is condemned to loneliness and chastity. The mother god and father god cannot come together.

Put another way, there are three birth myths. Autochthony is the original birth myth in which the self emerges from the ground of self – as delineated above. The second birth myth is maternal parthenogenesis whereby the infant is born from a mother without the participation of a father (the birth of Jesus is an example). The third birth myth is male parthenogenesis whereby the infant is born from a father but without the participation of a mother (Eve being born from Adam's rib). The infant's capacity to recognize that his or her birth resulted inescapably from genital intercourse represents the acceptance of and reconciliation with the fact of the connection between one's birth and parental intercourse. Thus, Western man's conception of the deity, whether maternal or paternal, is developmentally immature. The Infant as God deserves to be admitted to the holy pantheon, I believe.

I have now come full circle by pulling my extension of Freudian/Kleinian/Bionian theory into alignment with Jung's in regard to the numinous. Jung courageously maintained his belief in the spiritual, i.e., non-rational dimension of man as existing dialectically with his rational side. The concept of the numinous offers a dimension to our unconscious lives that is utterly missing in Freud. Now to the numen and to numinousness. According to one dictionary I consulted, "numen" means: "the presiding deity of a place." Other meanings were listed, but I wish to emphasize this one. It reminds me of the Hermes bars Athenians put on their doorways or the Mezzuzahs used by Jews for their doorways. Utmostly, it reminded me, trained as a physician, that the membrane of every cell in the body seems to have an ineffable presence or intelligence which selectively decides what gets through the membrane each way and what remains (selective permeability). That to me is a numen and is but a small example of the presence of numinous functions in our body alone, to say nothing of the mind – and the soul – and the spirit.

In Bion's (1992) paper, "Reverence and Awe," he states: "There is a great difference between idealization of a parent because the child is in despair, and idealization because the child is in search of an outlet for feelings of reverence and awe" (292). He also raises the subject of *faith* psychoanalytic respectability. In my own recent work, *Who Is the Dreamer Who Dreams the Dream?*, I suggest that the unconscious is populated by a numinous subject, "*the ineffable subject of the unconscious,*" who *is* the "dreamer who dreams the dream" (Grotstein 2000).

Faith, reverence, awe, "O," and the ineffable subject of the unconscious are our way of approaching the numinous.

References

Bion, W.R. (1992) 'Reverence and Awe', in *Cogitations*, pp. 284–92, London: Karnac.

Grotstein, J. (2000) *Who Is the Dreamer Who Dreams the Dream? A Study of Psychic Presences*, Hillsdale, NJ: Analytic Press.

Preface

Ann Casement & David Tacey

The idea of the numinous is often raised in psychoanalytic and psycho-dynamic contexts, but it is rarely itself subjected to close scrutiny. The numinous means something like 'awesome' and refers to the emotional quality of religious experiences, of being in the presence of the sacred. It has gained currency in the postmodern world, and even materialists and atheists are able to affirm a 'numinous' quality in nature and human experience, whereas before our time, the numinous (from *numen*, Latin for deity or divine will) would have been confined to religious discourses. Along with the concept of spirituality, which also exists outside formal religion, the numinous has been transformed, and is now included in humanist, secular and scientific views of the world.

In recent times, questions of soul and spirit are being raised in connection with the scientific exploration of the psyche, and especially in the context of psychotherapy. For instance, C. G. Jung wrote in a letter of 1945: 'the numinous is the real therapy', which has not been explored in any consistent way though it has led to increasing interest in the ways in which the concerns of therapy and religion overlap. The book will explore the intersection between clinical and religious interests, and indicate how this has led to the creation of a new, third area which is neither exclusively clinical nor exclusively theological. This third area has led to a discourse in which age-old questions are encountered anew. The spirit remains the same, yet its language and expression have changed.

The focus in this volume is not religion *per se*, but rather the 'religious attitude' in a variety of disciplinary and experiential contexts. Our title, *The Idea of the Numinous*, acknowledges a real debt to Rudolf Otto, whose major work, *The Idea of the Holy*, has pioneered a new approach to religious experience for nearly a hundred years. Contributors to the present book are interested in exploring the numinous in the human psyche, in clinical work, world events, anthropology, sociology, philosophy and the humanities. In other words, they are interested in tracking the diffuse awareness of the numinous in modern and postmodern life, through a multi-focal lens of different yet complementary perspectives. The originality of this volume is evident not only in its unique theme, but also in its range of approaches.

The contributors to the book originate from multi-disciplinary and multi-cultural backgrounds and represent diverse parts of the world, including Australia, Canada, Continental Europe, the United Kingdom, the United States of America, Latin America and Japan. They are: Jorge Ahumada, Paul Bishop, Lionel Corbett, John Dourley, Giorgio Giaccardi, Lucy Huskinson, Toshio Kawai, Mark Kuras, Roderick Main, Susan Rowland, Sonu Shamdasani and Murray Stein. The generous Foreword has been written by James Grotstein. It has been a great pleasure to work with such a distinguished list of contributors in the production of this exciting book and the editors would like to thank them wholeheartedly for contributing to it.

The editors also wish to express their thanks to Kate Hawes, our Publisher at Routledge, who is always quick to respond to, and encouraging of, creative ideas.

Chapter 1

Psychologies as ontology-making practices*

William James and the pluralities of psychological experience

Sonu Shamdasani

What is the contemporary relevance of *The Varieties of Religious Experience* for the study of psychology and its history? Already in James's time, the project for a unitary science of psychology, vigorously pursued from many sides, was collapsing into a chaos of ever increasing fragmentation, coupled with attempts to assert the ascendence of particular agendas for psychology through the hegemonic control of institutions. A hundred years later, this fragmentation has only increased. The disciplines of the psychology of religion and subliminal psychology which James vigorously championed collapsed and all but disappeared. Meanwhile through historical studies, the status of the terms 'psychology' on the one side and 'religion' on the other has increasingly come in for intense scrutiny, and the question has been raised as to whether these terms have any stable referents, or, on the other hand, whether their unitary designation is not designed to paper over the diversity and multiplicity of the conceptions and practices that they designate. In the light of these concerns, I would like to address the contemporary status of James's text by characterising his method of studying psychological experience, and by inquiring how this can help us comprehend the varieties of psychologies and the experiences which they generate. But first, we need to ask: *what was* psychology?[1]

In 1899, James remarked that the 'air has been full of rumours', and that 'we have been having something like a "boom" in psychology in this country'.[2] At the end of the nineteenth century, many figures in the West sought to establish a scientific psychology that would be independent of philosophy, theology, biology, anthropology, literature, medicine and neurology, whilst taking over their traditional subject matters. The very possibility of psychology rested upon the successful negotiation of these disciplinary crossings. The larger share of the questions that psychologists

* This chapter was originally published in J. Carrette (ed.), *William James and the Varieties of Religious Experience*. London: Routledge. Reproduced with permission.

took up had already been posed and elaborated in these prior disciplines. They had to prise their subjects from the preserves of other specialists. Through becoming a science, it was hoped that psychology would be able to solve questions that had vexed thinkers for centuries, and to replace superstition, folk wisdom and metaphysical speculation with the rule of universal law. The result would amount to nothing less than the completion and culmination of the scientific revolution. Several decades of work in science studies have demonstrated that there is no singular atemporal essence to science or notions such as 'the scientific method', or in other words, that 'Science' with a capital 'S' does not exist. As Isabelle Stengers notes, 'it is pointless to search for a noncontextual, general definition of the difference between science and non-science'.[3] However, this is not to erase all differences between disciplines classed as sciences and those that are not. Rather, as Stengers notes, it is to affirm that the question of the scientificity of a particular discipline 'only takes on meaning in the precise context in which it is posed'.[4]

There has been much discussion concerning the scientific status of psychology. Given the sacramental significance of the word 'science', it may be fruitful to speak more generally of ontology-making practices, which would include all disciplines that aim to construct general, universal ontologies.[5] The value of such a term is that it may help one to avoid falling into pre-given demarcations. The task is then one of differentiating and comparing the procedures of different ontology-making practices. Much of this work is already going on in science studies today.

In 1874, Franz Brentano proclaimed that psychology was the *science of the future*. It was to psychology that 'more than all other theoretical sciences, the future belongs', and which 'more than all others will form the future'.[6] To make this possible,

> We must strive to achieve here what mathematics, physics, chemistry and physiology have already accomplished . . . a nucleus of generally recognized truth to which, through the working together of many forces, new crystals will then soon adhere on all sides. In place of psychologies we must seek to place a psychology.[7]

Brentano's imperative sums up the aspirations of the 'new psychology' to form a unitary scientific discipline, modelled after how it imagined sciences like physics and chemistry to function. The mode in which psychologists sought to emulate – or simulate – the form of the prestigious sciences varied. However, the basic aspiration was to form a unitary science. Embedded within this conception was a distinction between two kinds of knowledge about human beings. The first was the scientific knowledge to which psychology aspired. This was to provide a certitude equivalent to the periodic table in chemistry. The second was 'all the rest', i.e. all other means by which human beings had sought to understand themselves philosophies, myths, religions, literatures, arts, moral systems, and so on. At best, this was seen to amount to a few lucky guesses. Psychology was to create a fundamental general ontology which would ultimately subsume all other forms of knowing about human beings. In this regard, James wrote to Hugo Münsterberg in 1890:

> The truth is that psychology is yet seeking her first principles, and is in the condition of Physics before Galileo or Newton. Nerve physiology has some laws, even of a quasi elementary sort; but of a law connecting body and mind, or indeed of what is the elementary fact of mind, we have not at present even the beginning of an hypothesis which is valuable.[8]

Thus for James, psychology's will to science implied that its business was to be one of discovering and formulating universal laws, and that these had yet to be found. Two years later he concluded his *Psychology: A Briefer Course* by saying:

> When, then, we talk of 'psychology as a natural science' we must not assume that means a sort of psychology that stands at last on solid ground. It means just the reverse; it means a psychology particularly fragile, and into which the waters of metaphysical criticism leak at every joint . . . it is indeed strange to hear people talk triumphantly of 'the New Psychology', and write 'Histories of Psychology', when into the real elements and forces which the word covers not the first glimpse of clear insight exists. A string of raw facts, a little gossip and wrangle about opinions, a little classification and generalization on the mere descriptive level; a strong prejudice that we have states of mind, and that our brain conditions them: but not a single law in the sense in which physics shows us laws, not a single proposition from which any consequence can causally be deduced. We don't even know the terms between which the elementary laws would obtain if we had them. This is no science, it is only the hope of science . . . But at present psychology is in the condition of physics before Galileo and the laws of motion, of chemistry before Lavoisier and the notion that mass is preserved in all reactions. The Galileo and the Lavoisier of psychology will be famous men indeed when they come, as come they some day surely will.[9]

One might do well to ask whether there could be a better description of the state of psychology today: gossip, wrangle, prejudices, but no single generally recognised law. Nevertheless, the frequency with which psychologists were likened (or likened themselves) to Galileo, Lavoisier and Darwin increased dramatically.

James's questioning of the presumption of writing histories of psychology before psychology was successfully founded bears consideration. From early on, histories of psychologies played an important part in attempting to define and construct the discipline of psychology and to demarcate it from other fields.[10] Throughout the twentieth century, histories of psychology have continued to play this role, whether intentionally or unwittingly. But what does the history of psychology consist in, if one leaves open the question as to whether psychology was ever founded? Rather than writing the history of the foundation of a discipline, one is writing the history of attempts by individuals in different disciplines to effect certain transformations in these disciplines through evoking the rubric of psychology.[11]

When challenged by James Ladd in 1892 concerning his assertion in *The Principles of Psychology* that psychology was a natural science, James replied that

> I have never claimed that psychology as it stands to-day, *is* a natural science, or in an exact way a science at all. Psychology, indeed, is to-day hardly more than what physics was before Galileo, what chemistry was before Lavoisier. It is a mass of phenomenal description, gossip, and myth, including, however, real material enough to justify one in the hope that with judgement and good-will on the part of those interested, its study may be so organised even now as to become worthy of the name of natural science at no very distant day . . . I wished, by treating Psychology *like* a natural science, to help her become one.[12]

There was a fine line between hoping that psychology would turn into a science by treating it like one, and – as was more generally the case – assuming that it already was a science, simply because it was talked about in a simulation of scientific rhetoric by sufficiently many people. Nevertheless, James invoked a distinction between a rational and practical science of the mind. Representatives of the former would be those German 'prism, pendulum, and chronograph-philosophers' whose methods 'could hardly have arisen in a country whose natives could be *bored*'.[13] By contrast, 'what every jail-warden, every doctor, every clergyman, every asylum-superintendent, asks of psychology is practical rules'.[14] It was James's increasing dissatisfaction with the meagre yield of laboratory psychology that led him to stress this distinction. It was towards a psychology that fulfilled this practical imperative that he was increasingly inclined. In conclusion, he argued that if one had to choose between the two forms of psychology, 'The kind of psychology which could cure a case of melancholy, or charm a chronic insane delusion away, ought certainly to be preferred to the most seraphic insight into the nature of the soul.'[15] In effect, psychology as a 'practical science of the mind' represented a psychology grounded in pragmatism as opposed to the positivist epistemology of experimental psychology. The *Varieties* represents the articulation of precisely such a psychology, and it is within this context that the question of religion – which had no place within the radically self-restricted domain of experimental psychology – arose.

Psychology's 'will to science' fuelled a profusion of activities. However, whilst there was no shortage of attempts to form the one general psychology, it became clear pretty soon that the sought-for unity was ever receding. The proliferation of variously styled psychologies demonstrated that there was little consensus as to what could be considered the aims and methods of psychology. In 1894, James wrote to Carl Stumpf: 'From all the psychologies either published or about to appear, there ought to be some sedimentary deposit of truth – I devoutly hope that it may be clearly discernable by all!'[16] A few years later, James lamented: 'there *is* no "new psychology" worthy of the name. There is nothing but the old psychology which began in Locke's time, plus a little physiology of the brain and senses and theory of evolution, and a few refinements of introspective detail.'[17] Thus the 'novelty' lay in the rhetorical mode in which psychology was increasingly presented. Not for the first time, an 'epistemological break' was to be created simply through proclaiming that it had taken place.

In 1900, the Berlin psychologist William Stern surveyed the new psychology. Aside from an empirical tendency and the use of experimental methods, he saw little in the way of common features. There were many laboratories with researchers working on special problems, together with many textbooks, but they were all characterised by a pervasive particularism. He noted that the psychological map of the day was as colourful and checkered as that of Germany in the epoch of small states, and that psychologists

> often speak different languages, and the portraits that they draw up of the psyche are painted with so many different colours and with so many differently accented special strokes that it often becomes difficult to recognize the identity of the represented object.[18]

Stern concluded: 'In short: there are many new psychologies, but not yet the new psychology.'[19] Thus the singularity of the term 'psychology' should not mislead one into thinking that such a discipline was ever successfully founded. Or that there is an essence to 'psychology' that could encompass the various definitions, methodologies, practices, world-views and institutions that have used this designation. Rather it indicates the massive significance that psychologists gave to being seen to be talking about the same thing. Indeed, psychology has come to mean many disparate and incommensurable things precisely because it had always been made up of them.

The formation of psychologies consisted in a parallel constitution of psychologies and their objects of study. The formation of an epistemological object consists in a process of purification, and fixity: taking an aspect of life and rendering it a suitable object of study, through imbuing it with the attributes of universality, ahistoricity, distinguishing between essential and non-essential attributes, and so on.[20] As we shall see, such aspects of this filtration of the ontology-making process were commented on by James himself.

For James at the time of the *Varieties*, psychology remained in a condition of aspiring to be a science. Hence none of its results – including those of his own psychology – had been sufficiently established to be universally binding. Thus psychologies could be considered to be optional ontologies, which had yet to join up with the general ontology which James considered science to be. The increasing gulf between the initial aspirations of the new psychology and the chaos and disunity that ensued forms one of the critical contexts of the *Varieties*. As we shall see, James's reformulation of psychology in the *Varieties* and after can in part be seen as a response to this.

DOES RELIGION EXIST?

One example of the dual constitution of psychologies and their objects of study is the psychology of religion. The formation of this discipline did not come about simply through applying the methods and conceptions of an existing discipline to a new area of study, or to 'naturally given' phenomena: rather, it was through constituting religion as an epistemological object that psychology aimed to constitute itself. The ubiquity of the term 'religion' and the longevity of so-called great world religions has led to the widespread notion that religion can be considered a *sui generis* category. From this perspective, it is surprising to consider that the modern concept of religion emerged only in the second half of the nineteenth century, and, furthermore, there are good grounds for dating its invention.

Contemporary scholars have questioned the status of the category 'religion', and posed questions as to whether it has any stable referent, and further, the uses which the term has served. Timothy Fitzgerald has argued that 'Religion cannot reasonably be taken to be a valid analytical category since it does not pick out any distinctive cross-cultural aspect of human life.'[21] Rather, he argues that the category of religion is itself a theological category, which he characterises as a liberal ecumenical theology. Thus the constitution of category of religion has led to the uncritical imposition of Judeo-Christian assumptions on non-Western data. In a similar vein, Richard King argues that the notion of religion is a 'Christian theological category' with a particular genealogy. He argues that 'the way the term has been employed results in the privileging of certain features of Christian and post-Christian Western culture and locates "other cultures" within an implicitly theological framework that transforms them as much as it attempts to make sense of them'.[22] Religion has generally been defined in a differential manner, that is to say, through being contrasted and set aside from the non-religious. Thus the formation of the concept of religion should not be seen as separate from the formation of a concept of the secular. Such an argument clearly has consequences for the history of the psychology of religion: the attempt to form a 'secular' science of the 'sacred' through constituting these very distinctions.

The questioning of the status of the term 'religion' thus converges with the questioning of the status of the term 'psychology'. If one can no longer assume that these terms have stable referents, one has to carefully study the uses that they serve in particular texts, practices and institutions. In reading the *Varieties* today – justly viewed as foundational in the psychology of religion – one has to consider how the text looks *after* 'religion' and *after* 'psychology'. What happens to the reading of the *Varieties* when we drop these terms, or rather, attentively track the work being done by them? If psychology never actually existed as a unitary enterprise, one has to look to its use in particular texts to determine its meaning, even in the case of a particular thinker.

I will first consider the consequences that follow from the suspension of the term 'religion' in the reading of the *Varieties*. One may commence with James's definitions of religion. In his work, one finds restricted and general conceptions of religion. In 1895, he proposed the following definition:

> when from now onward I use the word [religion] I mean to use it in the supernaturalist sense, as declaring that the so-called order of nature, which constitutes this world's experience, is only one portion of the total universe, and that there stretches beyond this visible world an unseen world of which we know nothing positive, but in its relation to which the true significance of our present mundane life consists.[23]

Traces of this restricted use of the term are to be found in the *Varieties*. In his chapter on 'The divided self', James writes: 'To find religion is only one out of the many ways of reaching unity; and the process of remedying inner incompleteness and reducing inner discord is a general psychological process, which may take place with any sort of mental material, and need not necessarily assume the religious form.'[24]

The *Varieties* begins with a generalised definition of religion: 'Religion, therefore, as I now ask you arbitrarily to take it, shall mean for us *the feelings, acts and experiences of individual men in their solitude, so far as they apprehend themselves to stand in relation to whatever they may consider the divine.*'[25] Additionally, James adds that 'we must interpret the term "divine" very broadly, as denoting any object that is god*like*, whether it be a concrete divinity or not'.[26] Thus we find a tension and oscillation in James concerning the term 'religion'. The source of this may be clarified if one simply considers the consequences of dropping the category in the reading of the *Varieties*. The question that follows is, what is it then a study of? Varieties of what? *It then may be considered to be a study of states of transformation*, based on a corpus of first-hand testimonials generally utilising Christian phraseology and iconography. This may explain the oscillation between the generalised and restricted concepts of religion in the text: the study of states of transformation (placing the emphasis on the subtitle of the book, *A Study in Human Nature*) would incline him to the generalised definition, whilst the specifically Christian conceptions in the transformation narratives would incline him to the restricted definition. The question of Protestant bias is one that James is more aware of than some critics give him credit for. In his preface to Starbuck's *Psychology of Religion* (1899) he wrote: 'The Volksgeist of course dictates its special phraseology and most of its conceptions, which are almost without exception Protestant, and predominantly of the Evangelical sort.'[27] (However, the shaping effect of the 'Volksgeist' is a theme that remains undeveloped in James.[28])

Considering James in this manner has some unexpected consequences. For over a century, criticisms have been made of James's conception of religion, along the lines of: James is not Durkheim, or Weber, or Freud, or a post-colonial feminist cultural critic, and so on. Such criticisms tend to counterpose other conceptions of religion or approaches to the topic.[29] A great number of such criticisms of James's treatment of religion dissolve as being as obsolete as the category of religion. If one accepts the legitimacy of James's attempt to study states of transformation in individuals, then the fact that he ignores institutional religion, the history of the church, dogmas and theologies, etc., appears to be simply beside the point. The text then becomes more contemporary than a number of the criticisms that have been directed towards it.

PSYCHOLOGY, OR HOW TO MAKE OUR IDEAS VAGUE

If the *Varieties* may fruitfully be considered to be a study of states of transformation, how does James intend to study them? In other words, what is the role and status of the term 'psychology' in the text?

In the introduction to the *Varieties*, James notes that he had initially intended the lectures to consist in two parts, a descriptive part on 'Man's religious appetites' and a metaphysical part on 'Their satisfaction through philosophy'. The growth of the psychological matter led to the second being 'postponed entirely' aside from a brief statement of his philosophical conclusions. Reading this at face value has led many commentators to consider the *Varieties* as a work of 'psychology' (however understood), and to neglect its imbrication in his philosophy of radical empiricism. Eugene Taylor has cogently demonstrated the inseparability of James's psychology from radical empiricism and demonstrated that, far from abandoning psychology, James's later work in part constituted a critique of the metaphysical basis of the new psychology, so as to reformulate it.[30] David Lamberth has excellently shown that James's descriptive psychology in the *Varieties* is closely connected with his unfinished philosophical project, and the manner in which this is subsequently articulated in *A Pluralistic Universe*.[31] Following Lamberth's reconstruction, I would like to go further and suggest that these two projects are in several important respects inseparable. Indeed, many paragraphs in which James is developing radical empiricism seamlessly interleave the discussion of the cases he introduces. Thus the nature of the descriptive psychology which James employs in the *Varieties* warrants closer consideration.

In this regard, James's mode of lengthy citation – which is strikingly out of temper with the predilection for paraphrase in the humanities today – is significant. In 1903, James wrote to his Italian translator, Guilo Cesare Ferrari: 'The book was written round the documents. I got them first, and poured in my connective remarks like a sort of galantine jelly to enclose them, and I confess that I should dislike to have any of them sacrificed.'[32] This form of composition is not incidental for two reasons. First, the documents are presented in an evidential manner. Whilst relying on first-hand testimonials, James makes available all the documentation on which he is basing his reading. The material is made public, and is therefore fully available for other researchers to judge James's constructions against the material he is using. This is in line with what he considered to be a necessary requirement for psychology to be a science. Second, it highlights the minimalism and secondary status of James's connective remarks. Descriptive psychology is now deliberately set in a minor key.

In the *Varieties*, James articulates his criticism of genetic explanation.[33] Elsewhere, he expresses his dislike of symbolic interpretation.[34] By contrast, the mode of 'descriptive psychology' which James pursues in the *Varieties* may be characterised as an attempt to bring to formalised articulation different attitudes and possible ways of living life. The narratives that James compiles show experiences of transformations of the self and its experience of the world. Here, his descriptive psychology simply provides comparative, formalised articulation of these and sorts them into a serial order.

In his reply to Pratt's questionnaire on the subject of religious beliefs in 1904, James spoke of his 'hospitality towards the religious testimony of others'.[35] This may be taken as a leitmotif of James's approach. His characterisation of the religion of the healthy-minded and the sick-minded characters is marked by this hospitality: whilst his sympathies are clear, no standpoints are dismissed.[36]

Two further features of James's descriptive psychology here may be highlighted. The first is the delimitation of explanation. As James puts it, psychology can describe, but not explain. For example, when discussing the shift of excitement, James notes:

> Now if you ask of psychology just how the excitement shifts in a man's mental system, and *why* aims that were peripheral become at a certain moment central, psychology has to reply that although she can give a general description of what happens, she is unable in a given case to account accurately for all the given forces at work.[37]

If psychology cannot explain, what then is the status of psychological language and description? He goes on to describe these shifts in terms of things being 'hot' and 'cold' to us, and how they form centres of dynamic energy. However, there is no attempt here to link this to an underlying neurophysiology – as he had attempted in certain sections of *Principles* – these centres are now simply metaphoric. He writes of his language use: 'Whether such language be rigorously exact is for the present of no importance. It is exact enough, if you recognize from your own experience the facts which I seek to designate by it.'[38] Thus the purpose of psychological language here is *evocation*. What is proffered by way of explanation – hot, cold, centres of dynamic energy, the 'hackneyed symbolism of a mechanical equilibrium', and so on – is not presented in an ontological sense, but in a metaphorical one. The use of language in a non-ontological manner shifts the status of psychology. It no longer sets psychology above what it sets out to study, in imitation of how sciences are imagined to function. Psychological language is not privileged in any way as a form of translation over the languages it studies – in this case, the first-hand testimonials. Richer and more articulate descriptions take the place of explanations. James makes this suspension of ontological language explicit in the following statement:

> When I say 'Soul', you need not take me in the ontological sense unless you prefer to; for although ontological language is instinctive in such matters, yet Buddhists or Humians can perfectly well describe the facts in the phenomenal terms which are their favourites.[39]

This suspension explains how James can go on to use terms such as 'consciousness' in his late writings even after his banishment of consciousness in 'Does consciousness exist?' His later usages do not represent a contradiction or recantation, rather they represent a different form of usage.

The second aspect to which I wish to draw attention are moments where James stands outside psychology and looks at its assumptions and modes of operation. In his discussion of conversion he refers to the 'vague and abstract language of psychology' as constituting 'our own symbolism'.[40] He then compares the views of psychology and religion:

> Psychology and religion are thus in perfect harmony up to this point, since both admit that there are forces seemingly outside of the conscious individual that bring redemption to his life. Nevertheless psychology, defining these forces as 'subconscious', and speaking of their effects as due to 'incubation', or 'cerebration', implies that they do not transcend the individual's personality' and herein she diverges from Christian theology, which insists that they are direct supernatural operations of the Deity.[41]

Here, he suspends the ontological hypostatisations of psychology, and looks on it as a system on a par with Christian theology, without privileging either. Each can be described from the outside as a self-enclosed symbolic system with its ontological postulate.

These elements of James's descriptive psychology are developed in 'The Energies of Men'. In its quest for what makes possible the renewal of energy, this essay can be considered a continuation of the *Varieties*. James opens this essay by distinguishing between structural and functional psychology. This corresponded to the difference between the analytical and the clinical points of view in psychological observation. Clinical conceptions are vaguer and more adequate, more concrete and of more practical consequence. He champions the value of functional psychology, and in particular, the 'vagueness' of its language use:

> The terms have to remain vague; for though every man of woman born knows what is meant by such phrases as having a good vital tone, a high tide of spirits, an elastic temper, as living energetically, working easily, deciding firmly, and the like, we should all be put to our trumps if asked to explain in terms of scientific psychology just what such expressions mean. We can draw some child-like psychophysical diagrams, and that is all. In physics the conception of 'energy' is perfectly defined. It is correlated with the concept of 'work'. But mental work and moral work, although we cannot live without talking about them, are terms as yet hardly analyzed, and doubtless mean several heterogeneous elementary things . . . it is obvious that the intuitive or popular idea of mental work, fundamental and absolutely indispensable as it is in our lives, possesses no degree whatever of scientific clearness to-day.[42]

The 'psychology' already present in 'intuitive or popular' ideas is championed over 'scientific clearness'. The task then would be one of making this implicit 'psychology' more explicit. Thus functional psychology simply renders everyday language use more articulate, rather than attempting, as does structural psychology, to translate it into the terms of an underlying fundamental ontology. One may pose the question: have structural, onto-logical psychologies always actually been functional psychologies, in James's terms, albeit impoverished ones, enabling people to transform their experiences and the languages for talking about them, despite their aspira-tions to form general universal ontologies? The conceptual frameworks of structural psychologies, whilst intended to have an explanatory power above that of everyday language, have been metaphorised and reabsorbed into the latter. Viewed functionally, the 'laws' of structural psychology become practical maxims and aphorisms. All that is left today of Mesmer's system of animal magnetism is the metaphoric description of personalities as 'magnetic' and 'mesmerising' – linguistic fossils of a grand monistic medical physics. A similar fate is now befalling psychoanalysis.

The question that then arises is whether this characterisation of James's procedure in the *Varieties* and after may have a wider validity in charac-terising the workings of psychologies. To take this up, one needs to con-sider the question of the malleability of experience in James.

JAMES AND CONTEMPORARY MIND-CURE

Given the multiplicity of disciplines and practices that have gone under the name of psychology, it is hazardous to attempt general statements and characterisations of 'psychology'. Thus in the following I am principally, though not exclusively, concerned with the psychotherapies: those contem-porary mind-curers who form the modern-day analogue and indeed the heirs of the mind-curers studied by James in the *Varieties* under the rubric of the religion of the healthy minded.[43]

From the outset of his interest in hypnosis, James was struck by the variability of trance states and the difficulty of constructing theories identifying the essential characteristics of the trance. He concluded his 1886 'Report on hypnotism' (written with Gouverneur Carnochan) by noting:

> Our experience has impressed upon us the variability of the same subject's trance from one day to another. It may occur that a phenom-enon met with one day, but not repeated, and therefore accounted a mere coincidence, is really due to a particular phase of the trance, realized on that occasion, but never again when sought for.[44]

Thus any attempt to make an epistemological object out of the trance was beset by its variability. The following year, he concluded 'Reaction-time in the hypnotic trance', by writing: 'The only lesson of the facts I report seems to be that we should beware of making rash generalizations from few cases about the hypnotic state. That name probably covers a very great number of different neural conditions.'[45] If the hypnotic state was actually a name for different conditions, its use would serve to conceal the fact that these conditions might call for distinct explanations – which was James's critique of the concept of the unconscious.

In *Principles*, James discussed the conflict between the late nineteenth-century hypnotic schools, which constituted the genesis of modern psychotherapy. Concerning differing theories of the trance state, he wrote:

> The three states of Charcot, the strange reflexes of Heidenhain, and all the other bodily phenomena which have been called direct consequences of the trance-state itself, are not such. They are products of suggestion, the trance-state having no particular outward symptoms of its own; but without the trance-state there, those particular suggestions could never have been successfully made.[46]

Whilst conceived in a realist mode, psychological theories actually created new forms of experience, due to the impressionability of the trance state. This enabled any theory to be 'realised'. James trenchantly points out the pitfalls that this held for the possibility of developing an objective account of hypnosis:

> Any sort of personal peculiarity, any trick accidentally fallen into in the first instance by some one subject, may, by attracting attention, become stereotyped, serve as a pattern for imitation, and figure as the type of a school. The first subject trains the operator who trains the succeeding subjects, all of them in perfect good faith conspiring together to evolve a perfectly arbitrary result.
>
> With the extraordinary perspicacity and subtlety of perception which subjects often display for all that concerns the operator with whom they are en rapport, it is hard to keep them ignorant of anything he expects. Thus it happens that one easily verifies on new subjects what one has already seen on old ones, or any desired symptom of which one may have heard or read.[47]

His discussions of theories of trance are not solely concerned with one phenomenon, but with the malleability of experience to conceptual reframing in general. This malleability explains the endless generation of multiple psychological and psychotherapeutic systems producing 'perfectly arbitrary results' – a history of psychotherapy in a nutshell. It explains the inevitable failure of such systems to form a universal psychology and general ontology. For James, the hypnotic schools had led to a potentially limitless proliferation of contradictory systems, each appealing to individual testimony as their proof.[48] His critique focused on their means for verification. There was no theory that could not be 'verified' by the procedures being used.

It is important to note that James's conception of the malleability of experience and its receptivity to conceptual remodelling is not part of a human/natural science division. Rather, it is an aspect of a more generalised modelling. As early as 1881, he wrote:

> While I talk and the flies buzz, a sea-gull catches a fish at the mouth of the Amazon, a tree falls in the Adirondack wilderness, a man sneezes in Germany, a horse dies in Tartary, and twins are born in France. What does that mean? Does the contemporaneity of these events with one another and with a million others as disjointed, form a rational bond between them, and unite them into anything that means for a world?
>
> Yet such collateral contemporaneity, and nothing else, is the real order of the world. It is an order with which we have nothing to do to get away from it as fast as possible . . . we break it into histories, and we break it into arts, and we break it into sciences; and then we begin to feel at home. We make ten thousand separate serial orders of it, and on any one of these we react as though the others did not exist. We discover among its various parts relations that were never given to sense at all (mathematical relations, tangents, squares, and roots and logarithmic functions), and out of an infinite number of these we call certain ones essential and lawgiving and ignore the rest. Essential these relations are, but only for our purpose, the other relations being just as real and present as they . . . the miracle of miracles, a miracle not yet exhaustively cleared up by any philosophy, is that the given order lends itself to the remodelling. It shows itself plastic to many of our scientific, to many of our aesthetic, to many of our practical purposes and ends.[49]

Psychologies have shown themselves remarkably successful at remodelling the chaos of the collateral contemporaneity of experience into serial orders. There are few aspects of experience that have not been multiply traversed by the encompassing arcs of rival psychological systems. Yet what is one to make of the collateral contemporaneity of psychologies, and what is the status of the appeal to individual testimony as their evidential support?

REVELATION AND VALIDATION

To take up these questions, one may consider James's discussion of mysticism in the *Varieties*. For a number of contemporary scholars, the status of the term 'mysticism' is as problematic as the term 'religion'.[50] Again, one can bracket out the problems surrounding the generic category of mysticism, and consider the types of experiences that James is studying: namely, experiences that are authoritative over the individuals who have them. In other words, James is concerned with experiences that are considered to be self-authenticating, such as states of transformation. Of such experiences, James writes: 'No authority emanates from them which should make it a duty for those who stand outside of them to accept their revelations uncritically.'[51] James's attitude towards such experiences is twofold: on the one hand, he affirms the reality of the experiences in question, but on the other, refrains from taking the conclusions drawn from them as legislative. He adds that those who don't have revelations must decide that as the various revelations corroborate incompatible theological doctrines, 'they neutralise each other and leave no fixed result'.[52] Thus if we embrace any one of them 'we do so in the exercise of our individual freedom'.[53] James here seems to sharply distinguish between what should be regarded as constituting general ontology – and hence recognised by all – and the optional ontologies (or 'overbeliefs', in James's expression) wherein everyone should be left free to make their own choices.

The theories of the various schools of psychotherapy provide a set of narratives concerning the cause of illness or distress and how its resolution may be effected, with plot templates in the form of case histories. These transformation narratives are in turn linked to what are claimed to be universal models of human functioning. The self-authenticating nature of the transformative experiences undergone by individuals is taken as the proof of the ontologies in question. Thus we are faced with the transformations of experience generated by the psychotherapies on the one hand, and, on the other, by the positing of ontologies (forces, mechanisms, structures of the chronically overpopulated inner world) in the continued pursuit of a unitary science. This has led to the efflorescence of multiple optional ontologies, which have been embraced by large-scale social groupings. However, in the main, these tend to the monistic form, akin to the absolute idealism critiqued in *A Pluralistic Universe*. As James suggests, those who have not had such experiences should be under no obligation to accept the legislative universalism of such revelations.

For James, evaluation is by way of pragmatism. In the *Varieties*, this features as the judgement of the validity of religious experiences. Pragmatism is often understood in an individual sense. However, it is important to note that the judgement of validity in the *Varieties* is not by the subjects themselves (which is not James's primary concern) but by others. Valuation concerns what *we* should make of their experiences. It is important to stress this social dimension of pragmatism. As James states in *Pragmatism*:

> The truth of an idea is not a stagnant property inherent in it. Truth happens to an idea. It becomes true, is made true by events. Its verity is in fact an event, a process: the process namely of its verifying itself, its veri-fication. Its validity is the process of its valid-ation.[54]

A process of validation or verification is a way of describing how *practices* establish their truths. In his discussion of pragmatism's conception of truth, James stresses that truth in science requires 'consistency with previous truth and novel fact'. Theories that work are those that 'mediate between all previous truths and certain new experiences'.[55] Thus the degree of rigour of the verification process of a particular ontology-making practice would consist in the extent to which it successfully enables this consistency and mediation.

As we have seen, James's critique of the hypnotic schools – which formed the template of modern psychotherapeutic schools – focused on the failings of their means of verification. The inability to provide any check or comparative framework, would, from this perspective, constitute a lack of rigour. However, viewed from a functional perspective, the multiplicity of systematised articulations of experience offered by psychologies is to be welcomed. James suggests as much in the *Varieties* in his consideration of the multiplicity of religious formations:

> Is the existence of so many religious types and sects and creeds regrettable? To these questions I answer 'No' emphatically. And my reason is that I do not see how it is possible that creatures in such different positions and with such different powers as human individuals are, should have exactly the same functions and the same duties. No two of us have identical difficulties, nor should we be expected to work out identical solutions.[56]

The same would then apply for the varieties of psychologies, understood in functional terms. They may be understood as vehicles which have provided systematised articulations of experience. Paradoxically, it is the very failure of psychologies to establish a general ontology, in a structural sense, that has given such functional utility to the efflorescence of optional ontologies which the self-same psychologies have generated.

Notes

1 Parts of this section were elaborated in the context of a work in progress on the historiography of psychoanalysis with Mikkel Borch-Jacobsen, whom I would like to thank. On the formation of modern psychology, see my *Jung and the Making of Modern Psychology: The Dream of a Science* (Cambridge: Cambridge University Press, 2003).

2 William James, *Talks to Teachers on Psychology and to Students on Some of Life's Ideals* (Cambridge, MA: Harvard University Press, 1983), p. 14. References to James's work are given to the Harvard edition, with the exception of the *Varieties*, where references have been given to *The Varieties of Religious Experience: Centenary Edition*, with a foreword by Micky James and new introductions by Eugene Taylor and Jeremy Carrette (London: Routledge, 2002).

3 Isabelle Stengers, *Power and Invention: Situating Modern Science*, trans. P. Bains (Chicago: University of Minnesota Press, 1998), p. 81.

4 Ibid., p. 82.

5 The stress on *practices* of ontology-making is linked to what Andrew Pickering describes as the shift from a representational to a performative tense in science studies (*The Mangle of Practice: Time, Agency and Science*, Chicago: Chicago University Press, 1995).

6 Franz Brentano, *Psychologie vom empirischen Standpunkt* (Leipzig: Felix Meiner, 1925), p. 36.

7 Ibid., p. 2.

8 27 August, ed. Ignas Skrupskelis and Elizabeth Berkeley, *The Correspondence of William James, Volume 7, 1890–1894* (Charlottesville: University Press of Virginia, 1999), p. 89.

9 James, *Psychology: A Briefer Course* (Cambridge, MA: Harvard University Press, 1984), pp. 400–1.

10 See, for instance, Max Dessoir, *Outlines of the History of Psychology* (New York: Macmillan, 1912); James Mark Baldwin, *History of Psychology: A Sketch and an Interpretation*, 2 vols (London: Watts & Co., 1913).

11 On this question see Roger Smith, 'Does the History of Psychology have a Subject?' *History of the Human Sciences*, 1, 1988, pp. 147–77; on the historiography of psychotherapy, see my review of Stanley Jackson, *Care of Psyche: A History of Psychological Healing*, *Medical History*, forthcoming.

12 James, 'A Plea for Psychology as a "Natural Science"', *Essays in Psychology* (Cambridge, MA: Harvard University Press, 1983), p. 270.

13 James, *The Principles of Psychology* (Cambridge, MA: Harvard University Press, 1981), p. 92.

14 James, 'A Plea for Psychology as a "Natural Science"', p. 272.

15 Ibid., p. 277.

16 24 January, *The Correspondence of William James, Volume 7, 1890–1894*, pp. 485–6.

17 James, *Talks to Teachers on Psychology*, p. 15.

18 William Stern, 'Die psychologische Arbeit des neunzehnten Jahrhunderts, insbesondere in Deutschland', *Zeitschrift für pädogigische Psychologie und Pathologie*, 2, 1900, p. 415.

19 Ibid.

20 On the denial of historicity to material objects and entities, see Bruno Latour, 'The Historicity of Things', *Pandora's Hope: Essays on the Reality of Science Studies* (Cambridge, MA: Harvard University Press, 1999), pp. 145–73.

21 Timothy Fitzgerald, *The Ideology of Religious Studies* (Oxford: Oxford University Press, 2000), p. 4.

22 Richard King, *Orientalism and Religion: Post-colonial Theory, India and 'The Mystic East'* (London: Routledge, 1999), p. 60.

23 James, 'Is Life Worth Living?', *The Will to Believe* (Cambridge, MA: Harvard University Press, 1979), p. 48.

24 James, *Varieties*, p. 139.

25 Ibid., pp. 29–30.

26 Ibid., p. 32.

27 James, *Essays in Morality and Religion* (Cambridge, MA: Harvard University Press, 1982), p. 103.

28 On the relation of the *Varieties* to contemporary 'religious-like' movements, see Clifford Geertz, 'The Pinch of Destiny: Religion as Experience, Meaning, Identity, Power', in *Available Light: Anthropological Reflections on Philosophical*

Topics (Princeton, NJ: Princeton University Press, 2000), pp. 167–86; and Ramón del Castillo, 'Varieties of American Ecstasy', in *Streams of William James*, 5(2), European Perspectives on 'The Varieties of Religious Experience', Guest editor Felicitas Kraemer, pp. 1–4, forthcoming. This volume also contains papers presented at the centenary conference.

29 On criticisms of James, see Carol Zaleski, 'Speaking of William James to the Cultured among his Despisers', in Donald Capps and Janet Jacobs (eds), *The Struggle for Life: A Companion to William James's 'The Varieties of Religious Experience'* (Society for the Scientific Study of Religion, Monograph Series 9, 1995), pp. 40–60.

30 Eugene Taylor, *William James on Consciousness beyond the Margin* (Princeton, NJ: Princeton University Press, 1996).

31 David Lamberth, *William James and Metaphysics of Experience* (Cambridge: Cambridge University Press, 1999), pp. 97–145.

32 25 February. *The Varieties of Religious Experience* (Cambridge, MA: Harvard University Press, 1985), appendix, p. 553.

33 *Varieties*, pp. 13ff. On this question, see Jeremy Carrette, 'The Return to James: Psychology, Religion and the Amnesia of Neuroscience', introduction to the centenary edition of the *Varieties*.

34 (Apropos of Freud.) James to Flournoy, 28 September 1909, Robert Le Clair (ed.), *The Letters of William James and Théodore Flournoy* (Madison: University of Wisconsin Press, 1966), p. 224.

35 Reproduced in Donald Capps, '"That Shape am I": The Bearing of Melancholy on James's Struggle with Religion', Donald Capps and Janet Jacobs (eds.), *The Struggle for Life: A Companion to William James's 'The Varieties of Religious Experience'*, pp. 105–6.

36 It is important to note that James's concept of character in the *Varieties* is not purely subjective, as subsequent psychologies would conceive it. Character here stands for a particular outlook on life, a particular philosophy.

37 James, *Varieties*, p. 155.

38 Ibid.

39 Ibid., p. 154.

40 Ibid., p. 166.

41 Ibid., p. 167.

42 James, 'The Energies of Men', *Essays in Religion and Morality* (Cambridge, MA: Harvard University Press, 1982), p. 144.

43 On the significance of late nineteenth-century mind-cure in the genesis of modern psychotherapy see Eric Caplan, *Mind Games: American Culture and the Birth of Psychotherapy* (Berkeley: University of California Press, 2001).

44 James, *Essays in Psychology*, p. 197.

45 Ibid., p. 203.

46 James, *The Principles of Psychology*, vol. 2 (Cambridge, MA: Harvard University Press, 1981), p. 1201.

47 Ibid., pp. 1201–2.

48 At the same time, James valued the therapeutic utility of hypnotism. On 26 November 1890, he wrote to his sister Alice James, 'If I were you, I would seriously try *hypnotism*, which might do you good.' *The Correspondence of William James, Volume 7, 1890–1894*, p. 114. In his review of Pierre Janet's work, James contended that the 'possible application to the relief of human misery' was the 'really important part of these investigations' ('The hidden self', p. 265). In the *Varieties*, James criticised the over-extension of the word 'suggestion': 'the word "suggestion", having acquired official status, is unfortunately

beginning in many quarters to play the part of a wet blanket upon investigation, being used to fend off all inquiry into the varying susceptibilities of individual cases. "Suggestion" is only another name for the power of ideas, *so far as they prove efficacious over belief and conduct*' (p. 91). In 'The Energies of Men' James offered the following definition of the action of suggestion: 'It throws into gear energies of imagination, of will, and of mental influence over physiological processes, that usually lie dormant' (p. 139).

49 James, 'Reflex Action and Theism', *The Will to Believe*, pp. 95–6. This gener-alised notion of the plasticity of experience is not grounded in ontological distinctions, such as the distinction proposed by Ian Hacking between 'inter-active kinds' and 'indifferent kinds', *The Social Construction of What?* (Cambridge, MA: Harvard University Press, 1999), which risks falling back into a classical dichotomy between the 'human' and 'natural' sciences, and one might add, into the dualisms which James sought to overthrow with radical empiricism.

50 See Richard King, *Orientalism and Religion*, p. 60.

51 James, *Varieties*, p. 327.

52 Ibid., p. 396.

53 Ibid., p. 397.

54 James, *Pragmatism* (Cambridge, MA: Harvard University Press, 1975), p. 97.

55 Ibid., p. 104.

56 James, *Varieties*, p. 376.

Chapter 2

Witchcraft: the numinous power of humans

Ann Casement

Introduction

Explorations of witchcraft have generated a considerable literature in anthropology where it is generally taken to denote the projection of supernatural evil by human instigation. Most anthropologists agree that witchcraft comprises a system of belief dealing with mystical power and thus is integral to the study and understanding of religion and cosmology. The modern anthropological concern with witchcraft is generally acknowledged to have begun with Evans-Pritchard's *Witchcraft, Oracles, and Magic among the Azande*, and most subsequent anthropological studies on the subject pay tribute to this original work. As the concepts of *witchcraft* and the *numinous* are central to this chapter, a brief definition of each will be attempted before moving on to a depiction of witchcraft amongst the Azande.

In *The Idea of the Holy* (1923), Rudolf Otto formulated the term *numinous* to depict the tremendous, awful, mysterious non-rational emotions that are generated by a recognition of something in the objective situation. Otto states that this experience cannot be transmitted, it can only be awakened 'as everything that comes "of the spirit" must be awakened' (Otto 1958: 7). He goes on to say that much can be taught by way of concepts and instruction but the numinous basis of this kind of experience cannot be handed down in this manner. It passes instead from mind to mind through 'a penetrative imaginative sympathy with what passes in the other person's mind' (Otto 1958: 60). In his study of witchcraft amongst the Azande, Evans-Pritchard's description of what they call *mbisimo mangu*, the soul of witchcraft, is psychic in action and 'bridges over the distance between the person of the witch and the person of his victim' (Evans-Pritchard 1976: 10). In all this, the numinosity of witchcraft is stressed, not the subjective feelings that accompany it. In other words, it is what Otto means by the 'feeling of the numinous' (Otto 1923: xvii) that refers to something in the objective situation awaiting discovery and acknowledgement.

Jung calls this phenomenon *participation mystique*, a term he took from the anthropologist Lévy-Bruhl, which denotes 'an unconscious identity in which two individual psychic spheres interpenetrate to such a degree that it is impossible to say what belongs to whom'. As Sonu Shamdasani points out in his meticulously researched book *Jung and the Making of Modern Psychology: The Dream of a Science*, Lévy-Bruhl was a key source for Jung's concept of archetypes. The anthropologist Paul Radin, who was well disposed to Jung's work on the whole was critical of his reliance on *participation mystique*. Shamdasani goes on to say this about what Lévy-Bruhl called primitive mentality: 'Thus while they didn't separate mind and matter in an Aristotelian fashion, it didn't mean that they didn't distinguish them – rather, that they assumed an interaction between the two' (Shamdasani 2003: 329). He is fair to Lévy-Bruhl in stating that he reversed his own conception of *participation mystique* later in life. However, it is the latter's reworking of Durkheim's concept of *collective representations* that influenced both Jung and Evans-Pritchard and the main thrust of this chapter is to illustrate the relationship of numinosity to collective representations through Azande witchcraft beliefs.

Evans-Pritchard's work is in part a refutation of Lévy-Bruhl's *participation mystique* in showing that the Azande are not permanently in a state of mystical union with the world around them. Even their belief in witchcraft appears to be 'just-so' and, on the surface at least, they are angered rather than awed when they find themselves its victims. However, this chapter will be attempting to show what Jung calls 'the numinous character of the reality in the background' (Jung 1964: 468) and Otto means by the 'feeling of the numinous' (Otto 1923: xvii) for both the Azande and Evans-Pritchard himself.

The bottom line 'c' of Jung's famous diagram from his late work *The Psychology of the Transference* (in Jung 1954: 221) might be the trajectory along which this kind of unconscious communication between witch and victim is transmitted. This would fit with recent speculation in psychoanalysis about right-brain to right-brain functioning linking it to unconscious communication, namely projective identification, splitting and denial. As a social scientist I do not feel qualified to write in depth about the brain. Interested readers are directed instead to papers on these links by Mark Solms and Jaak Panksepp, amongst others, from the Rome conference of the International Neuro-Psychoanalysis Society in September 2004.

Linking it to unconscious communication of the sort touched on above gives a psychological insight into the numinosity associated with witchcraft. This power may fly about by itself but is ineffective unless it has a human host. Witches are seen as subversive in embodying evil dedicated to undermining social structure and values. Their time for being active is the night, which is perhaps a metaphor for their activities that may be summarized as dark, evil, demonic, mystical. They may have an animal or spirit counterpart known as a 'familiar' in the language of English witch-hunting, which may accompany the witch or carry the projection of the witch's power on a mission of evil. Spreading disease is seen as a common activity of witches and a slow wasting disease is sure evidence of witchcraft. AIDS workers in various parts of Africa today have to assure people that HIV is not spread by witchcraft.

Financial misfortune is also associated with witchcraft as exemplified by migrant workers in African towns who ascribe falling into debt to having their credit cards bewitched by witches back in their home villages. Village folk may be envious of what they assume to be the greater affluence of their kin working in towns who are not sending sufficient funds back home. Amongst the African community in the UK there are periodic outbreaks of witchcraft accusations related to children. The media recently carried accounts of such outbreaks involving desperately poor asylum seekers from the Congo Basin (Kinshasa, Brazzaville, Northern Angola). The accused children were all related but not closely to the accusers who were having a difficult time supporting them. The practices and beliefs amongst this group are a synthesis of traditional and new – amongst the latter being possession by the devil accompanied by exorcism through corporal punishment.

Witches may engage in obscene practices such as cannibalism and vampirism, eating the flesh and drinking the blood of their victims and are universally associated with death – in some societies all deaths are deemed to be caused by witchcraft. Such is the case with the Azande. A point worth noting is that most anthropological accounts of witchcraft point to the fact that actual accusations decrease at times of stability and increase at times of social upheaval. This is the case amongst the Azande as evidenced by the following: 'the concept of witchcraft provides . . . a natural philosophy by which the relations between men and unfortunate events are explained' (Evans-Pritchard 1976: 18). Other instances of socio-cultural upheaval leading to the proliferation of witchcraft accusations may be seen at the time of the Reformation in England when church property was seized by the Crown and the poor were thrown onto the community at large to care for. This is well documented in Alan Macfarlane's *Witchcraft in Tudor and Stuart England*. A recent phenomenon is the witchcraft that is inherent in anti-Islamic sentiment, on the one hand, and overzealous accusations of racism, on the other.

The Azande material that follows will serve to underline this point and includes a description of the divinatory mechanisms that are often used if a witch is brought to trial. If this is followed by a confession or conviction then the usual punishment is recompense to the victim and treatment of the witch for removal of the power they possess.

AZANDE WITCHCRAFT

The way of life of the Azande has changed considerably since Evans-Pritchard's account of them was published in the 1930s but witchcraft beliefs in Central Africa remain undiminished. As a result, this part of the chapter will be written in what is known as the 'anthropological present' as its central focus is the place of witchcraft or *mangu* in Azande life.

By way of background, it is necessary to give a brief description of the Azande and their homeland. At the time that Evans-Pritchard lived and worked amongst them, they were a Central African people living in the watershed between the Nile and the Congo. Their traditional homeland, as with so many African tribal groupings, was divided between three modern African states: the Sudan, Zäire and the République Centrafricaine, all three of which were at that time under colonial domination. Although the latter inevitably had an impact on traditional practices focused on witchcraft, it nevertheless continued to be a central force in Azande society.

Evans-Pritchard largely concentrated his research on the Sudanese Azande. They were cultivators and hunters, growing corn, sweet potatoes, manioc, ground-nuts, bananas, legumes and hunting game which was in abundance. In addition, there were the annual swarmings of termites, which were eaten as a delicacy. They also kept domestic fowl which, as we shall see, played a large part in their techniques for controlling hostile forces but no cattle as their country was infested with tse-tse fly.

The countryside was dotted with homesteads each comprising a man and his family, while his neighbours were related to him by bonds of kinship or marriage. A highly organized indigenous political system grew out of this pattern of scattered residence and the Azande homeland in fact consisted of a number of tribal kingdoms, each of which was ruled by a different member of a single royal dynasty, the Avongara. In this society of aristocrats and commoners, the members of the Avongara were never accused of witchcraft as it would have brought the princely class into disrepute and undermined their authority. Nevertheless, they believed in witches as firmly as other people and constantly consulted the poison oracle to find out who was bewitching them, particularly their wives.

Witchcraft may be defined as a supernatural, mystical power innate in some people which enables them to work evil directly without the aid of magic. Amongst the Azande, it is thought to be a substance in the bellies of witches transmitted by unilinear descent, for example the sons of a male witch may be witches but not his daughters. Similarly, the daughters of a female witch may inherit her power but not her sons. Witches are also known by their red eyes which signify spiritual danger.

As Evans-Pritchard reports: 'Witchcraft . . . is so intertwined with everyday happenings that it is part of a Zande's ordinary world' (Evans-Pritchard 1976: 19). It is part of a chain of causation that accounts for the existence of a variety of phenomena. For instance, a boy knocked his foot against a stump of wood lying on the footpath. As a result, his foot was cut causing him pain that increased when it began to fester. The boy agreed that witchcraft had not put the stump in his path but it had caused him to knock his foot against it as he must have been bewitched at the moment when he did so and, as a result, did not see the stump. Furthermore, most cuts heal quickly but his had festered due to witchcraft. Azande say of witchcraft that it is the *umbaga* or second spear. When they kill game there is a division of meat between the man who first speared the animal and the man who plunged the second spear into it.

'Zande belief in witchcraft in no way contradicts empirical knowledge of cause and effect. The world known to the senses is just as real to them as it is to us . . . Belief in death from natural causes and belief in death from witchcraft are not mutually exclusive' (Evans-Pritchard 1976: 25). Nevertheless, for a Zande, witchcraft is a participant in all misfortune and, in that sense, witchcraft is misfortune. The notion of witchcraft enters into every aspect of Azande life and a witch is seen as one motivated by hatred, envy, jealousy and greed. In this way, the numinous power of witchcraft acts as a social leveller, as it does in many tribal societies, in keeping individuals from pursuing too much wealth or power or from displaying their talents or looks in too conspicuous a way. Interestingly, witchcraft also acts to keep individuals in their social place as a commoner would never accuse a nobleman of bewitching him, partly because it would be inadvisable to offend them but also because the two would have little social contact due to their different status.

As can be seen from the above, witchcraft articulates social as well as personal relations. It serves a third important function in that society, that of moral arbiter and Evans-Pritchard reports that a Zande may as often say something is bad when he means it is witchcraft. This is because witchcraft is not haphazard but is the planned assault by one individual on another. The Azande say that hatred, envy, jealousy, and so on go ahead and witchcraft follows on after. It is in the idiom of witchcraft that Azande moral rules find expression. However, an individual is only perceived to be a witch at the time of the misfortune and is not seen, even by his victim, as a witch for all time. In this way, Azande notions of witchcraft express dynamic relationships between individuals at times of misfortune.

Witch-doctors

Since witchcraft is seen as the chief cause of misfortune, particularly sickness and death, the Azande are keen to establish and maintain contact with this evil power in an effort to exert some form of control over it. The most important ways for so doing in serious cases are through the activities of witch-doctors, who are both diviners and magicians, and in consulting the poison oracle. A brief description of both follows.

The Azande witch-doctor is able to expose witches through his powers of divination and as a magician he has the capacity to thwart them. Evans-Pritchard obtained much of the esoteric information about witch-doctor practices through exploiting the rivalry between two noted practitioners. As he slyly puts it: 'When informants fall out anthropologists come into their own' (Evans-Pritchard 1976: 69). Witch-doctors dance and divine at séances held in public and are heralded and accompanied by drums. They adorn themselves with hats decorated with feathers, large hide bags containing skins, horns, magic whistles, belts, leglets and armlets made from various wild fruit and seeds. When they arrive at their destination, they discuss in low tones the affairs of the séance and prepare the ground for dancing. Members of the ruling classes never become practitioners as it would be undignified for them to dance in public nor do women take part in these dances, although some widows may be witch-doctors.

In describing a séance attention will be concentrated on one witch-doctor's performance but séances often have several taking part at a time. To begin with a large circle is drawn on the ground with white ashes sprinkled along it, which no layman is supposed to enter as it is reserved for the witch-doctor's dance. The witch-doctor lays out his medicines derived from trees and plants and gains his authority from his knowledge of these along with the supernatural power that resides in him. Before commencing to dance and sing, a witch-doctor will often select a group of small boys to act as a chorus. If they do not sing lustily enough, he may shoot a bone or black beetle into one of the boys to show his annoyance.

The warming-up process takes some time to get going but eventually a witch-doctor will begin to give such a spirited performance that he will get out of breath and have to stop for a while. This is the moment for an oracular reply when a member of the audience may put a question to him and he is able to point the person in the right direction to look for the witch. At times the practitioners dance themselves into a fury and gash their tongues and chests with knives and dance with them hanging out of their mouths to give themselves a ferocious look. The witch-doctor dances the questions that are put to him and these dances are spirited, violent and ecstatic signifying a symbolic fight against the numinous powers of evil.

According to Evans-Pritchard these séances appear to serve several functions at the same time. They have a social value in enhancing the reputation of the householder who has initiated one as they are a source of entertainment and provide material for comment and gossip for a long time afterwards. To quote: 'To the master of the homestead it is a means of finding out who is troubling his welfare; of warning the witch, who is probably present in person at the séance, that he is on his tracks; and of gaining public support and recognition in his difficulties, and esteem and publicity by throwing open his house to the countryside and by employing performers' (Evans-Pritchard 1976: 77).

However, he also states that 'witch-doctors believe in witches quite as firmly as a layman' (Evans-Pritchard 1976: 86). As a result, witch-doctors seldom divulge the names of witches in public but will name them privately to their client after the séance has ended. This is to protect themselves against witchcraft which could attack them when they are unprotected once out of their role of witch-doctor and off their guard. What is clearly indicated here is the numinous power of witchcraft at work.

The poison oracle

The greatest service that witch-doctors perform is to seek out and lay bare the many activities of a group of homesteads and in that way access any potential trouble spots before a major undertaking such as a group hunt. This is a joint venture that involves many individuals so that the welfare of a whole district is at stake. The witch-doctors' performance represents a public attack on any evil mystical forces that are around and in this way the atmosphere is cleared of witchcraft.

However, in matters of importance the witch-doctors may be consulted only in the preliminary stages before taking the matter to the great oracle known as the poison oracle. The latter known in Zande as *benge* is the most authoritative of the oracles to be consulted. 'In important collective under-takings, in all crises in life, in all serious legal disputes . . . on all occasions regarded by Azande as dangerous or socially important, the activity is preceded by consultation of the poison oracle' (Evans-Pritchard 1976: 121). Examples of typical situations about which the poison oracle is consulted are cases of adultery; a wife not conceiving; before undertaking long journeys or becoming a witch-doctor; or in the case of a prince before moving his court.

Zande rely completely on its decisions which have the force of the rule of law when obtained on the orders of a prince. The poison used is a red powder manufactured from a forest creeper and mixed with water to make a paste. Evans-Pritchard brought the paste back to England to be examined where it turned out to be a compound related to strychnine. The paste is squeezed into the beaks of small domestic fowl that generally have violent spasms after swallowing it, although some fowl are completely unaffected. Azande interpret the behaviour of the fowl, especially their death or survival, as providing answers to the questions that are put before the oracle.

'A visitor to Zandeland hears as much of the poison oracle as he hears of witchcraft, for whenever a question arises about the facts of a case or about a man's well-being they at once seek to know the opinion of the poison oracle on the matter' (Evans-Pritchard 1976: 121). Evans-Pritchard found that whenever a Zande acted in a rude or untrustworthy manner it was usually because of the dictates of his oracles as they were usually polite and reliable in normal circumstances. This discordant behaviour is hard to understand until their 'mystical notions' are taken into account and it is unnecessary for one Zande to explain his wayward behaviour to another as they take it as prudent behaviour to regulate conduct according to the directions of the oracles.

Poison oracle ceremony

The usual place for a consultation is far removed from the homesteads at the edge of the cultivated fields. This is for a variety of reasons, one of which is to ensure secrecy. Another is to avoid pollution by people who have not observed the prerequisite taboos such as eating elephant's flesh or fish, having sexual relations with women or smoking hemp. It is also imperative to escape witchcraft, which is less likely to be able to locate and corrupt the oracle in the bush. The heat of the day is avoided as the poison becomes particularly potent in the hot sun and eight to nine in the morning is the favoured time for a ceremony, although the night is sometimes resorted to for long séances. Any day is acceptable except the one after a new moon.

Only wealthy men posses more than half a dozen fowls at a time so though cockerels are best, chickens of all sizes and ages may be used instead. Fully grown birds are not favoured as they succumb easily to the poison whereas younger ones remain for a long time under its influence before expiring or surviving, so that the oracle has time to hear all the relevant details of the problem placed before it and give a well-considered judgement.

It is particularly the province of married men with households to consult the poison oracle as they are not only the ones in a position to resolve their personal problems but are also dealing with matters of public importance such as witchcraft and adultery. Young or poor men have to persuade a kinsman to consult the oracle on their behalf and this is one of the main duties of social relationships. Needless to say, women are debarred from anything to do with the poison oracle and the great advantage middle-aged men have over women and younger men is their ability to use it. As Evans-Pritchard puts it: 'being cut off from the main means of establishing contact with the mystical forces that so deeply affect human welfare degrades women's position in Zande society' (Evans-Pritchard 1976: 131).

There is only space here for a brief account of the proceedings at a poison oracle séance which typically consists of question and answer. If a fowl dies after having poison administered to it in the first test then another fowl must survive. The death of a fowl is not in itself positive or negative and depends entirely on the form of the question put to the oracle. The following is an example of the way a verdict is reached.

First Test. If X has committed adultery poison oracle kill the fowl. If X is innocent poison oracle spare the fowl. The fowl dies.

Second Test. The poison oracle has declared X guilty of adultery by slaying
the fowl. If its declaration is true let it spare this second fowl. The fowl
survives.
Result. A valid verdict. X is guilty (Evans-Pritchard 1976: 139).

The poison oracle has similarities with the Delphic oracle, although it is not
personified. Zande faith in its judgement is embedded in a coherent mystical
system that does not contradict sensory experience nor is it identical with it.
They explain its ability to see far-off things by saying that its *mbisimo* or
soul sees them and the numinous power of the poison oracle resides in the
naming of this soul.

FUNCTIONALISM

The above description of Azande witchcraft beliefs has been given at some
length to illustrate Evans-Pritchard's classical *functionalist* approach. Within
this theoretical framework, he was trying to show how a system of belief
functions to exercise a stabilizing influence on the social and moral order in
that society. *Functionalism* in anthropology derives from the work of the two
most prominent anthropologists in Great Britain during the earlier part of
the twentieth century, Bronislaw Malinowski and A.R. Radcliffe-Brown.
They developed it in reaction to two theories: the evolutionism that dominated nineteenth-century anthropology and the historicism of the early
twentieth century. Radcliffe-Brown's version was particularly influential on
anthropology as his theory derived from Emile Durkheim the view that
society far from being merely the sum of individuals is instead a system of
social forms. Functionalism in its turn was criticized for disregarding historical processes and for being circular in that human needs are cited as the
reason for the existence of social institutions, which in turn are used to
explain their existence. It eventually fell into disuse but not before it had
inspired a valuable and widely varied anthropological discourse on institutions and social relationships.
   Anthropologists found it useful in their day-to-day workings with the
people they were studying as it catered for the need to maintain an emotional distance from the belief systems of the people with whom they were
working. It is also the case that analytical psychologists need to cultivate a
certain objectivity in relation to their patients' material in order to maintain
analytic neutrality and to guard against accusations of suggestibility. In his
anthropological work, Evans-Pritchard was only too aware of this need,
particularly as he himself was a Catholic convert and a man of strong
religious belief. In his seminal account of Azande witchcraft he tried to
maintain this critical distance by rationalizing their belief system through

demonstrating its functional properties. At the same time, he tried to incorporate his religious belief in his work and there is a moment in the account when his anthropological stance breaks down into interpretative ambiguity as follows.

One night he had been sitting late in his hut writing notes when around midnight he decided to take a stroll before retiring. In the course of this, he noticed a bright light passing towards the homestead of a man called Tupoi. He decided to investigate and followed it until a grass screen obscured his view. At this point, he ran through his hut out to the other side in order to see where the light was going but lost sight of it. The response from everyone that he told about this incident the next day was that he had witnessed witchcraft. At the same time, news spread that a relative of Tupoi died that day. 'I never discovered (the light's) real origin . . . but the coincidence of the direction along which the light moved and the subsequent death accorded well with Zande ideas' (Evans-Pritchard 1976: 11).

In order to maintain his anthropological authority, Evans-Pritchard went on to try and explain this event rationally as someone answering the call of nature without recourse to the supernatural. The anthropological study of witchcraft, intertwined as the latter is with a belief system, presents special difficulties for anthropologists in the Durkheimian mould who are trying to study it as a 'social fact'. This is because it is a subjective and hence a personal experience and subjectivity brings the anthropologist into the realm of the 'inner life' of the people he or she is studying. This 'can collapse the distance between the anthropologist and the people he or she studies' (Engelke 2002: 3).

COLLECTIVE REPRESENTATIONS AND PARTICIPATION MYSTIQUE

Both Evans-Pritchard and Jung were influenced by Durkheim through their reading of the French anthropologist, Lévy-Bruhl. In particular, it was Durkheim's concepts of *collective representations* and *collective consciousness*, largely re-worked by Lévy-Bruhl in his 1910 work, *The Mental Functions in Inferior Societies*, that interested both men. The first concept denoted the beliefs and assumptions collectively held which individuals in a society unconsciously accept; whilst the second 'was made up of collective representations, which expressed how the group thought of itself' (Shamdasani 2003: 290). According to Lévy-Bruhl, 'primitive' mental functioning was dominated by a different type of collective representation – what he called 'mystical' – to the mental functioning of 'civilized' peoples. 'Lévy-Bruhl stressed the disjunction between primitive and civilized mentality . . . Consequently, he characterized "primitives" as living in a state of mystical participation' (Shamdasani 2003: 291).

It is this concept of *participation mystique* that exercised such an influence on Jung, as a quick look at the *General Index*, Volume 20 of the *Collected Works* will testify. This term was used to postulate a special 'primitive' cast of mind to explain apparently irrational beliefs as well as the fact that 'primitives' went about in a permanently mystical state. Although this theory was discredited decades ago, not least by Lévy-Bruhl himself, Jung continued to use it as do many of his followers to this day. Evans-Pritchard repudiated this theory whilst at the same time acknowledging Lévy-Bruhl's 'exceptional brilliance and originality' (Evans-Pritchard 1976: xxi) when it came to his insights into the nature of *collective representations*. It is these that Evans-Pritchard was at pains to highlight in his study of Azande witchcraft beliefs whilst at the same time questioning why humans should entertain metaphysical assumptions of any kind. The British anthropologist, Mary Douglas went further in pointing to the fact that witchcraft does not require the existence of any mysterious spiritual beings – only the mysterious powers of humans. Although Evans-Pritchard belongs in the *functionalist* tradition and Mary Douglas in the *structuralist*, what they have to say here resonates with Jung even though he traces his descent from the *idealist* tradition. Douglas states a further point as follows:

> The belief is on the same footing as belief in the conspiracy theory of history, in the baneful effects of fluoridation or the curative value of psychoanalysis – or any belief that can be presented in an unverifiable form. The question then becomes one about rationality.
>
> (Douglas 1970: xvi)

Another great French anthropologist, Lévi-Strauss, also criticized Lévy-Bruhl's concept of primitive mentality and claimed that the latter had set up a false antimony between logical and pre-logical mental functioning. He states:

> The savage mind is logical in the same sense and the same fashion as ours . . . contrary to Lévy-Bruhl's opinion, its thought proceeds through understanding not affectivity, with the aid of distinctions and oppositions, not by confusion and participation.
>
> (Lévi-Strauss 1966: 268)

Lévi-Strauss was equally dismissive of Jung as we can see from his statement that it is possible to 'dispose of theories making use of the concepts of "archetypes" or a "collective unconscious"' (Lévi-Strauss 1966: 65). As an adherent of the French *rationalist* tradition, Lévi-Strauss was critical of anything that might be thought of as 'mystical'.

Archetype, numinosity, collective representations, participation mystique

In exploring concepts from Jung, Evans-Pritchard, Otto, and Lévy-Bruhl, this chapter is attempting to link various non-rational aspects of social life that continue to have significance today. For Jung, these concepts come together in the *psychoid* nature of the archetype that points to his own unification theory or, as he put it, *unus mundus*, the unitary world 'towards which the psychologist and the atomic physicist are converging along separate paths' (Jung 1964: 452). He goes on to say: 'The psychoid archetype has a tendency to behave as though it were not localized in one person but were active in the whole environment . . . Animals and primitives have a particularly fine nose for these things' (ibid.). And further: 'As soon as the dialogue between two people touches on something fundamental, essential, and numinous, and a certain rapport is felt, it gives rise to a phenomenon which Lévy-Bruhl fittingly called *participation mystique*' (ibid).

On the one hand, Jung suggests that the numinosity generated by archetypal motifs plays itself out in the witchcraft beliefs of 'primitive' humankind which he finds 'very interesting and very sensible – actually more sensible than the academic views of modern science' (Jung 1964: 11). He points out that this numinosity is to be seen at work in the demons of sickness that possess modern humankind – both physical and psychological. On the other hand, Jung goes on to marvel at the striking difference between the 'prelogical' state of mind and 'our' own conscious outlook as attested to by Lévy-Bruhl and gives an example of witchcraft belief as 'a perfect example of that capricious way of explaining things which is characteristic of the "prelogical" state of mind' (Jung 1964: 52). Although he concludes that: 'primitive man is no more logical or illogical than we are. Only his presuppositions are different . . . he does not examine his assumptions. To him it is an unquestionable truth that disease and other ills are caused by spirits or witchcraft' (Jung 1964: 52).

It is this assumption on Jung's part, deriving from his uncritical espousing of Lévy-Bruhl's theory of *participation mystique*, that is called into question in this chapter, viz. that 'primitives' live in a constant state of numinosity ungrounded in the profane world. This misapprehension was commonly held to be true at one time so that 'primitives', psychotics and children were portrayed as solely inhabiting the archetypal realm. Evans-Pritchard's work is a corrective to this misapprehension with his direct observation through on-the-ground fieldwork of Zande witchcraft beliefs. He demonstrates instead that the Azande are perfectly capable of reality testing as follows: 'Zande belief in witchcraft in no way contradicts empirical knowledge of cause and effect. The world known to the senses is just as real to them as it is to us' (Evans-Pritchard 1976: 25). Their belief in death from natural causes and belief in death from witchcraft are not mutually exclusive. Instead they supplement each other, and, as was said above, witchcraft is called the *umbaga* or second spear so that if a man is killed by an elephant Azande say the elephant was the first spear and witchcraft was the *umbaga* and that together they killed him.

RETURN OF THE REPRESSED

It may be seen from the above section that Jung tended to both idealize and denigrate 'primitive' society in relation to modern social life. The former was seen to be only 'prelogical' and numinous versus the scientifically based civilized world which was portrayed as logical but with a concomitant lack of the numinous. In the latter instance, Jung was certainly on to something when he pointed to the loss of the numinous which is increasingly evident in today's secular world. As a result, there is a real craving for that dimension which is not being met by organized religion. The response from the latter is a hollow offering of the same old rituals that have lost their numinosity and power to inspire. The other response is an alarming increase in fundamentalism in the three major world religions of Judaism, Christianity and Islam. David Tacey's (2004) book *The Spirituality Revolution* is an exploration of this whole area.

What is also on the increase is the growth of witchcraft accusations and the proliferation of conspiracy theories which point to the contamination of the numinous by the power principle. For an example of the former, one may turn to Elizabeth Loftus's book *The Myth of Repressed Memory* where it is expressed as follows:

> In Salem, Massachusetts, three hundred years earlier, and in Europe during the sixteenth and seventeenth centuries, sane and rational people convinced themselves that witches were performing black magic and consorting with the devil. Now, at the close of the twentieth century, sane and rational people were getting hysterical about rumors that a murderous satanic cult had infiltrated their communities.
>
> (Loftus and Ketcham 1994: 258)

With regard to conspiracy theory, one has only to think of how that has been constellated around the death of Princess Diana.

As Tacey's book shows, there is a rise in the number of self-proclaimed witches who trace their roots to paganism and nature. This is compensating for the loss of the numinous in the religion of the West with its one-sided focus on a transcendent God in a distant heaven. 'The realm of nature must be rediscovered as a major site for sacred celebration and religious worship' (Tacey 2004: 103). What Tacey means by 'the realm of nature' is akin to what Jung meant by the inner quest for the numinous located in the natural realm within the psyche. Witchcraft, with its connection to evil, suggests that the numinous has become contaminated by the desire for power. As a result, the numinous arises in the West saturated with unconscious forces such as complexes (as in the return of the repressed) and manifests negatively in an increase in witchcraft and conspiracy beliefs. This is accompanied by an abandoning of the reality principle which could help ground and constructively shape these beliefs. Until the West can turn its attention wholeheartedly inwards to the numinous power in the psyche, the latter will continue to express itself in negative ways and swamp the much-needed consciousness that must accompany such an inner quest.

References

Douglas, M. (ed.) (1970) *Witchcraft Confessions, and Accusations*, London: Tavistock.

Engelke, M. (2002) *The Problem of Belief in Anthropology Today*, Oxford: Blackwell.

Evans-Pritchard, E.E. (1976) *Witchcraft, Oracles and Magic among the Azande*, London, Oxford, New York: Oxford University Press.

Jung, C.G. (1954) *The Practice of Psychotherapy*, vol. 16, London: Routledge & Kegan Paul.

Jung, C.G. (1964) *Civilization in Transition*, vol. 10, London: Routledge & Kegan Paul.

Lévi-Strauss, C. (1966) *The Savage Mind*, Oxford: Oxford University Press.

Loftus, E. and Ketcham, K. (1994) *The Myth of Repressed Memory: False Memories and Allegations of Sexual Abuse*, New York: St. Martin's Press.

Otto, R. (1923) *The Idea of the Holy*, London: Oxford University Press.

Otto, R. (1958) *The Idea of the Holy*, London, Oxford, New York: Oxford University Press.

Shamdasani, S. (2003) *Jung and the Making of Modern Psychology: The Dream of a Science*, Cambridge: Cambridge University Press.

Tacey, D. (2004) *The Spirituality Revolution: The Emergence of Contemporary Spirituality*, Canada, UK, USA: Brunner-Routledge.

Chapter 3

On the importance of numinous experience in the alchemy of individuation

Murray Stein

In a letter to P.W. Martin (20 August 1945), the founder of the International Study Centre of Applied Psychology in Oxted, England, C.G. Jung confirmed the centrality of numinous experience in his life and work:

> It always seemed to me as if the real milestones were certain symbolic events characterized by a strong emotional tone. You are quite right, the main interest of my work is not concerned with the treatment of neuroses but rather with the approach to the numinous. But the fact is that the approach to the numinous is the real therapy and inasmuch as you attain to the numinous experiences you are released from the curse of pathology. Even the very disease takes on a numinous character.
>
> (Jung 1973, 1: 377)

If one holds the classical Jungian view that the only genuine cure for neurosis is to grow out of it through pursuing individuation, then treatment based on this model would seem necessarily to include "the approach to the numinous," as Jung states so firmly in this letter. The individuation process, as proposed by Jung and his followers, typically includes experiences of a numinous nature.

The question is: How are such momentous experiences related to and used within the context of analysis and the individuation journey, and how do they contribute to the overall process of individuation? On the answer to this complex question rests the difference between psychological individuation and the development of spirituality. While the psychological hero(ine) of the individuation journey is by no means identical to the spiritual hero(ine) of the journey to God (however this term may be defined), it is not always easy to tell where their paths diverge, precisely because Jung placed such central importance on numinous experience for individuation. And yet they do diverge, and decisively.

ON HEALING AND NUMINOUS EXPERIENCE

We can begin by investigating how attaining to numinous experiences releases a person from the curse of pathology, as Jung claims in his letter to P.W. Martin. Generally speaking, an "approach to the numinous" is considered a religious undertaking, a pilgrimage. The "attainment to the numinous experiences" that Jung speaks of refers to religious experiences of a quasi-mystical nature. By itself, this attainment might well persuade a person that life is meaningful. Numinous experience creates a convincing link to the transcendent, and this may well lead to the feeling that character flaws like addictions or behavioral disorders are trivial by comparison with the grand visions imparted in the mystical state. The pathological symptom can be interpreted as an incitement to go on the spiritual quest, or even as a paradoxical doorway into transcendence, and this can donate meaning to the malady itself. Perhaps some degree of pathology is needed, in fact, in order for a person to feel strongly enough motivated to set out on a spiritual quest to begin with. In this case, attainment to numinous experiences would bring about a change in the feeling that pathology is a *curse*, even if it did not result in curing the pathology itself, although it might lead to this as well   .

For modern and psychologically astute people, however, such a spiritual development might not signify more than a temporary sticking plaster and by no means a definitive solution to the problems created by neurosis. For such people, who tend to be the ones who seek out analysis rather than spiritual guidance or religious pilgrimages, spiritual awareness by itself is not enough. So how would an approach to the numinous and the attainment of numinous experiences contribute to the more far-reaching psychological project of individuation? This becomes a much more complicated matter than the purely religious realize.

To begin with fundamentals, one cannot conceive that Jung (or the Jungians following him) would possibly entertain the notion that achieving freedom from the curse of pathology for oneself or for the people one works with in analysis can be separated from living a full life, that is from engaging to the fullest extent possible in the process of individuation. Going on spiritual quests or having numinous experiences may be part of the route to individuation but by themselves are not enough to establish, let alone to complete, an individuation process, although they may create a profound change in attitude and personality as in the case of Paul on the road to Damascus (cited by Jung in *Psychology and Religion* (1937)). Generally speaking, however, a numinous experience is a "hint," as Jung defines it in several passages. It is a hint that larger, non-egoic powers exist in the psyche, which need to be considered and ultimately made conscious. High on the agenda of the individuation *opus* is making the psyche conscious, and this far-ranging enterprise can be described minimally as multifaceted because of the complexity resident within the Self. Treating pathology is not a partial undertaking in Jungian psychotherapy. Specific symptoms cannot be isolated from more general questions of consciousness and wholeness, that is from individuation issues of a profound and far-reaching nature.

To get more deeply into this discussion, we should recall the basic two-phase movement of the individuation process, analysis and synthesis. The development of consciousness and the realization of the complete person-ality's identity, i.e., individuation, requires initially that a person break the unconscious identity with the persona on the one side and with the anima/animus on the other (see Stein 2005a). The attachments and identifications with these structures and their contents must be loosened through conscious reflection and analysis. After that, a process of inner dialogue ("active imagination") can take place through which the gap is opened wider between ego consciousness and these other psychic structures. This defines the analytic movement in the individuation process. Through it, consciousness comes to resemble less a static set of objects and patterns, like a painting, and more something like a mirror through which objects can float freely into and out of view but do not remain permanently in residence. This movement of analysis includes dissolving the attachments to religious objects, tradi-tional practices, and childish theologies. It is one of the primary achieve-ments of individuation to arrive at this type of fluidity in consciousness and to gain a measure of freedom from identities that were created early in childhood and adolescence and then became cemented in place through ongoing attachments, loves, loyalties, and the need to belong and to be one of the group, a member of the collective. If this project resembles a spiritual quest, it is one by way of a *via negativa* (the way of negation), such as Zen Buddhism espouses. If one thinks about the psyche structurally, as above, one understands readily enough that identification with the persona and the anima/animus blocks individuation by cluttering the personality's ego with foreign objects, i.e., introjects and other unconsciously acquired and maintained contents. Consciousness must be freed from this contamination if a person is to gain individuality and true uniqueness.

Experientially, it is the affectively charged "voices" or "images" em-bedded in these psychic structures, which back them up and make auth-oritative demands, that cause the problem. In these are represented the figures with whom one is identified or to whom one is bound emotionally by affective ties – parents, mentors, lovers, community leaders, enemies, "ghosts," etc. The reality of psychological life requires that in analysis we confront voices and images that communicate feeling and emotion; we do not confront inner structures as such. To speak structurally introduces a level of abstraction that is theoretically necessary but not in and of itself clinically useful or descriptively accurate. It is in considering the voices and images as they are experienced concretely within the psyche, which influ-ence and at times even take possession of consciousness, that we come upon the mythic dimension, which is only a small step away from the experience of a *numen*.[1] In the analytic movement of individuation, the ego's unconscious identification with such figures, including archetypal ones, becomes subject to ana-lysis (dissolving, taking apart). One must become free of their power and influence. Detachment and separation, not union, are the central themes of this movement.

To put this discussion into an historical perspective, Jung's interest in mythical figures of the unconscious psyche began around 1909 and found its first major published statement in the two-part work, *Wandlungen und Symbole der Libido* (1912) (first translated into English in 1916a as *Psychology of the Unconscious*). Taking off from a text written by Miss Frank Miller, "Some instances of subconscious creative imagination," and published with an introduction by the Swiss psychologist Théodore Flournoy,[2] Jung unearthed the mythical background concealed in this American woman's fantasies. For him, this investigation exposed a deeper layer of the psyche than the purely personal. There are voices and images active in the unconscious that occupy a space located at a non-personal level. At first Jung termed these "primordial images;" later he named them "the archetypes of the collective unconscious." A careful investigation of consciousness, especially through the analysis of daydreams, waking fantasies, and dreams, uncovers archetypal images at work that have a controlling influence over waking thought and feeling. As Jung poked into these hidden recesses, he discovered the influential power of the primordial images over consciousness, and for him their determinative authority for psychological life became irrefutable. Stuck behind and within the personal inner voices and images, Jung discovered "the gods." These impersonal forces and energies of massive dimension and of both primitive and sophisticated quality are not only disturbers of consciousness, however; they are also the carriers of culture, of spiritual values passed down through generations, and of patterns of instinct and imagination that can be found in all cultures and at all times of human history. Ultimately, their images embody and represent humankind's experience of the divine on the one hand, and of the instincts (such as sexuality, hunger, creativity, etc.) on the other.

This profound realization of the psyche's archetypal foundations led Jung to the view that pathological symptoms also contain (and often conceal) an archetypal element. Human psychopathologies are not only individual and personal acquisitions. They appear cross-culturally and universally, and their appearance and statistical manifestation are relatively unaffected by social and cultural circumstances. They are typical outcomes of human interaction with environments of many types, and they disguise or represent basic human needs, including spiritual ones. A person must address these needs directly and take them on board if life is to achieve balance and wholeness. Individuation depends on making this move toward consciousness and integration.

Numinosity enters this discussion in relation to the role that archetypal influences play in pathological states of mind. As Jung writes in a letter, dated 30 January 1961, to William Wilson, co-founder of Alcoholics Anonymous: "His [i.e., Roland's, Jung's patient] craving for alcohol was the equivalent on a low level of the spiritual thirst of our being for wholeness, expressed in medieval language: the union with God" (Jung 1973, 2: 624). In Bill W's case, as Wilson is referred to in the literature of AA, the approach to the numinous and the attainment to numinous experiences changed him when he was able to free himself from the notion that opening himself to the numinous would oblige him to go back to the familiar religion of his childhood and to its prescribed teaching and dogmatic structures. Since he could not do this, his path to the integration of the numinous was blocked. For Bill W, his religious tradition had become, as it has for modern people generally, Procrustean. The key came in the spontaneous advice from an alcoholic friend who had found a way to spirituality: "Why don't you choose your own conception of God?" (Alcoholics Anonymous 1976: 12) Giving the ego choice and responsibility, rather than insisting on submission to dogma, was the answer to his religious conflict. Becoming freed to find his way to the numinous as an individual – this is the essential point for modern people – changed Bill W in such a fundamental way that the illness corrupting the physical and psychological body could be overcome. From this forceful realization that the numinous element in spirituality can heal, an individual was freed from his addiction to alcohol and a worldwide self-help organization was born. Once the true underlying craving for spirit was effectively addressed and integrated into daily life, the desire for alcoholic ecstasy could be held in check.

Are not all addictions, one wonders after having seen such a wide variety of them in clinical practice, a search for something so elusive as to be considered somehow "of the spirit"?

RUDOLF OTTO, CREATOR OF "THE IDEA OF THE NUMINOUS"

Because Jung weighted numinous experience with such great significance for individuation, it is instructive to know something about this terminology and where it came from. The German theologian Rudolf Otto (1869–1937) developed the use of the terms *numinosum*, numinous, numinosity in his famous work, *Das Heilige* (translated into English, somewhat unfortunately, as *The Idea of the Holy*), in order to describe "the Holy" in such a way as to keep it distinct from other theological and philosophical or ethical renditions, such as "the good" or "goodness." He writes: "For this purpose I adopt a word coined from the Latin *numen*. *Omen* has given us 'ominous', and there is no reason why from *numen* we should not similarly form a word 'numinous'" (Otto 1917: 6–7). Otto set out to describe the human experience of "the Holy," not the theological concept of holiness. His work introduced a strong psychological and emotional component into the study of religions, in contrast to other comparative and historical approaches and above all to the theological enterprise, which often treats almost exclusively only received doctrines and offers a rational (in the sense of an organized and systematic) explication of traditional teachings and texts (i.e., "revelation").

For a Protestant like Otto, of course, "faith" was generally taken to be the central fact of religious life, not numinous experience. This can often take the form of intellectual and therefore quasi-rational assent to doctrinal propositions. Otto, on the contrary, wanted to speak about the nature of religious experience and to demonstrate the fundamental importance of the irrational in religion, hence his book's subtitle: "*Uber das Irrationale in der Idee des Göttlichen und sein Verhältnis zum Rationalen*" ("On the Irrational in the Idea of the Divine and its Relation to the Rational"). While obviously not desiring to abandon the rational elements of theology (see ibid.: 1–4), he creatively set forth the non-rational quality of religious experience and especially its strong emotional overtones. For Otto, the human encounter with "the Holy," as image, ritual, or sound, could only be accurately described with strong words like *mysterium tremendum et fascinans* (an awe-full and fascinating mystery), a phrase that he explicates meticulously and profoundly in his exposition of numinous experience. To enter into the presence of "the Holy" was for him to be shaken to the foundations by the power and awesome magnitude of the Other who is confronted in this experience. To describe this, he uses words like "shudder," "stupor," "astonishment," and "blank wonder." As a student of the world's mysticisms, he also related this to the "void" of Buddhist mystics (Otto 1917: 30). This universal religious moment is primarily an experience of feeling, whereas theology is above all an exercise of thinking and reflection.

It is not altogether clear how Otto arrived at his position, whether through the influence of early teachers and ministers, or of philosophers like Kant and Fries whom he studied deeply, or from Christian theologians like Schleiermacher who also emphasized the crucial importance of feeling in religious life and teaching, or by taking into account his own experiences of the Holy (see Alles 1996: 62–3). Perhaps his psychological typology also played a big role. His preference for feeling over thinking set him apart from his theological fellows. Whatever the reasons, he was gripped and fascinated by the power of numinous experience. In some of his letters written back home during his travels Otto describes two impressive incidents that some scholars have regarded as decisive for his deep appreciation of the numinous. These offer a vivid account of what he means by "numinous experience." The first occurred on a visit to Mogador in 1911, some six years before the publication of *Das Heilige*. His account is dated simply "On the Sabbath":

> It is Sabbath, and already in the dark, incredibly filthy vestibule we hear the "blessings" of the prayers and the scripture readings, those half-sung, half-spoken nasal chants that the synagogue bequeathed to both the church and the mosque. The sound is quite pleasant, and it is soon possible to distinguish certain, regular modulations and cadences, which follow one another like leitmotifs. At first the ear tries to separate and understand the words in vain, and soon one wants to quit trying. Then suddenly the tangle of voices resolves itself and . . . a solemn fear overcomes one's limbs. It begins in unison, clear and unmistakable:
>
> Qādôš qādôš qādôš 'ĕlōhîm ădoňāy ṣebāôt
>
> Māle'û haššāmayim wehāāreṣ kebôdô![3]
>
> I have heard the *Sanctus, sanctus, sanctus* of the cardinals in Saint Peters, the *Swiat, swiat, swiat* in the cathedral in the Kremlin, and the *Hagios, hagios, hagios* of the patriarch in Jerusalem. In whatever language these words are spoken, the most sublime words that human lips have ever uttered, they always seize on in the deepest ground of the soul, arousing and stirring with a mighty shudder the mystery of the other-worldly that sleeps therein. That happens here more than anywhere else, here in this deserted place, where they resound in the language in which Isaiah first heard them and on the lips of this people whose heritage they initially were.
>
> (Alles 1996: 80–1)

Here we find the religious shudder and the strong emotional response that Otto will later analyze in *Das Heilige*. This memorable experience must at the minimum have contributed importantly to the experiential ground for writing about the numinous with personal conviction. For the authorship of his remarkable book, the gift of intellectual creativity and courage had to play a major role.

The second such impressive numinous experience occurred some eleven years after *Das Heilige* appeared in print and added further confirmation to what Otto had been writing about for the past decade and more. This he recounted in a letter dated 4 January 1928 and postmarked Bombay:

> From our balcony we can see the wonderful Bombay Harbor. Right nearby sits the proud "Gateway of India", and left of that we see the mountainous island of Elephanta. We went there three days ago.

Visitors climb halfway up the mountain on magnificent stone steps, until on the right side a broad door opens in the volcanic rock. It leads into one of the biggest cave-temples of ancient India. Heavy pillars, carved from the rock, bear the roof. Slowly, one's eyes become accustomed to the dim light; then they can make out marvelous representations from Indian mythology carved on the walls. Eventually one's eyes find their way to the massive, main niche. Here towers an image of the deity that I can only compare with certain works of Japanese sculpture and the great images of Christ in old Byzantine churches: a three-headed form, depicted from the chest up, growing out of the rock, three times the size of a human being. To get the full effect, one must sit down. The middle head looks straight ahead, silent and powerful; the other two heads are shown in profile. The stillness and the majesty of the image is complete. It portrays Śiva as the creator, the preserver, and the destroyer of the world, and at the same time as the savior and bestower of blessings. Nowhere have I seen the mystery of the transcendent expressed with more grandeur or fullness than in these three heads . . . To see this place would truly be worth a trip to India in itself, and from the spirit of the religion that lived here one can learn more in an hour of viewing than from all the books ever written.

(Alles 1996: 94–5)

These deeply moving experiences of religious objects not his own (the one Jewish and the other Hindu) contributed to Otto's conviction that all religions are founded upon such strong impressions of "the Holy." The spiritual ground beneath the temples and the cathedrals of all religions, supporting their rites and rituals and their Sacred Scriptures, is made of numinous experiences, and is therefore psychological. For Otto, this forms the universal, foundational bedrock of all world religions: "From the very beginning religion is experience of the Mysterium, of what breaks forth from the depths of our life of feeling . . . as the feeling of the supersensual" (Alles 1996: 52, n. 44). Otto's grounding of religion in the experience of the Mysterium was fully compatible with Jung's view: "The idea of God originated with the experience of the numinosum. It was a psychical experience, with moments when man felt overcome. Rudolf Otto has designated this moment in his Psychology of Religion as the numinosum, which is derived from the Latin *numen*, meaning hint, or sign" (Jung 1988: 1038).

As a student of world religions, Otto could see the universality of humankind's experience of the *numinosum* and of numinous objects. Since time immemorial, humans have noted the "feeling of the supersensual" that Otto refers to in his definition. This is the experiential basis of religions, high and low, near and far. All are on an equal footing in this respect. In this sense, Otto was an apologist for religion as such, not specifically for his own tradition, Christianity (see Alles 2001). Appreciating the value of religious experience universally freed him from the narrow confines of his orthodox Lutheranism, and as a result he entered energetically and enthusiastically into dialogue with members of other religious communities, founded a "Religious League of Humanity," and proposed a parliament of world religions to be "made up of official representatives of the various religions" (Alles 1996: 147). For his liberal attitude he paid a high price at home in his German university at Marburg, where he received harsh and even abusive criticism and ridicule from the neo-orthodox Christian students and a variety of other theologians,[4] notably from his arch rival Rudolf Bultmann (see Alles 1996: 4).

While Otto considered all religions to share a common basis in the experience of the *numinosum*, he did retain the view that the Christian tradition offers the highest form of spirituality attained to date by humankind. This was not an unusual position for an identified Christian theologian to take in his time, although today it seems quite provincial and is certainly no longer "politically correct" in liberal religious circles. Nevertheless it is instructive to see how Otto argued in favor of this view, as in the following passage from *The Idea of the Holy* that also, curiously enough, anticipates by some thirty-five years some features of Jung's interpretation of the Bible in "Answer to Job":

> For what makes Christ in a special sense the summary and climax of the course of antecedent religious evolution is pre-eminently this – that in His life, suffering, and death is repeated in classic and absolute form that most mystical of all the problems of the Old Covenant, the problem of *the guiltless suffering of the righteous*, which re-echoes again and again so mysteriously from Jeremiah and deutero-Isaiah on through Job and the Psalms. The 38th chapter of Job is a prophecy of Golgotha. And on Golgotha the solution of the problem, already adumbrated in Job, is repeated and surpassed. It lay, as we say, entirely in the non-rational aspect of deity, and yet was none the less a solution. In Job the suffering of the righteous found its significance as the classic and crucial case of the revelation, more immediately actual and in more palpable proximity than any other, of the transcendent mysteriousness and "beyondness" of God. The cross of Christ, that monogram of the eternal mystery, is its completion. Here rational are enfolded with non-rational elements, the revealed commingled with the unrevealed, the most exalted love with the most awe-inspiring "wrath" of the numen, and therefore, in applying to the Cross of Christ the category "holy", Christian religious feeling has given birth to a religious intuition profounder and more vital than any to be found in the whole history of religion.
>
> (Otto 1917: 172–3)

Here we see how Otto used his idea of the numinous and the irrational to explicate the symbolic heart of Christianity.

JUNG AND OTTO

Jung did not share in this type of ranking of religious symbols or consider the Christian one to be the "highest," although he did find in the cross a profound symbol for the central burden of individuation, i.e., holding and suffering the tension of the opposites. Jung's concern with healing and with the psychological process of individuation was entirely other than Otto's primary focus, which was exclusively centered on the religious aspects of life and on worship of the Holy. Otto was only minimally involved in psychological healing and treatment, and the notion of psychological individuation did not play a part in his thinking. His primary interest lay in describing and analyzing the encounter with the numinous. Jung, on the other hand, personally engaged the "God within" in a wholly psychological manner, and while he related to the *imago Dei* with the same passion and feeling for its mystery and awesome emotional power as did Otto, he related to it psychologically and not worshipfully, and with the caution befitting the psychotherapist. The passion for the spiritual, like all passions, can easily tip over into pathos and extreme alienation of other parts of the Self, as we see so well today among religious fundamentalists and fanatics. The goal of individuation, unlike that of the religious quest, is not union with the divine or salvation but rather integration and wholeness, the forging of the opposites inherent in the Self into an image of unity and integrating this into consciousness.

It is regrettable, however, that Jung did not have personal contact with Otto to carry on this type of discussion. From the early 1930s onward, Jung made extensive use of Otto's terminology to refer to a variety of psychological phenomena, mostly those having to do with manifestations of the archetypal images of the collective unconscious. The potential for fruitful dialogue would have been great, partly because the two men shared a common cultural and philosophical background (unlike the insurmountable differences in this respect between Jung and Fr Victor White, the Dominican expert on Thomist theology, with whom he did have extensive discussions between 1945 and 1955 – see Stein 2005c, also Lammers 1994), partly because they both had a deep and abiding interest in world religions and mystical traditions (see Otto's *Mysticism East and West* (1962) and Jung's *Psychology and Religion: West and East* (1958)), and above all because they both attended to experience rather than to doctrine or "faith" as the primary object of inquiry. Their paths nearly crossed in Ascona, Switzerland around the founding of the Eranos *Tagungen* in 1932–3, which were dedicated to the dialogue between East and West and featured world-class scholars from around the world. Unfortunately, Otto was too ill by that time to participate in the first meetings of this circle of intellectuals, but the name Eranos was the result of his suggestion to the founder, Olga Froebe-Kapteyn (see Hakl 2001: 92–9). Jung attended and lectured at Eranos regularly throughout the 1930s and 40s. Otto and Jung also shared a close acquaintance with the Sinologist Richard Wilhelm, whom Otto visited in China and with whom Jung collaborated extensively (see Stein 2005b), and with the Indologist Wilhelm Hauer, with whom both men broke off relations, in Otto's case on account of Hauer's negative views on Christianity (see Alles 2002) and in Jung's because of Hauer's extreme pro-German and Aryan political views (see Shamdasani 1996: xlii).

With his book *Das Heilige* and the use of the term "numinous" to describe the nature of religious experience, Otto introduced a major psychological dimension into the scientific study of religion, even though this may not have been his primary motive (see Alles 2001). Jung, on the other hand, picked up on Otto's terminology to highlight what he already knew to be the important religious dimension of the psyche and of aspects of psychotherapeutic and developmental processes. There is much overlapping of views in their published writings with respect to the nature of numinous experience, even though their fundamental points of reference are quite different. Otto would certainly have objected to Jung's broad use of the term numinous to cover a wide range of psychological experience, while he himself limited it exclusively to the religious.

Jung, for his part, borrowed and transformed Otto's terminology for his own purposes. By the time he began to use the word numinous in the 1930s, *Das Heilige*, published in 1917, was already a classic and Jung was well advanced in his psychological theorizing. Jung effortlessly equated numinous experience with the manifestation of unconscious contents, the personal complexes as well as impersonal archetypal images. Here is Jung speaking in a lecture delivered in Zurich at the Swiss Federal Institute of Technology (ETH) on 5 May 1934 and repeated shortly thereafter at Bad Nauheim, Germany, at the Seventh Congress for Psychotherapy:

It will no doubt be remembered what a storm of indignation was unleashed on all sides when Freud's works became generally known. This violent reaction of public complexes drove Freud into an isolation which has brought the charge of dogmatism upon him and his school. All psychological theoreticians in this field run the same risk, for they are playing with something that directly affects all that is uncontrolled in man – the *numinosum*, to use an apt expression of Rudolf Otto's. Where the realm of complexes begins the freedom of the ego comes to an end, for complexes are psychic agencies whose deepest nature is still unfathomed. Every time the researcher succeeds in advancing a little further towards the psychic *tremendum*, then, as before, reactions are let loose in the public . . .

(Jung 1934: para. 216)

We see from this passage that for Jung "the *numinosum*" and "the psychic *tremendum*" – terms drawn straight out of Otto's work – translated into contents of the unconscious without further specification as to their nature or quality. For Otto, the theologian, these terms were reserved for religious experiences whose ultimate object would be considered metaphysical (i.e., the Divine), a transcendent reality mediated to people through religious symbols such as icons, statues, rituals, or sounds that related to acts of worship. For Jung, the psychologist, on the other hand, the object of a numinous experience was a content of the unconscious psyche that needed to be made conscious.

Jung nevertheless shared with Otto the "religious musicality" (Max Weber's term) to resonate to the numinous in the presence of religious symbols and ideas. Otto wrote that this sensibility couldn't be taught, it must be evoked (Otto 1917: 7). As with the appreciation and creation of art, some people have a genius for it while others have less, little, or no talent in this area (ibid.: 177). Jung had this gift to an extraordinary degree. His accounts of firsthand numinous experiences appear in several of his writings – *Memories, Dreams, Reflections* (1963), "Septem Sermones ad Mortuos" (1916b) and above all in the famous *Red Book* (forthcoming). These writings demonstrate that Jung's receptivity to numinous experience was profound and extensive. For this reason, he has been recognized by many as a true *Homo religiōsus*. It should be noted that Jung's accounts include purely "inner experiences," such as dreams and visions, as well as the more extroverted type that Otto describes in the letters quoted above.

NUMINOUS EXPERIENCES AND INDIVIDUATION: HINTS AND SIGNALS FOR INTEGRATION

For Jung personally these numinous experiences were of critical importance, as he states in the letter to P.W. Martin cited above. In the late work, *Memories, Dreams, Reflections*, he is referring to them when he writes: "The years when I was pursuing my inner images were the most important in my life – in them everything essential was decided" (Jung 1963: 199). This is a reference to the "Red Book" period, 1913–28, when he made his closest approach to the numinous. And then he makes the telling comment: "It was the *prima materia* for a lifetime's work" (ibid.). In other words, the attainment to numinous experiences, while significant in itself, was not of final import; rather, it provided the essential ingredients for further stages of the individuation *opus*. These experiences were something to work on. They offered the material out of which he could wrest his psychological theory and forge his final identity: "Out of it [i.e., the concluding numinous dream in a long series, the famous Liverpool dream] emerged a first inkling of my personal myth," and "That [i.e., the whole series of numinous images and experiences] was the primal stuff . . . and my works are a more or less successful endeavor to incorporate this incandescent matter into the contemporary picture of the world" (ibid.). This, in brief, is a thumbnail sketch of the psychological *opus* of individuation. It is an operation of sublimation, which raises the spiritual to the level of the psychological and renders numinous experience practical and useful. They become integrated into psychological functioning and assimilated into the contemporary world.

The psychological explanation for numinous experiences like those Otto reports lies in the phenomenon of projection, whereby unconscious contents are "found" in the physical objects, rituals, or sounds that elicit them. In religious experience, the psychologist claims, the ego is experiencing a content of the unconscious in projection. The stronger the experience, the more archetypal is the content. Such experiences link consciousness to the unconscious and offer "hints" that may be deciphered as communications. These hints can lead to a deeper perspective on life from the viewpoint of the collective unconscious and are essential for the psychological process of individuation if they can be brought forward and made conscious. This transformation from one state (the spiritual) to another (the psychological) falls under the name of a process called sublimation. To cite von Franz: "[Sublimation] comes from alchemy. Freud took it out of alchemy, out of chemistry. For example, when you boil water, it becomes steam. Steam is sublimated water. It is another aggregate state. Chemically, steam is not different from water. But qualitatively it manifests itself in another way. It has a higher potential. In steam, the water molecules are more alive; they whirl more about and therefore give the impression of steam instead of water" (von Franz 2004: 167). Sublimated, the archetypal images become woven into the fabric of a person's conscious identity. They become integrated. Thus, as sublimated spirit and transcendence, they offer healing. They release a person from the limitations of the purely immediate and time-bound framework of the ego and thereby contribute essentially to the formation of what Jung termed "the transcendent function" (1916c), a psychological structure of identity made up of personal and archetypal elements (see Stein 2005a).

"It is altogether amazing how little most people reflect on numinous objects and attempt to come to terms with them," Jung exclaims in his famous theological outburst, *Answer to Job*, "and how laborious such an undertaking is once we have embarked upon it. The numinosity of the object makes it difficult to handle intellectually, since our affectivity is always involved" (Jung 1954: para. 735). Sublimation and integration of this type is a difficult task but absolutely essential to the *opus* of individuation.

One must take care in discussions like this one to observe Jung's often repeated definition of "the unconscious" as: "the unknown." Otherwise a radical type of reductionism becomes inevitable. To say: "Religion is based on 'nothing but' projected unconscious contents (i.e., the numinous experiences of the *Mysterium*)" could be taken to reduce the study of theology and religion to a sub-department of psychology where the business would be to demonstrate how personal conflicts, etc. generate religious defenses and pseudo-solutions to life's problems. Some schools of psychology would doubtless applaud this demotion of the religious to the psychological. Not so with Jung and Analytical Psychology, however. In this approach, the psychological embraces (i.e., takes up, integrates) the religious in such a way that its spiritual value is not damaged or reduced. It is sublimated. In fact, the spiritual becomes confirmed and amplified through the psychological. Psyche is not seen as limited to brain chemistry, early childhood, or learning potentials. It is rather an ultimate term with an infinite horizon, which does not in principle exclude the metaphysical grounding of unconscious contents. Unconscious contents are all those factors of the world that lie beyond the ego's awareness and control, either because they have been repressed (as the result of conflict between incompatible images or ideas) or because they have not yet become fully conscious (everything else that has not yet been psychized, or sublimated, and integrated). To say that the object symbolized by religious experience is a content of the unconscious does not rule out its possible metaphysical standing. It only states a limit on human knowledge. This is therefore a statement of epistemological caution on the scientist's part, but not a claim that religious symbols and numinous objects have no further ontological basis. The metaphysical cannot be established or disconfirmed by scientific methods. It must remain hypothetical.

The "hints" Jung speaks of repeatedly in reference to numinous experiences may be taken as similar to what the sociologist and student of modernity, Peter Berger, has in mind with his phrase, "signal of transcendence": "To speak of a signal of transcendence is neither to deny nor to idealize the often harsh empirical facts that make up our lives in the world. It is rather to try for a glimpse of the grace that is to be found 'in, with, and under' the empirical reality of our lives" (Berger 1977: 212). Berger speaks from the perspective of faith, however, while Jung holds to the neutral, observational position of the psychologist.

SHADOWS OF THE *NUMEN*

In several passages in *The Idea of the Holy*, Otto acknowledges the dark side of the *numinosum*, which is the source of the "shudder" and "dread" found in accounts of religious experience worldwide (see for instance Otto 1917: 15–19). Jung, as a psychiatrist, was understandably highly sensitive to the destructive power of the unconscious and also aware of the negative potential fallout from numinous experience at many levels. Archetypes can profoundly disturb consciousness (see Jung's essay on Brother Klaus (1933) for an example of near-psychotic proportions), as important as the experience of them may be for linking the ego to the transpersonal reality of the Self.

In *Memories, Dreams, Reflections* (1963), Jung comments on the distorting effect that numinous ideas and images can have on cognition. In one remarkable passage, where he is offering an account of his encounter with Freud during the early years of his career as an analyst, he writes:

> Wherever the psyche is set violently oscillating by a numinous experience, there is a danger that the thread by which one hangs may be torn. Should that happen, one man tumbles into an absolute affirmation, another into an equally absolute negation . . . The pendulum of the mind oscillates between sense and nonsense, not between right and wrong. The numinosum is dangerous because it lures men to extremes, so that a modest truth is regarded as the truth and a minor mistake is equated with fatal error.
>
> (Jung 1963: 151)

Jung observed that Freud was in the grip of a numinous power, sexuality: "My conversation with Freud had shown me that he feared that the numinous light of his sexual insights might be extinguished by a 'black tide of mud.' Thus a mythological situation had arisen: the struggle between light and darkness. That explains its numinosity, and why Freud immediately fell back on his dogma as a religious means of defense" (ibid.). Jung concludes that the numinosity of sexuality had distorted Freud's normally incisive thinking capacities. Numinous contents of the unconscious pull thinking magnetically into an orbit where it becomes merely ingenious rationalization, as brilliant as it may be. This is what one commonly finds in people who are absolutely convinced of a religious teaching. Filled with faith and belief, their thinking is clouded by an archetypal image of massive but largely unconscious proportions, which lends its related privileged ideas a sort of triumphant, dogmatic certainty. One step further and one finds the martyr, whose identification with the archetypal image is so extreme that life itself loses priority. Needless to say, this is the exact contrary of the individuation project, which is to make the numinous content as conscious as possible, to sublimate and integrate it, and to bring it into relation with other quite different aspects of the Self, thereby relativizing it.

Jung applied this same critique to national politics in his 1936 paper on Wotan, where he offers a psychological analysis of the distorting power of numinous images in the churned up political and social processes tearing apart the cultural fabric of Germany and central Europe at that time. In this instance, he observed, the numinosity of the newly constellated old Germanic god, Wotan, had mesmerized an entire nation and was driving Germany to an (at that time) unknown and irrationally determined goal. Archetypal possession in a collective invests certain ideas and policies with defensive certainty and denies the legitimacy and standing of doubt. Contrary thoughts and images are savagely repressed. This was the case with German collective psychology at the time. There was no space for reflection, for questioning, for serious debate, never mind contrary views. Conviction based on archetypal backing seemingly cuts off circulation to the neo-cortex and fires the emotions. The old reptilian and limbic brains take over and rule.[5]

When the curtain came down on the final scene of "The Third Reich" and the theater in which it played lay in ruins, there remained little appetite for myth and symbol in the land. (The same was true for Japan, where the cultural myth of the divine Emperor was shattered by the military defeat and occupation.) There had been too much of the numinous afoot in the collective psyche, and it had contributed to the devastation. Numinosity was cancelled as a cultural option, and irony and rationality took charge of the culture. While defensive, this also represented a return to sanity. The result, however, has been a resolutely militant "modernity" that harshly rejects the need for meaning, which requires some sort of transcendent reference and relation to the numinous. In this seared cultural context, it became almost impossible to look upon the mythic without grave suspicion and bitter memory. Understandably enough, once badly burned, twice shy.

This wariness about the grand enthusiasms generated by religion, ideology, or mythopoetic hermeneutics has also introduced an uneasy suspicion of Jung's psychology and classical Jungian perspectives on dream interpretation and the hermeneutical methods of amplification and active imagination. These enter too deeply for comfort into the taboo territory of myth and symbol. What is lost thereby is the realization that the numinous experience offers a "hint:" that human life has a link to transcendence and that the individual is a "soul" with potential to come into relation with the spiritual in a wholly natural way that does not tip over into madness. In contemporary German art, this has begun to come to the fore again in the boldly symbolic paintings of Anselm Kiefer and in the later films of Wim Wenders, where hints and signals of transcendence shine through the fabric of everyday life.

THE INDIVIDUATION HERO(INE)

The psychological journey of individuation traverses the realm of the *numinosum*, where the hero(ine) listens intently to the "hints" offered in such experiences, but then its path *leads out of it* again. This journey does not find its final resting place in "the Holy" or its sanctuary. It is not, therefore, tantamount to a mystic journey, which prizes the experience of union with God or the vision of the *Mysterium tremendum* as the apex. Individuation does not culminate in an act of worship. Nor is it identical with the resolute *via negativa* of Zen. It has elements of both – experiencing the numinous and cleansing the mirror of consciousness – but it includes these as two movements within a greater *opus*. For the spiritual hero(ine), all else is a falling away from this high point. For the individuation hero(ine), on the other hand, the numinous experiences are "prima materia" for the *opus* of individuation, which goes on indefinitely. To remain or "get stuck" in the land of the *numen*, whether defined as full or empty, would amount to becoming assimilated to the unconscious (Jung 1935: paras. 221ff.), which means a pathological state of grandiose inflation, loss of ego boundaries and integrity, and possibly even entrapment in a paranoid psychotic defense. Such "states of possession" are generally destructive for individuals and to groups.

For the psychological process of individuation, however, the attainments to the numinous experiences, if sublimated and integrated by consciousness, are major milestones and often constitute sharp turning points on the journey. Most importantly, they go into the creation of the "transcendent function." The individuation task is to make them conscious and to bring them into relation with other aspects of the Self, and thereby to attain approximate wholeness.

To conclude, we can say that the psychological hero(ine) works to shed the personal identifications and complexes without succumbing to the seductive lure of archetypal ones. A personality can be suffused with experiences and knowledge of the numinous, but not be possessed by it or rely on it for defensive purposes. The psychological hero(ine) may achieve a measure of freedom from the complexes and the gods and also a hint of transcendent identity. Yet there remains a healthy measure of respect for all the powers, for it would be absurd to believe that one can be delivered from them altogether.

Notes

1 From **nūmen** -inis, n. (nuo), a nodding with the head, a nod. As an expression of will, command, consent. Of a deity, the divine will, divine command. Hence, the might of a deity, majesty, divinity. *Cassell's New Latin Dictionary*.

2 "Quelques Faits d'imagination créatrice subconsciente," *Archives de psychologie* (Geneva), V (1906): 36–51.

3 "Holy, holy, holy Lord God of hosts; heaven and earth are full of your glory" – a liturgical adaptation of Isaiah 6.3: "Holy, holy, holy is the Lord of hosts; the whole earth is full of his glory."

4 Alles (1996: 4) cites Paul Tillich's recollections: "During the three semesters of my teaching [in Marburg 1924–5] I met the first radical effects of the neo-orthodox

theology on theological students: cultural problems were excluded from theological thought; theologians like Schleiermacher, Harnack, Troeltsch, Otto, were
contemptuously rejected; social and political ideas were banned from theological
discussions."
5 Jung's archetypal analysis of Germany in the 1930s does not valorize or in any
way justify the social and political situation, as some have claimed. To say "a god
(e.g., Wotan) is behind it" does not make it good or noble. It only says that it is
unconsciously driven and controlled: Consciousness is not in charge here!

References

Alcoholics Anonymous (1976) *Alcoholics Anonymous*, 3rd edn, New York: Alco-
holics Anonymous World Services.
Alles, G. (ed.) (1996) *Rudolf Otto: Autobiographical and Social Essays*, Berlin and
New York: Mouton de Gruyter.
Alles, G. (2001) "Toward a Genealogy of the Holy: Rudolf Otto and the Apolo-
getics of Religion," *Journal of the American Academy of Religion*, 69(2): 323–42.
Alles, G. (2002) "The Science of Religions in a Fascist State: Rudolf Otto and Jacob
Wilhelm Hauer during the Third Reich," *Religion*, 32: 177–204.
Berger, P. (1977) "New York City 1976: A Signal of Transcendence," *Facing Up to
Modernity: Excursion in Society, Politics, and Religion*, New York: Basic Books.
Hakl, H. (2001) *Der verborgene Geist von Eranos: Unbekannte Begegnungen von
Wissenschaft und Esoterik*, Bretten: Scienta Nova, Verlag neue Wissenschaft.
Jung, C.G. (1912) *Wandlungen und Symbole der Libido* (1916a) trans. Beatrice M.
Hinkle as *Psychology of the Unconscious*, New York: Dodd, Mead and Co.
Jung, C.G. (1916b) "Septem Sermones ad Mortuos," in *Memories, Dreams, Reflec-
tions* (1963), New York: Vintage Books.
Jung, C.G. (1916c) "The Transcendent Function," *CW* 8, Princeton, NJ: Princeton
University Press.
Jung, C.G. (1933) "Brother Klaus," *CW* 11.
Jung, C.G. (1934) "A Review of the Complex Theory," *CW* 8.
Jung, C.G. (1935) *The Relations between the Ego and the Unconscious*, *CW* 7.
Jung, C.G. (1936) "Wotan," *CW* 10.
Jung, C.G. (1937) *Psychology and Religion*, *CW* 11.
Jung, C.G. (1954) "Answer to Job", *CW* 11.
Jung, C.G. (1958) *Psychology and Religion: West and East*, *CW* 11.
Jung, C.G. (1963) *Memories, Dreams, Reflections*, New York: Vintage Books.
Jung, C.G. (1973) *C.G. Jung Letters*, selected and ed. Gerhard Adler with Aniela
Jaffé, 2 vols., Princeton, NJ: Princeton University Press.
Jung, C.G. (1988) *Nietzsche's Zarathustra: Notes of the Seminar Given in 1934–1939*,
ed. James Jarrett, Princeton, NJ: Princeton University Press.
Jung, C.G. (forthcoming) *The Red Book*, ed. Sonu Shamdasani.
Lammers, A. (1994) *In God's Shadow: The Collaboration of Victor White and C.G.
Jung*, New York: Paulist Press.
Otto, R. (1917) *Das Heilige*, trans. John W. Harvey (1923; 2nd ed., 1950), *The Idea
of the Holy*, Oxford: Oxford University Press.
Otto, R. (1962) *Mysticism East and West: A Comparative Analysis of the Nature of
Mysticism*, New York: Collier Books.

Shamdasani, S. (1996) "Introduction," *The Psychology of Kundalini Yoga: Notes of the Seminar Given in 1932 by C.G. Jung*, Princeton, NJ: Princeton University Press.

Stein, M. (2005a) "The Work of Individuation," *Journal of Jungian Theory and Practice*, 7, 2.

Stein, M. (2005b) "Some Reflections on the Influence of Chinese Thought on Jung and his Psychological Theory," *The Journal of Analytical Psychology*, 50(2): 209–22.

Stein, M. (2005c) "The Role of Victor White in C.G. Jung's Writings," The Guild of Pastoral Psychology, Guild Lecture No. 285.

Von Franz, M.-L. (2004) "Conversations on *Aion*" (with Claude Drey), in B. Hannah and M.-L. von Franz, *Lectures on Jung's Aion*, Wilmette, IL: Chiron Publications.

Chapter 4

Varieties of numinous experience: the experience of the sacred in the therapeutic process

Lionel Corbett

> We may be outraged at the idea of an inexplicable mood, a nervous disorder, or an uncontrollable vice being, so to speak, a manifestation of God.
>
> (C.G. Jung 1935/1966: 238)

Introduction

During a period of despair, a man had the following waking vision:

> The vision that came to me felt unlike any daydream. I was seeing as if my eyes had been turned backwards and I was looking at something taking place within me. A huge thick curtain slowly came down and surrounded the back walls of a large space in my mind. I was lifted up and stood on a high mountain peak with large rock outcroppings. I could not see over the edge. The space was at once open and contained. The mountain was ancient and felt volcanic. Surrounding me, sitting among the rocks, were the shadowy forms of the hosts of heaven. I knew they had gathered there in order to meet me. They seemed to be expecting me and to delight in my presence. A soft, white glow radiated around me and I felt a deep warmth and sense of belonging . . . for that moment in time, I was heaven's agenda.

I hardly need to mention the restorative effect of this vision. But what is the clinician to make of such an experience when it is brought into the consulting room? In this chapter, I will make a case for my own belief that such numinous experience is an authentic experience of the sacred.[1]

Initially the onus is often on the clinician to recognize the nature of numinous experience, since the patient is often bewildered or simply unsure of its significance. This is especially so when the experience does not take a traditional Judeo-Christian form. We therefore need some kind of criteria for recognizing the presence of the numinosum, such as those of Otto (1958). The experience is mysterious, tremendous, and fascinating. The important factor is the affective quality of the experience rather than its specific content. In its grip, we feel we are facing something quite outside our usual experience, something awesome, uncanny. Sometimes the event is dreadful or terrifying, at other times profoundly peaceful or joyful. Often the experience inspires worship, or a sense of atonement or blessing. It may produce a religious conversion, or simply awaken a spiritual disposition in the soul that has so far remained dormant – an important factor if we take seriously Jung's notion that the development of a religious attitude (not necessarily based on a creed) is vital in the second part of life.

William James (1958: 292–3) noted four characteristics of such experiences. 1. They are ineffable – they defy expression in ordinary conceptual language. Unless one has experienced something like it, one is incompetent to understand such experience. 2. They have a noetic or cognitive aspect, in that they produce an overwhelming sense of understanding or clarity; we know something we did not know before, such as the unity nature of reality or its ground of love. This knowledge carries with it an extraordinary sense of authority, so that the experience is self-authenticating. 3. The experience is transient, usually less than half an hour and rarely more than a few hours, at which point everyday consensual reality supervenes. 4. Whether such experience is induced or spontaneous, during the experience one is passive; one's own will is in abeyance, in the grip of a superior power.

Important to the psychotherapeutic context is the fact that contact with the numinosum may have a healing effect (Jung 1973: 377). In what follows, I would like to describe a variety of manifestations of the numinosum, point out the ways in which they are healing, and discuss the relationship of such experience to psychopathology and character structure. Finally, I will indicate some of their effects on the therapeutic relationship.

VARIETIES OF NUMINOUS EXPERIENCE

Numinous experience occurs through a variety of channels, perhaps related to innate factors such as temperament, or to the various ways we may experience the unconscious based on our typology. In this chapter I will describe manifestations of the numinosum within dreams and visions, in the body, in nature, within the individual's psychopathology, and induced by means of entheogens. Hardy (1997) offers a much more elaborate classification of a large number of numinous experiences. Regardless of the subject's personal religious and cultural background, numinous manifestations may contain imagery from any religious tradition, and often their content is entirely novel. However, they are always specifically tailored to the psychology of the individual, which makes numinous experience relevant to psychotherapeutic practice rather than solely the province of professional theologians.

THE NUMINOSUM IN DREAMS

The classical Jungian literature is replete with examples of numinous dreams, but these tend to be demonstrations of the positive aspects of the numinosum. However, the numinosum may also appear in a terrifying manner, often depicting the archetypal core of a complex, or clearly linked to the dreamer's psychopathology, as the following dream illustrates:

> I'm in a maze of stairs, doors and ramps, something like an Escher drawing. I am running from the giant, severed head of my mother. Streaming from her head are tentacles that move like snakes and allow her to chase me. I perceive her as a monster. I am afraid of and disgusted by her, and I do not want her to touch me. She is laughing, as if it is silly that I am running from her because there is no way I will ever escape. To tease me, she occasionally catches up to me and touches me with a tentacle, just to let me know that I cannot outrun her. I run to a door and slam it behind me, shutting her out. But then I turn to see that there are only more ramps, stairs, and doors, to which she has as much access as I do. I am crying in frustration. She laughs.

Here the numinosum appears as the Gorgon or terrible Mother. Equally as darkly numinous is the following dream of a young man:

> I am tied to the stake at the base of a high gilded throne, on which sits a huge woman with large teeth and long flowing hair. Blood flows like a river down the steps in front of her. This is a hazy, bloody scene. I cannot talk as my energy drains; another woman is sucking blood from my neck and arm. I'm terrified, but too weak and helpless to do anything.

This dream combines the mythology of the vampire with a Kali-like[2] image. This kind of imagery led Jung to say that the experience of the archetype strikes at the core of one's being. Such dreams contribute to the individuation process, but can hardly be said to have a visible healing effect. Yet numinous dreams clearly may do so, as the following demonstrates.

A woman lost her 21-year-old son in a drowning accident, suddenly and unexpectedly. This tragedy almost destroyed her mental and physical well-being. She was filled with pain, anguish, and guilt. Although deeply religious, she could find no solace in her tradition. Nevertheless, she would pray to ask where her son was. She believes that her prayer was answered in the following dream, in which she felt as if she were fully awake:

> A magnificent panoramic view appeared before me. There was no sun, only a soft twilight glow in the atmosphere. As I looked from left to right, I saw hundreds of people of all ages settled in small groups. I felt that this must be the place where my son was located. I searched through the crowd but could not find him. I began to panic, and called out to him "Michael, Michael, where are you?" Suddenly, out of nowhere came a three-year-old child on a tricycle laughing out loud and riding in and out of the crowds. As he came nearer, I saw that he was Michael as he was during his childhood. My fear quickly turned to joy and thanksgiving.

As a result of this dream, she was convinced that life continues on another plane of existence. From that moment, her pain, guilt, and her death anxiety were greatly alleviated. This is obviously not the kind of dream that needs much analysis if we take it at face value. It could of course be reduced to a defensive operation in the face of intolerable grief, or simply seen as the emergence of a joyful, young aspect of the dreamer. However, like all numinous encounters, this type of dream carries a sense of such authority and authenticity that I am convinced that it is a message or statement rather than a defense. I hear such dreams not uncommonly after a death has occurred, and I suspect they are fairly frequent but rarely discussed, except in the privacy of a therapeutic situation. I realize that, should they be defensive, I may be colluding, unable to tolerate the patient's pain. In practice, I find no need to maintain an artificial professional persona that insists on a quasi-scientific skepticism or a hermeneutic of suspicion. Rather, one has to rely on one's human response in such a situation and not fall back on metapsychology, a belief system that is often as meta-physical as one's commitment to spiritual realities. In fact, a spiritual commitment may be solidly based on personal experience, whereas meta-psychological concepts are often based simply on hearsay. Our theories are based on abstract thought, but authentic mystical experience reveals the deep structures of reality. The very fact that numinous experience is considered to be rare, or is rarely spoken of in polite conversation, illustrates the distance between that reality and the western ego.

THE NUMINOSUM IN VISIONARY EXPERIENCES

Many psychotherapists and psychoanalysts, steeped in the tradition of western science, equate visionary experience with some kind of pathology, either organic or psychogenic. The materialistic assumption underlying this tradition is that there cannot be any such thing as an authentic spiritual experience, because reality is only physical. In this view, metaphysical in its own right, a visionary experience must have a physical or psychological explanation; it cannot be an authentic experience of another realm of being.[3] Because of this cultural bias, visionary experiences are the least likely to be brought into the consulting room. The patient is often afraid that he or she will be thought to be insane, using drugs, hysterical, or just endowed with too vivid an imagination. Accordingly we have no idea of the true incidence of visions. In an effort towards correcting this cultural bias, I would like to focus particularly on this type of numinous experience.

Prior to the following experience, a senior nursing administrator had just resigned her position as a result of "severe compassion fatigue" and a bitter power struggle with an unsupportive administrator. All her life she had been a caretaker, and was very identified with professional success. Wanting to be in a helping position, she now found herself in an adversarial role rather than being a voice for patient care. In colloquial terms, she was "burnt out," and painfully obsessed with her failure to meet her own high standards. Awake one night, ruminating about her career, feeling helpless and wondering what to do with her life, she had the following experience:

Suddenly I was aware of a pinpoint of light at the foot of the bed. I became alarmed as it expanded in size to about a six-inch oval, floating mysteriously in the dark. I was fearful and fascinated, awestruck by the weird presence of something other than me in my bedroom. I was sure I was not dreaming. The oval of light spoke wordlessly and identified itself as the Compassionate Heart (I thought of Jesus and Buddha). A loving presence filled the room and flooded me. The oval of light shot a beam of light directly to my heart. In that moment I saw myself with divinely compassionate eyes and was filled with a sense of forgiveness, unconditional love, and complete self-acceptance. I did not need to do anything, the silent voice instructed; I just needed to be as I was in this love-filled moment. My heart felt so expanded that I began to experience tremendous chest pain. I thought of calling for help but I was paralyzed. After this moment of true terror, I experienced such peace that I thought I had died. In that moment of surrender I saw the most loving moments of my life and the ones when I had constricted the impulse of love. I saw the moments when I had judged myself as lovable only because I had tried to live from a conscious standard of love and service. I surrendered to my death and remembered nothing more.

This vision initiated a process of self-discovery, during which she realized that her work had been largely a masochistic exercise. She realized how much she was the victim of a judgmental superego, and she became clearer about the childhood origins of her need to care for others instead of herself. This experience opened up an authentic capacity to love, not based on a professional persona. Eventually she left nursing and entered the ministry.

The following vision occurred to a woman who had been severely abused in childhood. She had suffered all her life from feeling alone, unloved and unable to love, only able to make a close connection to the family dog but not to people. Accordingly, she has an intense need for relationship, but this remains "the most elusive and difficult aspect of my life." During a particularly painful period:

A figure appeared dressed in a long, heavy, dark, brown-hooded robe, and stood on my pelvic bones facing me. I felt her presence and saw her clearly, although she was silent and virtually weightless as she stood on my body. My heart pounded and I was unable to move, but I did not feel afraid. I sensed her deep caring and her intention to help me. She leaned forward and with her index finger she touched the place between my breasts adjacent to my heart. As she did so, she drew up her finger and began to withdraw a heavy, rough cord from around my heart. I could feel the sensation of it unbinding my heart and felt an ease and relief as the weight and heaviness of the rope was drawn away. As she continued for many minutes, the heavy cord progressively diminished in size, becoming like coarse homespun, then a finer weave, finally emerging as a very thin, silver-white gossamer thread. As she withdrew the fiber, she was simultaneously weaving a cloth that fell to the floor and so covered a large, dark puddle that was beside me. This experience permeated me so deeply that I was profoundly touched, shaken, and moved.

She realized that the "heart" meant the ability to love and be loved, to live in relationship, and to feel a sense of belonging with others. A student of mythology, she associated the weaver with the figure of Clotho, the spinner of life in Greek mythology, one of the Fates who determined the course of human lives. Clotho opened her heart by progressively unbinding the protective barriers against love. The thread that had bound her heart was woven into a way to cross the murky waters of her chronic depression. The fact that this figure was weightless suggests that the whole experience occurred at the level of the subtle body rather than the physical body. The world's esoteric traditions all describe a spiritual body that cannot be seen with ordinary vision, presumably based on this kind of experience. Why therefore should we assume that this experience is merely allegorical? Here one could invoke the notion of the *imaginatio* or the *mundus imaginalis*, which, as Corbin (1972: 7) tells us, is ontologically as real as the world of the senses and the intellect. He also points out that the noetic and cognitive power of such perception – the information that it imparts – is as real as that of the five senses and the intellect.

One of the standard critiques of mysticism in general is that mystics tend to bring the particular theology of their tradition into their experiences. I suspect that this situation is more apparent than real; unorthodox or non-traditional manifestations of the numinosum are either dismissed as demonic, reported in a way that distorts the phenomenology of the experience,[4] or simply not reported at all, in order to avoid conflict with ecclesiastical authorities. Contemporary individuals who are committed to the Christian tradition may still experience the numinosum with a Christian content, but I have spoken with many Christians who experience highly unorthodox or even heretical manifestations of the numinosum. For this reason, religious establishments do not encourage mystical experience. It is not unusual, for instance, to dream of Jesus as a woman. The following experience, which begins with a traditional Christian content, ends in a way that furthers the subject's spirituality.

I awoke with an overwhelming sense of a presence in my home. There was also a vacuous, eerie silence. I sat up in bed. Suddenly a very quiet, low, rumbling tone began. A tiny white light appeared. As the tone's volume increased, so did the size of the light, becoming a ball that increased in circumference. The tone grew so loud I could hardly tolerate it. By this time the globe of light was about five feet in diameter, and difficult to look at because of its brightness. The light became a golden color, and upon it appeared a symbol I did not understand. From the center of the light I heard a voice say "Jesus" as the ball of light moved towards me, striking me with a force that gently rocked me. Then everything disappeared; the room became quiet and dark. Within a second, a second tone and dot of light appeared, which also grew in volume and brightness. Upon it was a different unknown symbol, and this time the voice said "Christ" as the light flew into me and dispersed.

> Following a brief moment of dark and silence, a third tone and dot of light appeared. The light grew as before, but when it flew into me it was silent. Finally, the room returned to normal, leaving me awestruck.

Intuitively, the subject realized that the third light represents that aspect of the divine that cannot be named or spoken of, taking him into a non-conceptual experience of Silence.

I occasionally hear of contemporary numinous experience that spontaneously repeats or affirms some of the world's most powerful spiritual imagery, which makes me suggest that some of our classical spiritual metaphors originally arose as visionary experiences. During an intensely lonely period of his life, the following happened to a 17-year-old boy with no knowledge of eastern spiritual traditions. He reported the vision to me thirty-five years later, when it was still clear; the memory was indelible.

> Out of the darkness, faintly at first then with increasing clarity, the thin strands of a web appeared. It seemed to be a huge spider's web stretching out over an unimaginable void. The silken threads reached out endlessly in all directions. There was no center to this web, or everywhere was the center. Wherever my eyes roamed, wherever my gaze settled – that was the center. The strands of the web, its warp and woof, seemed to be space and time themselves. Wherever they intersected, at every juncture, there was a single dewdrop. Each drop contained within itself a spark of Light. There was a great stillness, a pregnant expectancy. Suddenly, as if tapped into motion, the jeweled web exploded into a dazzling display of light. Each drop sparkled and flashed, piercing the darkness, every drop dancing with the colors of its own light and reflecting the dance of all the other drops. Waves of motion coursed throughout the breadth and depth of the web, each drop linked to every other through delicate strands, each drop responsive to every other, finally settling back into stillness.

Not until many years later did this man come across a description of Indra's Net, a metaphorical depiction of reality from the *Avatamsaka Sutra*, the Flower Garland Sutra of Buddhism, written around the first century CE. Here, instead of dew drops, at each connecting knot of the web lies a jewel in which can be seen the reflection of every other jewel – an image of the interdependent, mutually co-arising universe in which every part reflects the whole. What puzzled him was that Indra's net is not usually said to be in motion. Much later, he associated the movement with the idea of the Music of the Spheres, an archetype of Apollonian mysticism, of harmonic rhythms and relationships, which informs western consciousness and contemporary science. This vision seems to be a profound syzygy of eastern and western archetypal images of reality.

The following experience, reported to me by a middle-aged ministerial student, occurred when she was a young child, but remains fresh in her memory.

> I was walking on a beach with my family, on a misty day. I had trailed behind the others, and so was running to catch up with them. Suddenly a horrible thing happened. The whole world disappeared. There was a black, shining surface that was really a vast, immeasurable void, sort of like a transparent lens over nothingness, and a vast nothing above it. This vastness was horrible; it was alive and I could feel it, but it was not like a creature or being of any kind. As I opened my mouth to scream, nothing came out. I could not make a sound. I looked below my feet and saw that I was standing on nothing. I looked at my mother, walking ahead of me with her friend; they were suspended over "the nothing," but they did not seem to realize it. They did not realize that "the nothing" was the only thing there. I ran to the tent, sobbing. My mother was angry when I tried to tell her about it, and accused me of being silly. But I believed that if you did not know about "the nothing" you were safe, because then the illusion of all the solidness in the world would keep you from seeing the emptiness, the vast, deep void. Since I knew, I stayed in the tent.

Obviously, this experience could be explained away as the result of some kind of abandonment or separation terror. However, it happens to correspond perfectly to Buddhist notions of the Void, the ultimately empty nature of all phenomena.

Another "teaching" example is provided by the following, in which a vision follows a dream with the same theme. In the relevant part of the dream, which occurred during a period of loss and desolation, a woman meets the figure of Death. He is tall and black-robed, his face covered with a long veil. When she tries to run, he follows her, and she realizes that she must not panic or he will pursue her aggressively. She thinks of lifting his veil to look directly at his face and ask him what he wants of her, but she is too afraid to do so. In the next few months she was haunted by this dream image. She often attempted active imagination with the figure, but would receive no response. Then:

One night I awoke to a vision of veiled Death standing in the corner of my bedroom. I felt curiously calm and yet driven to know this figure more fully. In a strikingly autonomous active imagination, I approached Death to throw back his veil. As I did so, I was met with a blinding white light that receded just enough for me to make out the featureless face. Neither male nor female, Death was a shining, white-skinned fetus, unformed and yet formed, lacking any human particularity yet awesomely beautiful in its unborn potential. As I realized that Death was life ever poised between being and non-being, Death bent towards me gently and tenderly laid its cheek against mine – a gesture like a benediction. I was flooded with an overwhelming sensation of bliss and love. My heart and brow seemed to open and teem with an exquisite energy. The experience of being touched by this figure was profound . . . it had the potential to be any being, all beings or no being. The touch of its skin was the most amazing sensation, moist and malleable and positively teeming with life, as if I could feel its cells dividing, changing, and dancing beneath the surface.

The dreamer felt that this encounter was an "intimation of immortality." I suggested to her that the experience points to the fact that birth and death are, at a deep level, aspects of the same archetypal reality or process; she agreed that this might account for the tremendous feelings of both dread and longing that were evoked.

A numinous experience may tell us something we already know cognitively, but the information is given in a way that is so powerful one cannot resist its impact. The following happened to a woman who had experienced an extremely deprived childhood.

One night, when the moon was dark and my bedroom lay in inky blackness, I sensed a presence in the corner of the room. I was afraid. The presence grew and grew, until, pulsating, it filled the entire room, throbbing within the confining walls. The whole room seemed to tilt, as if accommodating itself to another dimension. I lay in terror, with my eyes tightly closed. A voice, deep and gentle, said to me: "Love. The whole thing is love." Slowly, the energy ebbed from the room, leaving me in paralyzed terror in the darkness.

She went on to say that there had been many occasions in her life when she wanted to give up, to be "small and hard and raging." But, she went on, the memory of that night "calls me back to life," and to the challenge of discovering what "love" might be. Obviously, to hear that "the whole thing is love" is not a new idea in the history of spirituality. However, that sounds like a useless platitude to a person whose character structure and developmental history do not allow love. But this intense experience opened the possibility for this individual.

THE NUMINOSUM IN NATURE

A further genre of numinous experience occurs to people who find the sacred within the natural world. Some traditional religionists were nature mystics, but today this sensibility is mostly found in the guise of political movements such as the environmentalists. What often drives them, however, is a profound feeling for the numinosity of nature, so that to desecrate the land is tantamount to sacrilege. One can recognize such individuals when they have this type of experience:

> Hurrying to a class at the university, because I was late I had to cross an expanse of lawn. As I ran across the grass, I had the most amazing and horrible experience. I could feel that each blade of grass had a life force, that the ground had a life force, that everything was bound together in this wonderful dance. I could feel my feet crushing the blades of grass, I could hear the crunch, I could feel the pain the grass felt. From this experience of expanded consciousness and oneness – which came totally unbidden and unexpected at that moment – I realized that I was something more than this pocket of flesh and mind, wondering and searching.

THE NUMINOSUM IN THE BODY

In the West, the body is a neglected source of numinous experience because of the generally negative stance taken towards it by our religious traditions. Nevertheless, it may be a vehicle for sacred experience.

> Immediately following an intense meditation practice, I lay down to relieve pain that had developed. I experienced sensations of extraordinary energy, light, and movement in my body. I heard a voice say that this was an experience of, and an opportunity to observe, Eros and its energy. It entered from above my body

through a point mid-way between the pubic area and the navel, as a column of white light with radiating yellow/gold light at its base. The sensations of this energy were simultaneously exciting, sensual, sexual, powerful, hot, vibrant, radiating, expansive, enlivening, and frightening. It was like observing Eros in a pure and intense form, like watching electrical energy, but seeing it as an energy of the heart. My initial reaction was to jolt myself out of the experience, but recognizing its power and importance, I was able to maintain a silent, still awareness for some time. As I became self-conscious and also exhausted, the energy receded and left. Later in the retreat, I experienced an extraordinary sense of both being, and being enveloped by, a completely opened heart that was all-expansive and all-encompassing. It left me with an amazing sense of joy and peace, and a feeling of being wholly part of the cosmos.

Unfortunately, the western religious traditions have ignored what many eastern cultures have understood; sexuality is an important vehicle for the expression of our spirituality. As Jung (Jung 1978: 105) put it, sexuality is "a genuine and incontestable experience of the divine, whose transcendent force obliterates and consumes everything individual." Sexuality can allow ecstatic union with the sacred, during which our sense of being separate individuals disappears – an experience of enlightenment. Following an intense night of lovemaking, a young woman described a heightened state of spiritual awareness, during which:

I stood outside of time. It was as if time normally flowed in a horizontal plane, and I had somehow stepped out of this horizontal flow into a timeless state. There was absolutely no sense of the passage of time. To say there was no beginning or ending of time would seem irrelevant. There was simply no time . . .

(Feuerstein 1992: 29)

This woman clearly transcended her ordinary personality during this experience, which is the state of mind to which so much spiritual practice is devoted.

ENTHEOGENS AND THE NUMINOSUM

There is controversy about whether entheogens, or psychedelics, produce authentic spiritual experience or whether their effects are simply the result of a disordered brain. Based on the following type of experience, I believe that these compounds affect brain functioning in a way that allows us to experience realms of reality that are not normally accessible to us.

Suddenly I became aware of a presence that was enormously powerful and nurturing. It/She reassured me that I could surrender to the experience. I had an odd sensation of separating from my body, and suddenly felt myself floating, exquisitely light and free. I seemed to exist as pure consciousness within brilliant light, and felt blissful peace and joy. I became aware of two beings composed almost entirely of light. We discussed my path in life, significant events and their relevance to my life's purpose. The deep wisdom and compassion of these beings helped me understand and accept several painful life events, and feel forgiveness towards people who had hurt me. I felt relief and emotional healing. Next, they led me to a golden platform that ascended seven levels, like a stepped pyramid. At the top was a blaze of brilliant, diamond light, radiantly clear, sparkling with flashes of color. I was awed, and sensed that this was a divine presence. The light coalesced into the form of a goddess with an Asian face. No words were exchanged, just unspeakable reverence and devotion on my part, and unfathomable love on hers. I knew her to be Kuanyin. She smiled at me, then turned her gaze at what appeared to be the earth far below, surrounded by the darkness of space. As I looked at the planet, I saw countless drops of light, which I knew represented every living being on the earth. My heart opened as I experienced an incomparable love for all life, and the deepest compassion I have ever known. I felt unconditional love for all, including rapists and murderers, whom I loved with the sadness of one who sees their suffering. I knew them as lost souls who had forgotten their true nature, and I felt a deep desire to help guide each one towards their birthright. Looking at Kuanyin, I realized that my experience was simply a reflection of her divine nature, shared with me at this moment.

Needless to say, this experience was directly relevant to the subject's developmental history. She had been raised in an abusive household, and was often beaten, shamed, and ridiculed by her mother. Kuanyin is the archetype of a loving, compassionate, divine mother, of the kind that she did not have as a child. The vision was therefore extremely helpful. Again, depending on the therapist's personal commitment, one could dismiss the experience as defensive, merely a fantasy released by the drug, or as a healing contact with the numinosum. I believe that the high level of spirituality revealed in this experience, together with its coherence, are evidence that it was authentic.

THE EFFECTS OF NUMINOUS EXPERIENCE ON THE THERAPEUTIC PROCESS

The therapist's response to a numinous encounter that is brought into psychotherapy may have a profound effect on the therapeutic process, for good or ill. We tend to describe these effects in terms of our therapeutic orientation and philosophy of treatment, but the therapist's belief system is also a crucial factor. As we have seen, the healing value of numinous experience may lie simply in its content, because the numinosum addresses a specific aspect of the patient, either a wound, a developmental difficulty, or a current problem. The therapeutic task is then to help the patient understand and integrate the experience. However, the therapist's attitude and response to the patient's experience of the numinosum is also very significant, whether or not the content of the experience can be understood. If the therapist is dismissive or reductive, the patient may be very hurt. If the therapist responds in an attuned and sensitive manner, the patient feels that his or her experience is valued and validated. This enhances the self–selfobject tie, whose healing effects are themselves numinous.

Notes

1 For the sake of space I will not discuss the ways in which this proposition may be justified or refuted, in the latter case by insisting that such experience is simply a fantasy or a defense arising from personal levels of the unconscious that have nothing to do with transcendent reality. The argument also hinges on whether numinous experience arises from transpersonal levels of the psyche, in which case the objective psyche would be responsible for what we call "God," or whether the psyche simply transmits the experience of a divinity that lies beyond it. For a fuller discussion of these questions, see Corbett (1996, 2000a, 2000b), and Schlamm (1994).

2 In Hindu mythology, Kali is a ferocious aspect of the Divine Mother. She is the goddess of death as transformation, necessary for the renewal of the life force.

3 For example, the visions of Hildegard of Bingen (1098–1180) have been described as the result of migraine because they are strikingly similar to the visual auras that accompany that illness (Singer 1958; Sacks 1992). However, to dismiss them as *only* due to migraine is to ignore the possibility that severe migraine, like any disorder of the brain, may open a window onto a spiritual dimension. A severe illness, especially one that affects brain functioning, reduces the hegemony of the ego. One function of the ego is to maintain a barrier or gate between consensual reality and the larger order of Reality. Once the ego is weakened, the veil between this reality and spiritual reality becomes much thinner. That is, Hildegard's many illnesses – not all of which were migrainous in nature – *allowed* her to talk to the angels rather than *causing* her to do so. (Sacks himself, although committed to the medical paradigm, does point out that a diagnosis of migraine does not mean that her visions did not allow authentic insight into spiritual reality.)

4 See, for example, Jung's (1969) description of the case of Brother Klaus, whose non-traditional experience of the numinosum that included the divine feminine had to be reinterpreted to fit Trinitarian Christian theology.

References

Corbett, L. (1996) *The Religious Function of the Psyche*, London: Routledge.

Corbett, L. (2000a) "A Depth Psychological Approach to the Sacred", in D. Slattery and L. Corbett (eds.), *Depth Psychology: Meditations in the Field*, Zurich: Daimon.

Corbett, L. (2000b) "Jung's Approach to the Phenomenology of Religious Experience: A View from the Consulting Room", in R. Brooke (ed.), *Pathways into the Jungian World*, New York: Routledge.

Corbin, H. (1972) *"Mundus Imaginalis* or the Imaginary and the Imaginal", in *Spring*, New York: Spring Publications.

Feuerstein, G. (1992) *Sacred Sexuality*, New York: Jeremy Tarcher.

Hardy, A. (1997) *The Spiritual Nature of Man: A Study of Contemporary Religious Experience*, Oxford: Oxford University Press.

James, W. (1958) *Varieties of Religious Experience*, New York: The New American Library, a Mentor Book.

Jung, C.G. (1935/1966) "Two Essays on Analytical Psychology" (p. 238), *CW* 7.

Jung, C.G. (1969) "Brother Klaus", in *Psychology and Religion: West and East*, *CW* 11, Princeton, NJ: Princeton University Press.

Jung, C.G. (1973) *Letters*, vol. 1, ed. G. Adler and A. Jaffé, trans. R.F.C. Hull, Princeton, NJ: Princeton University Press.

Jung, C.G. (1978) *Psychological Reflections*, ed. J. Jacobi and R.F.C. Hull, Princeton, NJ: Princeton University Press.

Otto, R. (1917/1958) *The Idea of the Holy*, trans. J.W. Harvey, London: Oxford University Press.

Sacks, O. (1992) *Migraine: Understanding a Common Disorder*, Appendix 1, *The Visions of Hildegard*, Berkeley: University of California Press.

Schlamm, L. (1994) "The Holy: A Meeting-Point between Analytical Pscyhology and Religion", in J. Ryce-Menuhin (ed.), *Jung and the Monotheisms*, London: Routledge.

Singer, C. (1958) *From Magic to Science: Essays on the Scientific Twilight*, New York: Dover Publications.

Chapter 5

Numinosity/femininity

Mark Kuras

> The clinical practice of psychotherapy is a mere makeshift that does its utmost to prevent numinous experiences.
>
> (Letter to Kirsch, May 1953; quoted in McGuire 1974: 118)

In "Flying Saucers: A Modern Myth," Jung defines numinosity as the "actual and immediate experience of spiritual reality" (Jung 1958: 342). Classically, spiritual reality is the contrary of material reality, a difference noted by Jung in another theoretical context as two kinds of thinking, directed and fantasy thinking, a parallel to Freud's distinction between the primary and secondary process. I will argue that Jung's idea of fantasy thinking harbors an important quality not active in Freud's construction of the primary process: fantasy thinking is meant to represent the intrinsic logic of spiritual reality, a discourse which, as it works through distinct grammatical structures in the psyche (archetypes) "compensates for the barrenness and emptiness of traditional forms" (ibid.) that are established through directed thinking, an event felt as numinous.

The transition from primary process to fantasy thinking, the entry into the numinous, occurs through the attainment of a certain attitude. Jung defines an attitude as "an *a priori* orientation to a definite thing" (Jung 1921: 414). This implies that an experience of the numinous that becomes clinically effective requires that a certain sensibility gets established, a sensibility that Jung feels is thwarted by traditional clinical models. I will attempt to engage Jung's radical contention through the following hypothesis: I will assume numinosity to be the affective presence of spiritual reality, the "thinking" not thought from or in the ego-complex. The experience of this autonomous process, which Jung calls variously "religiosity" and the "original behavior of psyche," eventually is one of intense solidity and containment, an event which initiates a sensual appreciation for the aims of this thinking and so progressively introduces a functional distinction between the ego-complex and consciousness. This distinction is, to me, the defining feature of Jung's clinical technique, which is both in continuity with primal methods of psychological healing and exceptionally responsive to the unprecedented strains of psychological distress in this postmodern phase of psychological life.

Postmodernity has been described as "the final penetration of the rationalizing impulse of modernity into the inner sanctum of the subject" (Eagleton 1996: 69–92). This has yielded an assault upon "absolute truth, objectivity, timeless moral values, scientific inquiry and a belief in historical progress. It calls into question the autonomy of the individual, inflexible social and sexual norms and the belief that there are firm foundations to the world" (Eagleton 2003: 17). Postmodernism "puts its trust in pluralism – in social order that is as diverse and inclusive as possible" (ibid.: 18). In this sense, "culture" assumes the position once reserved for religion, with the difference that whereas religion was able to "link fact and value, the routine conduct of everyday life with matters of ultimate spiritual importance, culture divides these domains down the middle" (ibid.: 99).

There are numerous theories about the genesis of the postmodern; particularly compelling are those that link it to enhancements of capitalism and innovations in media – these both effect and in turn are affected by developments in the structure of the ego-complex (Kuras 2003). There my emphasis was on the relationship between the ego-complex and consciousness, a relationship that was psychically cast in the idiom of dominance and submission. Immersed in a virtual reality, a digital world, consciousness seemed to lose autonomy, or, stated differently, was prevented from engaging in certain psychological sensitivities. To the degree that contact with these dynamic powers waned, everyday life became devoid of any "spiritual" significance, resulting in an exacerbation of certain phenomena in narcissism, and in paranoia, and summarily in a unique depressive affectivity that is, arguably, the infrastructure of the specific distresses that are now termed character pathology. Translated into Jung's terminology, character pathology references the absence of the dynamic reverberance of symbols, or alternatively, registers the predominance of signs whose dynamic properties are very different.

Jung, in compensation, crafted a therapeutic response to this movement. More directly, Jung's model of psychological healing is a response to the enhancements of the ego-complex exacerbated through psychoanalytic techniques which, through the mutually reinforcing environment of capitalism and the media, catalyzed the strict and peculiar psychological spaces now termed postmodernity. This manifests in dynamic psychology as new forms of resistance, unprecedented upgrades in the capacity to oppose the categorical factor of the numinous, whose deepening absence yields an experience of unremitting remoteness. Transferentially, this manifests in great frustrations, a mutual pessimism about the power of analytic work. This pessimism ends up being conflated with insight and depth and then constructs a very peculiar alliance, a pleasure manifest in simultaneously being exceedingly visible and not seen.

This odd "postmodern" state exposes an abiding disparity between ego-consciousness, and what could be called consciousness-in-self. Already in this distinction is the difference between two dynamic planes of association (ego-complex/self) that consciousness can be on, and resultantly two distinguishable "bodies" consciousness can be in and act from. In the ego-complex, what reflects to consciousness is that it is made, manufactured, causally constructed by conditional and thus conditioning (usually traumatic) events; on the associative plane called self, consciousness is tautened, constantly re-receives itself as having a distinct order that not only comes prior to, but abides through, any contingency. This associative act of conservation is experienced as a dynamic fact (soul? daimon?) – always present is this centripetal force toward this "self" no matter the contingency, a centering or grounding power that Jung framed out in his notion of individuation, a power, in what amounts to the late phase of Jung's theorizations, which unveils as the god-image, the contemporaneous personification of spiritual reality, the evanescent grasp of numinosity.

The relationship between these two dynamic planes is customarily cast as conflictual: conscious/unconscious, mature/primitive, etc. What Jung was able to apperceive was that in this unconscious, this primary process, was associative activity that proved to be beyond regulatory reflexes and more than self-protective displacements and condensations; there was a "thinking," an intelligence, proved out through the way this thinking offset seduction. In other words, Jung uncovered the way that some "deep" process (psyche) was acting to secure consciousness amidst this commanding postmodern sensibility. Within the orient of clinical process, I assume that the postmodern sensibility is correspondent to the dynamic maturity of the ego-complex, which I liken to what Jung called "midlife" (Kuras 2003). At this crucial point, consciousness is abducted, falls into an increasingly fallow dynamic and what was just a moment before the generative conflict between the ego-complex and the instinctive unconscious now develops into the dominance of the ego-complex over the associative sensibility of these primary processes – this being the essential structure of character disorder. In other words, consciousness is *given* an identity that is secured through a process of suppression (impression), e.g., the determinism of social constructivism, the contemporary face of suggestion, and simultaneously *loses* the intelligence that would otherwise act to maintain consciousness (in essence) amidst the hounding impositions that characterize the postmodern field.

Postmodernity is then the accelerating foreclosure of an intelligence, one that would not repress or even disable the discriminative (and finally dissociative) acts historically specific to the ego-complex, but is capable of comprising it. I believe that Jung's recognition of the possibility of these actions, spurred through a therapeutic technique, is what lifts his theory of symbol formation to mythic proportion: whereas Freud *ends* in the intractable conflict between eros and death, in the borderline dimension of idealization and devaluation, Jung, in his distinctive sense, *commences*: the essential disclosure in Jung's *Memories, Dreams, Reflections* (1961a) is clinical, outlines the means to the numinous, to the affective presence of spiritual reality, to that associative dimension needed now to think through the conceits of the now matured ego-complex, to address its unprecedented, but not unanticipated, influence on the psyche as a whole.

Through the concept of numinosity, I am engaged with the trajectory of Jung's consummate sensuality. In very certain terms, Jung's personality, as it is received now, is a drama, the resuscitant struggle for contact with numinosity, its capacity to modulate the present influence of the ego-complex on consciousness. In this sense, the numinous, as a higher order plane of association, is correspondent to what psychological-mindedness is obliged to be in postmodernity. More, numinosity would then conserve the validity of a conception of neutrality, a position from which consciousness still believes in the possibility of achieving a criticality not possible in the epistemological/ontological fields bestowed through the ego-complex. Notably, this neutrality is not "distant," it is not constituted through the repression of certain psychological qualities (e.g. affect); rather it is a sensuality to certain field-phenomena. This sensuality of the numinous presences exhibits itself as an increased capacity for personification and amplification. This is something related to, but also an upgrade from, what Freud called evenly hovering attention. Evenly hovering attention refers to the subjective attitude the analyst must obtain in order to sensually engage the unconscious, the psyche. This consists of suspending everything which *usually* focuses attention, that is the executive functions comprising the ego-complex. If accomplished, the subjectivity of the analyst embodies a stance that "makes use of everything."

This attitude is picked up in Jung as "intuition," and will mature, in analytical psychology, into what is also explicated as a sensuality that is first conceived through Jung's concept of intuition, and will mature into what Jung will call "trancing" (Douglas 1997b: 155) or where there is "no epistemological criticism" (Jung 1954: 274), later active imagination (Jung 1955: 526), and what Schwartz-Salant has called "imaginal field experiences" (Schwartz-Salant 1998: 63).

A particularly apt description of this analytic attitude is evoked, perhaps not surprisingly, from a poet, Walt Whitman: "I do not make poems of separate parts; I make songs of the ensemble" (quoted in Hirshfield 1997: 215). I evoke Whitman because more than most he unveils that the more consciousness is "on the plane" of the numinous the more it is engaged with a perplexing immersion in "eros," in Freud's sense. In his description of symbol formation (Jung 1921: 479), Jung describes how establishing a symbol rests upon a degree of composure with the numinous which presences, in postmodernity, in a particular form of eroticism.

This eros offers to consciousness refined states of empathy nascent in the primary process. More, this immersion in eros is functionally equal to a carrying of those dynamic processes that have traditionally through mythopoiesis been gendered as feminine.

It is important to situate this term: by femininity I mean an imaging of dynamic quality which has characteristics comparable to Freud's id and Freud's eros, specifically the way both these function without negation, termed above as "ensembling." This is an attribute that is as imagistically "feminine" as it is affectively "numinous." This coupling of numinosity and femininity is definitively Jungian, and comes through an optic that Jung's work persistently attends to and steadfastly attempts to refine. From the *Symbols of Transformation* (Jung 1911–12) through *Visions* (Jung 1930–1934), on to an arrival at *Mysterium Coniunctionis* (Jung 1955–1956) is a reverberant concern opening a progressive movement from the hysterics of Ms Miller through the fitful prospective imaginings of Ms Morgan to Mysterium's revelations of the structural provisions in the psyche functioning to conserve individuation – the subject's originality and imperviousness to suggestion. Ms Miller is an infirm femininity, penetrated, suggestible, dominated by the masculinity of directed thinking (the embedded heroic mythology of the ego-complex); Ms Morgan is the femininity of intuitive thinking gyring around what is surfacing as its own center (which is where Jung "is"); Mysterium is this femininity infusing consciousness: consciousness now positioned in a femininity that is critically alert to its bonding/bondage in/through/by the ego-complex.

The latter experience is, evidently, strenuously resisted by the ego-complex, a reflex-reaction that, I contend, is the core dynamic of transference and countertransference in analytic work with postmodern psychopathology. In other words, what, at a collective level, is this postmodern deconstruction of all unity-constituting presences, is, on the individual level, personified as misogyny.

> I have no small opinion of fantasy. To me, it is the maternally creative side of the masculine mind.
>
> (Jung 1931: 45)

Through this amplification of fantasy and mother, Jung substantiates his rationale for departing from the standard developmental-reductive perspective that theoretically informs most analytic work. Taken as mythology in the best sense, developmental models which presume to narrate the relations between mother and child are, from this point of view, imaging the now pronounced fusion between consciousness and the ego-complex and how this affects the status of "fantasy" (personification/amplification) in postmodern psychological life.

Fantasy to Jung is multi-valent; he links it to an anchoring: "In the normal course of things, fantasy does not easily go astray; it is too deep for that, and too closely bound up with the tap-root of human and animal instinct" (ibid.: 45), as the means through which consciousness can dis-identify from the ego-complex (ibid.: 48), because "fantasy" is the direct experience of the activity of a supra-personal process:

> we need to have not only a personal, contemporary consciousness, but also a supra-personal consciousness with a sense of historical continuity. However abstract this may sound, practical experience shows that many neuroses are caused primarily by the fact that people blind themselves to their own religious promptings because of a childish passion for rational enlightenment. It is high time that the psychologist of today recognized that we are no longer dealing with dogmas and creed but with the religious attitude *per se*, whose importance can hardly be overrated.
>
> (ibid.: 46)

Fantasy as "mother" follows from Jung's observations that at a particular depth, at a particular level of freedom, fantasy feels like a kind of "centering" process, centering in the sense that it has, in its autonomy, a "peculiar purposefulness" (ibid.: 50). It is important here to juxtapose Jung's other findings, linking the centering and purposefulness with another, albeit cryptic term, "wholeness," and to further amplify this with the mandala, and lastly with Jung's specific notion of symbol. This cluster of observations points toward processes that are perpetually directed toward "unity" in a dynamic sense, points into a sensuality, a perceptivity not dependent on repression as an organizing factor. I think this is the deep distinction between directed thinking and intuitive/fantasy thinking.

In this depth of fantasy thinking, Jung experiences a "mother" whose acts definitively place her not behind the ego-complex but beyond it. As noted earlier, these unity-constituting acts, in order to be what they are, constantly take account of the attitude of consciousness toward themselves – in our time this is a critique of the ego-complex, one that unavoidably exposes its limitedness and discriminative aggressivity and acts then to embrace it, to provide, in symbol, an inclusive structure, the compassion, that consciousness may then enter to hold them.

Jung intuits that the unity-constituting processes have been infantilized by ego-consciousness, played down, decreased in scale, so that they can be consumed through the signature means of the ego-complex. In response to these aggressive reductive processes, Jung initiated his self-analysis which began to yield clinical methods (to actively supersede a developmental-reductive interpretive posture) that aided the distinction between consciousness and the ego-complex (Jung 1946: 190–9), which in turn proceeded to reveal that these unity-constituting processes, as distinct from, say, Freudian notions of homeostasis and constancy and the death-instincts, end up in the radical structures of inclusivity catalogued in *Mysterium Coniunctionis*.

Now, the critique of this will be that it sounds utopian. Granted, it is optimistic, and so in contrast with Freudian pessimism (cf. *Civilization and its Discontents* (1930)), but this optimism, the stimulation of these unity-constituting processes, this numinosity, lies through the necessary perimeter of the ego-complex – I mean the experience of this numinosity (and, in turn, the numinous reaction to our grasp of the numinous: unity after unity) is enhanced through the fact that there now could be a consciousness that has come consciously through the ego-complex and can now touch numinosity in this way for the first time.

> The symbol-producing function . . . is an attempt to bring our original mind back to *(ego-)*consciousness, where it has never been before, and where it has never undergone critical reflection.
>
> (Jung 1961a: 258)

In my experience the struggle to resuscitate the "original mind," which Jung re-states as "original behavior," constitutes the predominant transferential-field in the work with the steadfast narcissism/paranoia/depression (i.e. the remoteness) that typifies character pathology. This is the skirmish Jung initially referenced in his pioneering claims regarding psychological incest. Recall that Jung came to feel that the structural aspects embedded in the incest motif referred to some historical or phylogenetic event, but marked a reiterative psychological task: in *Symbols of Transformation* (Jung 1911–12) it is Ms Miller's exodus from her encapsulated consciousness into her "larger" personality. Ms Miller's fantasies, and even more especially Jung's (and Flournoy's) interpretation of this text, emphatically display the incredible resistances to having consciousness journey outside the epistemological borders of the ego-complex, and go forth to the autonomous dimensions of "fantasy." This is the incest taboo, that "bulwark against the occult," the prohibition of "mother."

So now I posit this "inside" of the analyst in postmodernity – the embellished ambivalence toward the numinous; cast in terms of incest, this reconnoitering with mother/fantasy is made tantamount to psychosis. The paradigmatic instance of this confrontation with mother/femininity is construed (from a consciousness encapsulated in the ego-complex) as an instance of the ego-complex's decompensation: *Schreber*.

The Schreber case comprises *The Memoirs of my Mental Illness*, written by Daniel Schreber (Schreber 1903/1988), a prominent judicial figure from a celebrated family, who suffered a psychotic breakdown. The psychological form and contents of this rupture were meticulously documented by Schreber, and amounted to an elaborate philosophic (delusional) system, in which he (Schreber) would submit to be penetrated by a paternal God, and through that act be "feminized," impregnated and so enabled to populate a new and improved world.

So both in content (the transmutation to the feminine) and form (being penetrated by "psychotic" process), the Schreber case is a medium through which Jung, by juxtaposing it with the Miller Fantasies, follows the redemptive concept of femininity (McGuire 1974: 213J), which is different than Freud who, in the same encounter with this text, reduces it through a proposed intimacy between paranoia and latent homosexuality. This divergence is, I think, one of the first instances of an unbridgeable difference between analytical psychology and psychoanalysis. It is also, to my mind, another amplification of this postmodern transferential *impasse*. The "feminization" that Schreber engages is the face of an encroaching numinosity. Schreber's transit to this femininity is definitely catalyzed by an unprecedented intensity of ego-consciousness (via his "father" and Doctor and God, as shall be seen), and is the doppelganger of what will be Jung's own passage, especially in relation to Freud then and "classical" analytical psychology's relation to psychoanalysis still, a dynamic order depicted unswervingly in *Memories, Dreams, Reflections* (Jung 1961a).

As an example of psychotic process, the Schreber case first appears in analytical psychology in 1906 in *On the Psychology of Dementia Praecox* (Jung 1907), and is used multiple times by Jung as a primary example of what we would term today as acute symptoms of a paranoid schizophrenia. As an instance of psychotic decompensation, Schreber's case resides in the same clinical terrain out of which Jung's theory initially emerged, this in distinction to Freud, who, to this point, had grounded his theory in the dynamics of neurotic symptomotology. Jung and Freud discussed the Schreber case in 1910, coincident to Jung's engagement with the Miller Fantasies (presumed as another account of psychotic process) which also coincides with Freud's engaging mythology from a psychoanalytic perspective, an exchange which would lead to the structural postulates promulgated in the Wolfman case (Freud 1918), on to *Totem and Taboo* (Freud 1913) and so straight into the complex issues of inbuilt psychic structure, archaic vestiges and mythologems, which then shift attention from developmental trauma to the depths of metapsychology.

This discourse on archaic psychic structure is based on the phenomenology of psychic dimensions/processes that ooze beyond the mechanical abstractions that guide Freud's reflex-arc/homeostatic models; what would finally arrive in psychoanalysis as *eros*, is what, through his probe into fantasy thinking /mythology, Jung is opening to: those psychic dynamisms that autonomously and simultaneously forge psychological contents (symbols) and a psychological subject (non-ego consciousness) acting for what Freud called pleasure, what Jung called meaning. I believe Freud and Jung see the same phenomena; but Freud customarily reads this process as desirous of homeostasis, absence of tension, seeking a zero-point, nirvana, all states that exist prior to, and so are sensually more primitive than, the defining tensions of ego-consciousness. Jung, on the other hand, enters through the guiding encounter with a mediumistic femininity (Prieswick (cf. Jung 1902) and Miller, and his psychic mother, if that is not seized as a literalism), that is to say with an upgraded grasp of the hysteric issue, and sees this as a dynamism seeking what he called "superior character" or "the larger personality," which I take to mean a sensuality of a higher logical type, a criticality or psychological-mindedness, a sensibility to symbol, able to flit past the epistemological bindings (the literal-mindedness) titivating the ego-complex.

To Jung this was best appreciated in mythic style: then, juxtaposing Schreber (in his desire to be feminine) and Prieswick (in her transferential idealization of Jung) and Miller (and her lover Chiwantopel), "finds" the masculine and the feminine (now as categorical processes: directed thinking/ intuitive thinking) hysterically lurching toward a union (then this will become *Mysterium Coniunctionis*).

By late 1910, Jung is becoming more sensitive to this structural dimension (or, perhaps it is possible to say that Freud's influence places Jung in the psychological position of Schreber/Prieswick/Miller), and so able to entertain the idea that the Miller Fantasies "really add up to a redemptive system" (McGuire 1974: 213J), an attitude whose radicalness cannot be underestimated; this stirred him to reassess the memoir, leading to an appreciation for the "greatness of Schreber's mind."

Freud's response to all this is revealing: with Jung now immersing himself in mythology (and to anticipate, I emphasize that the immersion is into a "thinking" – intuitive/fantasy – thinking), Freud intensifies his epistemological commitment: "I didn't even read half the book . . . but I have fathomed the secret. The case is easily reduced to its nuclear complex" (McGuire 1974, L: 213J). To Freud, the essence of the Schreber case eddies around an infantile conflict with the father; Freud assumes that Schreber's delusional system – his losing his masculine definition (his fragmentation/ dissociation) equated with a creeping infusion of "feminine voluptuousness" – is the imagistic expression of a homosexual desire, a wish to be penetrated by an ideal man, his father, his doctor, his god. The Freudian bias is to see this femininity as the absence of masculinity, as a pathological regression, not a redemptive progression.

Jung's appreciation for Schreber's mind, its redemptive currents, its numinosity, stimulates authorities in himself that will lead to his going through Freud's theoretical model. I am not making this Jung's personal journey; I am in one swish minimizing his imperiousness by raising this transit into a theory of therapeutic action (viz. enhancement of numinosity).

But first there is what can be termed a field-phenomenon, one imaged in the dynamics of directed thinking and intuitive thinking or, in more mythic casting: a Freud and a Jung. The influx of numinosity occasions a taboo, a resistance. In the correspondence between Freud and Jung in a footnote to Jung's rather bland response to Freud's interpretation, it is noted that Jung "had a vivid dream which left him with a feeling of humiliation" (McGuire 1974, L: 215, n.1), which he connected to his work on the Miller Fantasies and the "intense inferiority feeling" (ibid.), accompanying this engagement. In other words, as Jung begins to emerge past Freud's causal-reductive mode of interpretation, finding it too restrictive, Freud responds in an ego-dominated, patriarchal manner, a dynamic that persists throughout the remaining two years of their collaboration, and arguably still exists today in analytical psychologists who attempt to begin in Jung's "mysticism", and, against grave resistance, endeavor to engage the femininity equal to the autonomy of psyche.

So, the equation Jung = Schreber/Freud = Father gives off the idea of how sensitive consciousness can be to the numinous, given the reductive epistemology of the ego-complex. As Jung noted, the sensitivity is coarse, the numinous coming first symptomatically, as an inferiority per the presiding ego-ideal, which then accelerates the functions of the ego-complex; this inferiority of Jung's stands off against this enhancing of the ego-complex proffered by Freud, and mimics the relation between Schreber and his "father."

Schreber's father was a prominent physician and educator, particularly influential in child care/developmental theory. He created a system of child-rearing tied excessively to the Enlightenment premises of late nineteenth-century thought.

> Our entire effect on the direction of the child's will at this time will consist in accustoming it to absolute obedience . . . the thought should never occur to the child that his will could be in control, rather should the habit of subordinating his will to the will of his parents or teachers be immutably implanted in him . . . There is then joined to the feeling of law a feeling of impossibility of struggling against the law; a child's obedience, the basic condition of all education.
>
> (Quoted in Breger 1981: 92)

More, Father Schreber designed elaborate machines to "position" the human body, concretizing the idea that a "straight body" thinks right thoughts. In Schreber's system he describes this as "soul murder."

> A second novel feature of the Doctor's approach is the use of all sorts of mechanical devices and contraptions that are applied to the child to mold, strengthen and moralize his body . . . There are belts to tie children in one position while they sleep, metal bars to keep them sitting straight, harnesses and springs to pull the shoulders back, and

straps that bind the head and keep it upright by pulling on the hair. The Doctor obviously did not believe that the human body could move, sit, stand or lie down in the "correct" way without mechanical assistance.

If the child is strapped into a bed by a "scientific" instrument, the parent does not so directly feel the pain he is causing. The machine separates him from his own potential empathy.

(ibid.)

Mythopoiecally, the methods portrayed are the "unconscious" aspect of Enlightenment intents, in general, and are a vampy rendition of the classical psychoanalytic technique in particular. Schreber and Jung, respectively, find themselves in the nucleus of this cultural complex, in the den of this harsh patriarch, in consort with the dynamics of hysteria, that lamentation for receding feminine eroticism, for intuitive thinking, for numinosity.

In *Analytical Psychology: Notes on a Seminar Given in 1925*, Jung speaks about the "subjective" aspect of *Psychology of the Unconscious*, stating that the latter work can be "taken as myself . . . my own unconscious," which, he also is aware, "forecasts the future" (Jung, 1989: 27).

Jung goes on:

the book begins with a statement about two kinds of thinking: . . . intellectual or directed thinking, and fantastic or passive automatic thinking. In the process of directed thinking thoughts are handled as *tools*, they are made to serve the purposes of the thinker; while in passive thinking thoughts are like individuals going on about on their own . . . Fantastical thinking knows no hierarchy: the thoughts may even be antagonistic to the ego.

I took Miss Miller's fantasies as such an autonomous form of thinking, but did not realize that *she stood for that form of thinking in myself* . . . fantasizing was a mental process that was directly repellant to me. As a form of thinking I held it to be altogether *impure*, a sort of *incestuous intercourse* . . . It shocked me . . . to think of the possibility of a fantasy life in my own mind; it was against all the intellectual ideals I had developed for myself, and so great was my resistance to it, that I could only admit the fact in myself through the process of projecting my material into Miss Miller's. Or, to put it even more strongly, passive thinking seemed to me such a weak and perverted thing that I could only handle it through a diseased woman.

(Jung, 1989: 27–8, emphasis added)

Jung raises Schreber's discourse – the "sick woman" is revealed and received as a style of thinking, an associative action, indigenous to a structural dimension in psyche and experienced as "depth." This analogic and imagistic thinking is seen by Freud as a primitive process serving the peremptory modes of discharge existing prior to the binding inhibitions of an ego-structure. Jung angled in differently, and found, through a link to mythopoiesis brought out through Schreber and Ms Miller, that in this picture-language were disclosures that were primary, but not primitive, "thoughts" of a subject who was perceptually broader than the subject proffered through the ego-complex. At that moment, Jung can proscribe a definitional perimeter for the "symbolic" absolutely distinct from the allegoric. The allegoric is meaning moving horizontally, from the surface of one text to another, as when trinity becomes triangularity becomes Oedipal: this collapses meaning into an operative but dead structure; the Oedipal, in Freud's allegory can show where the psyche has been, or where it's fixated, but not where it is going. The symbolic, alternatively, moves in a decidedly hierarchical space: the analogic and imagistic work is not obfuscatory, but exposes what, from the ego-complex, is experienced as a transgressive striving for a critical perspective on the ego-complex, a standpoint from which to catch sight of the ego-complex's specialized unconsciousness. So, by raising the Oedipal from the allegoric to the symbolic, Jung sees that the Oedipal is less a working-past and more a *working-toward* the primal scene, which, in its turn, is the *working-up* of a point of view through which the masculinity of the ego-complex critically comprises the ever-striving-to-encompass femininity of the mother. This categorical opposition, between the dominant complex encapsulating consciousness and the psyche's femininity, relentlessly abides in the symbolic, and so the interactions between the players of this opposition are always when all's said and done religious: every transitory resolution of the opposition is experienced as numinous.

And this awareness is honored unevenly, even sheepishly: on one hand, Jung personally experiences that acquiring access to this thinking (which forms the basis for his technical recommendations regarding active imagination in its broadest sense (Jung 1916/1958, 1928, 1955)) brings consciousness into intimacy with the redemptive cycles which, for Jung, define "psyche," but that these processes, on the other hand, constellate paranoia in Schreber/inferiority in Jung, both indicating the desired but still fitful posture within which consciousness may religiously experience this femininity now boldly sensitive to its domination in the ego-complex.

Clinically, I contend that this presence rouses novel and intense resistances to reductive interpretation informed by developmental theorization that conflate therapeutic progress with confining consciousness to an identity established through the "cultural" values of the ego-complex. This femininity experiences this reduction as an assault upon the setting requisite to symbol formation. As stated earlier, this penetration into the "inner sanctum" of the subject has the effect of constellating an attitude that sees signs (culturally derived contents) for symbols (emergent acts of inclusivity); this stance comes under the dynamic protection of an ego-complex and, as such, can become functionally dominant. I mean that, now, in post-modernity, contents that function in a symbolic way cannot be taken for granted; the idea of default self-regulation, i.e. compensation, is outmoded.

To restate, it is the waning of these processes that coincides with the psychological events appearing clinically in the insular transference/countertransference fields associable to character pathology. To situate, and clinically engage, this waning retrospectively, reductively, is to dominate, and mute, the femininity that alone would, prospectively, seek an as yet forged phase of empathy that would thrust consciousness past the constructed isolation and anomie of the ego-complex. A developmental perspective, if made primary, if not critically recognized as an expedient cultural fantasy, serves to increasingly encapsulate consciousness in a psychic surround that lacks eroticism; active fantasy, which aggressively strives for forms that widen consciousness, is degraded into passive fantasy, making consciousness now defenseless against the suggestions of its cultural surround. Consciousness, as it is reduced to its ego-identity, truncated, becomes more solipsistic, opinionated, resistant to intimacy, also presents as more acculturated, dominated by sociality. What is being lost is the effects of the "actual and immediate experience of spiritual reality."

Jung anticipated this (Jung 1957) and began to forge means to reattach to these processes, which traditionally, yet still daringly, implies that consciousness can still reclaim a degree of sufficiency apart from the acculturative infrastructure of the ego-complex; this is no claim to a statuesque (a non-dynamic) truth, but desire for a "body" acclimated to an eroticized world (imaged in shamanism and alchemy as femininity). In this initiatory literature (shamanic, meditative, hallucinogenic), engagement with this spiritual reality, this eroticism, has a remarkably stable and stabilizing effect: consciousness experiences a thisness, granted by a differentiation from its contingent identity (ego-complex); this is a sensual body with an exquisite sensitivity to, and yet minimal deformation by, the quotidian. This is a decisive clinical event, as this prompts a movement on a few levels: subjectively, it means one now works from fantasy as distinct from memory, and relationally, it means that the discourse moves from being cast as a relation between ego-complexes to what Freud called unconscious to unconscious communication, what Jung took up as the alchemical field, the emergence of a sensuousness, an intuitive thinking, marked by the presence of personification and amplification: mythopoiesis.

Suppose that to be "mother." Suppose that the immediate relations between consciousness and this mother is the decisive scene to which analysis attends. And finally suppose, here in a heuristic sense, that this is the inmost register of an analytical psychology. Then our myth is this transit from the lowliness of Ms Prieswick to the eccentricities of Ms Miller, and is a step which opens analytical psychology up to the insight that Schreber's model is only, on one side, a paranoid capitulation to paternal dominance, and is, on the outlying side, a revelation of the structural process, the archetypal intiatory structure of death/rebirth, an insight which catapaults analytical psychology into the dawning aptitudes of Ms Morgan, exposed now to what has been called the "archetypal feminine rite of intiation" (Douglas 1997b), which I would rephrase to be the postmodern rite of initiation to the feminine, to the "maternal side of the masculine mind," to numinosity and the resuscitation of the perceptivities lurking in active fantasy (Jung 1921: 428).

This active fantasy is what Jung received not as regressive, but as the progression coming on through the reentry of the categorical numinous in a post-ego consciousness (Jung 1961a: 258). This progression toward "wholeness" brings on an inferiority that has lately derailed analytic researches into the non-ego states that empirically ground the signature insights of analytical psychology. Admittedly wholeness sounds tender-minded, and so it must be referenced, as Jung constantly tried to do, to an empirical process, which, in personification/amplification, blooms in a familiar idiom: attachment to the mother. But Jung does not read this text in the specific terms of ego-development, but as the text through which consciousness comes to terms with the ego-complex's mature tendency to prohibit maternal attachment, with maternal here being the image of the numinous. In my view, Jung's work attempts to empirically detail a progressive intimacy with the numinous, the core dynamic of the postmodern patient: this succession from the inferiority of the hysteric to the provisionalities of the anima to the certitudes of the self.

Just as Schreber's femininity is not equitable with the loss of his masculinity, so consciousness of numinosity is not a forfeiture of ego-consciousness but its initial redemption, the inaugural whisper of this empathic composition (this Self) capable of embracing the ego-complex's inherent, heroic, differentiating violences.

This act remains the forefront of the numinous experience: ruthless self-exposure of the ego-complex's "culture," in a field of loving (this Self).

This theory of therapeutic action, fitted to postmodernity, age of the maturity of the ego-complex, age of character pathology, attempts to undertake the transit from the hysteric and her conversions to the borderline "character." And so Jung's (and analytical psychology's) theoretical body enfolds this "sick woman," sympathetically goes in and out of her constant thrashing on the borderlines between light and dark, idealization and devaluation, thrashing, in wholly Gnostic action, for some shard of the numinous, her self-mutilations a ceremonial attempt to get to something that might bear the violences of ego-consciousness. It isn't that this borderline or Schreber or Prieswick or Miller depict more genius than madness; surely each fractured (as did Jung) under these dynamisms, but each of their scenes, and Jung's scene with Freud too, loop around the common theme of postmodern psychopathology and the correlated form of therapeutic action as in the *Visions* seminar, in my view the initial text of postmodern therapeutic process.

Jung's work with Ms Morgan steadfastly values and so pursues numinosity and the "religious attitude" resulting from an intimacy with its processes; intuitively, Jung senses himself as coupled with a dynamic feminine presence, which, in effect, relativizes the working-model of the "masculine," in his psyche. "It is the prerogative of our times to discover that woman has a psychology, and that there is another viewpoint outside the masculine world" (Jung 1930: 527).

References

Breger, L. (1981) *Freud's Unfinished Journey*, New York: Routledge & Kegan Paul.

Douglas, C. (1997a) *Translate This Darkness*, Princeton, NJ: Princeton University Press.

Douglas, C. (1997b) "Introduction" to *Visions*, Princeton, NJ: Princeton University Press.

Eagleton, T. (1996) *The Illusions of Postmodernism*, Cambridge, MA: Blackwell.

Eagleton, T. (2003) *After Theory*, New York: Basic Books.

Freud, S. (1913) *Totem and Taboo*, New York: Norton.

Freud, S. (1918) "From the History of an Infantile Neurosis'," *Collected Papers*, vol. 3, New York: Basic Books.

Freud, S. (1930) 'Civilisation and its Discontents', *SE, 21*.

Hirshfield, J. (1997) *Nine Gates*, New York: HarperCollins.

Jung, C.G. (1902) "On the Psychology of So-Called Occult Phenomena", *CW* 1.

Jung, C.G. (1907) "On the Psychology of Dementia Praecox", *CW* 3.

Jung, C.G. (1911–12) *Symbols of Transformation, CW* 5.

Jung, C.G. (1916/1958) "The Transcendent Function", *CW* 8.

Jung, C.G. (1921) *Psychological Types, CW* 6.

Jung, C.G. (1928) "The Technique of Differentiation between the Ego and the Figures of the Unconscious", *CW* 7.

Jung, C.G. (1930–34) *Visions*, ed. C. Douglas, Princeton, NJ: Princeton University Press.

Jung, C.G. (1931) "The Aims of Psychotherapy", *CW* 16.

Jung, C.G. (1946) "On the Nature of the Psyche", *CW* 8.

Jung, C.G. (1954) "The Philosophical Tree", *CW* 13.

Jung, C.G. (1955–56) *Mysterium Coniunctionis, CW* 14.

Jung, C.G. (1957) "The Undiscovered Self", *CW* 10.

Jung, C.G. (1958) "Flying Saucers: A Modern Myth", *CW* 10.

Jung, C.G. (1961a) "Symbols and the Interpretation of Dreams", *CW* 18.

Jung, C.G. (1961b) *Memories, Dreams, Reflections*, New York: Random House.

Jung, C.G. (1989) *Analytical Psychology: Notes on a Seminar Given in 1925*, ed. W. Mcguire, Princeton, NJ: Princeton University Press.

Kuras, M. (2003) "Therapeutic Action in Postmodernity: Analytical Psychology in its Essential Departure from Psychoanalysis", paper presented at "Science and the Symbolic World: New Paradigms in Psychoanalysis and Analytical Psychology", Charleston, South Carolina, 23–27 April 2003.

McGuire, W. (1974) *The Freud/Jung Letters*, Princeton, NJ: Princeton University Press.

Schreber, D. (1903/1988) *The Memoirs of My Nervous Illness*. Trans. I. McAlpine and R.A. Hunter, Cambridge: Harvard University Press.

Schwartz-Salant, N. (1998) *The Mystery of Human Relationship*, New York: Routledge.

Chapter 6

Vagaries of numinous experience: two questions to George Steiner

Jorge L. Ahumada

According to the *The Shorter Oxford English Dictionary* the term numinous, which entered English usage in the seventeenth century, derives from the Latin *numen*: to nod the head. It refers to the divine or spiritual and extends to the awe-inspiring, the aesthetically appealing and the uplifting. Now, is there some unity to such panoply of themes? What, if anything, can psychoanalysis add? Mainly, can clinical work instruct us on the legitimacy or falsity of felt numinosities, an issue as old as the Book of Genesis?

Freud memorably depicted himself to the pastor Oskar Pfister as 'a godless Jew' (Jones 1955: 458): it stands that in his opinion his method of psychic enquiry did not pierce the walls barring access to the divine. Over a century ago, more famously still, following on the themes of the disenchantment of the world and the death of man, Nietzsche (1882: 167) proclaimed in *The Gay Science*: 'God is dead'. The prominence this assertion gained does not bode well for the current status of numinosity as it relates to divinity.

THE OPACITIES OF THE NUMINOUS IN THE CLINICAL SETTING

Despite exceptions, psychoanalysis and religion have met uncomfortably. Freud's atheism, notably in 'The Future of an Illusion' (1927), fits the picture, but it further happens that religion is often left out clinically as being the analyzand's private realm. That when drawn into the process religious phenomena shed their numinosity signals built-in antagonisms between in-depth enquiry on psychic realities, and numinosity as religiously envisaged.

My clinical example is a woman approaching 40 in an acute psychotic episode, attended years ago. When first contacted she stood on her head in a corner of her seclusion room, legs angled in a V propped up against the walls; though little was graspable in her confused mumblings, I retained a reference to 'a lady surrounded by flowers'. Gradually I grasped that she felt she was undergoing a transcendent religious episode she was reluctant to speak about. During the ensuing months, as she pulled herself together, it turned out that 'the lady surrounded by flowers' was none other than the Virgin Mary, and that her bizarre bodily posture when first met witnessed her being in the holy process of giving birth to a Son of God. In turn this happenstance was a delusional attempt to reverse the guilt ensuing from an infidelity lived as a *coitus cum demone*, as a sexual relationship with the Devil, which had unlocked the psychosis. This uneasy mix of the erotic and the religious was replicated in the treatment situation in a delusional erotized transference, insisting once and again on having sexual relationships with me as the only road to a cure. That she often called me 'my guru' evinced that such erotized numinosity belonged to the holy, not the aesthetic. The issue peaked in an attempt to come to my house: not finding me there, she went to a small bistro at the corner, bought the biggest sandwich and left it in front of my door. And thereby, on my supposed ingestion of the hyperbolic sandwich – iconically equated to herself – she relinquished her erotic transference as done and satisfied, evidencing that the numinosities at stake belonged in an impossible world where ingestion and sexual consummation did each other's job, in line with the equivalence of sexual relationship and cure. In such universes religious feelings enmesh into the psychotic ongoings and do not gain autonomy.

HAPPENSTANCES OF NUMINOSITY, FROM THE 'EXILE FROM EDEN' TO THE 'HOUSE OF LANGUAGE'

Notwithstanding declamations on the death of both God and man, numinosity might well have shifted, from the cosmos as home to the gods, to our sublunar realms, switching persons, functions and places. Though the term comes from the theological, it is amply professed in literature and philosophy that it has now gained new homes.

Indeed, a shift in the numinous to aesthetics and politics started in literature as the eighteenth century closed, and then caught philosophy. Blurring the limits between the literary and the philosophical marks the Romantic revolution, on a par, in the frame of the disenchantment of the world, with a huge shift of the properly human from our prosaic lives into the future tense, seeking a metamorphosis that recaptures the plenitude of Eden. In the words of the Catalonian scholar Antoni Marí there is in Romanticism a nostalgia for an ancient, primordial state or space, the nostalgia of a lost paradise where contraries coexist and multiplicities compound a mysterious unity (Marí 1998: 11–12).

The Oxford historian of ideas Isaiah Berlin takes up this tidal change in the functions and personification of numinosity quoting Lenz, a core voice of the literary *Sturm und Drang*: 'God brooded over the void and a world arose . . . Clear a space! Destroy! Something will arise! Oh God-like feeling!' (Berlin 1975: 230). In turn Nietzsche sought in dance and in song 'the mysterious Primal Unity' whereby man 'feels himself a god' (Nietzsche 1872a: 956). Promptings to incarnate the deity on the side of literary men and philosophers boost Collingwood's argument that myths – contemporary ones not excluded – take their shape in the form of theogonies (Collingwood 1946).

Hölderlin's poetic language, forwards the noted literary critic George Steiner, sought after the numinous, perhaps sacred *Grund des Wortes* where words find their ground: despite its huge psychological risks – which ultimately drove him into madness – Hölderlin's sacrificial mythical dialectics is to Steiner a paradigmatic heroic guide both for the absolute poet and for anyone seeking his human essence. In an agonistic confrontation as *antitheos* in the steps of Oedipus, Antigone and Ajax, this sacrificial dialectics invades the 'space of the gods' challenging it in collision and even in mutual destruction, amounting to blasphemy, suicidal *hubris*, and ultimate assertion of the dialectical reciprocity of existence of men and gods. Antigone's invocation of 'My Zeus', he avows, is an act of arbitrary appropriation, an incursion into the 'absent' realm of divine justice, and a desperate affirmation of the relevance of that realm to the survival of mankind and society (Steiner 1975: 347–8).

Upholding language as the House of Being, Steiner argues that Hölderlin's genius realizes itself in his translations because the clash, mediation, and dialectic fusion of ancient Greek and German enacted tangibly the collisions of being. The poet, he says, brings his native tongue into the field of force of another language invading and striving to break open the core of alien meaning, annihilating his own ego in an attempt both peremptory and utterly humble to fuse with another presence. He posits that these hermeneutic motions of the poet/translator are akin to Antigone's trespassing on the sphere of the gods (but, can challenges at appropriation-fusion with the gods in blasphemy and suicidal *hubris* be exemplar of humbleness? Aren't they better thought of as moved by an intolerance to the nothingness and despair issuing from the disenchantment of the world?).

Long before the Romantics, the literary/poetic way to numinosity was convoked by the German tradition of the *Dichter*: taking his foothold there Steiner later expounds in 'A Reading against Shakespeare' that the term 'poet' purveys no place for its Adamic dimensions, the gap between *Dichter* and poet amounting very nearly to an abyss. The sacrality of the literary act provides the poet/writer, he deems, a salvational, prophetic-didactic role of 'counter-creation to the divine or the unknown'. Confrontation with nothingness is here acknowledged: perceiving nothingness, the *Dichter* 'shall endure to save others from it' (Steiner 1986: 122).

That the authentic *Dichter* be of the rarest should be no surprise given the might summoned by the premise of an *ab initio* Adamic contract between word and world:

True *Dichtung* bears witness. It 'object-knows' in the concrete sense in which Adam's nomination of living forms in Eden corresponded precisely to the truth, the substantive being and signification of these forms. Like Adam, the *Dichter* names that which is, and his naming defines, embodies its veritable being.

(Steiner 1986: 121–2)

Such 'object-knowing' is deemed to differ strictly from pedestrian and scientific ways of knowing, so he underlines – after Heidegger – that the *Dichter* 'speaks being': he is the 'shepherd of being' assuming – in the Romantic fashion – that man's veritable humanness is not found among us but is in trust of the future. 'It is in the custody of the *Dichter* that man comes nearest to being what he is (what he could be if he is to be man)' (Steiner 1986: 122–3). In defence of the *Dichter*'s truth-telling he joins Wittgenstein in that Shakespeare – unmatched *Sprachschöpfer*, incomparable wordsmith as he was – did not reach such summits.

Which fits Freud's work. Useful and in a way revolutionary as his method and findings are when put to good use, Freud was an enquirer, not a 'shepherd of being' or a prophet. When, notably in 'Civilisation and its Discontents' (1930), he opined on weighty cultural and societal issues, he did not slide into the *Dichter*'s shoes. In his words:

I have not the courage to rise up before my fellow-men as a prophet, and I bow to their reproach that I can offer them no consolation: for at bottom that is what they are all demanding – the wildest revolutionaries no less passionately than the most virtuous believers.

And he goes on:

The fateful question for the human species seems to me to be whether and to what extent their cultural development will succeed in mastering the disturbance of their communal life by the human instinct of aggression and self-destruction.

(Freud 1930: 145)

Freud was no Romantic: when self-destruction or unleashed aggression come to task, a Romantic worth his salt promptly harnesses these for the emancipatory enterprise.

THE DEATH OF MAN AND THE EMANCIPATORY RETURN OF THE NUMINOUS

Example of such harnessing, where the exile from Eden leads to an oscillation between self-destruction and unleashed aggression, is, decades after

Hölderlin and at the start of Nietzsche's *oeuvre*, a 1871 tract published posthumously, *Philosophy in the Tragic Age of the Greeks*. Counterpoising his own devitalized, tame, mediocre times and the ancient Greek masters' free, numinous culture, and convinced that with their fall indescribable riches were lost, he forwarded his goal:

> To get past Hellenism by means of deeds: that should be our task . . .
> My aim is to generate open enmity between our contemporary 'culture'
> and antiquity. Whoever wishes to love the former must *hate* the latter.
> (Nietzsche Werke X, 410, Leipzig: Naumann,
> 1894. Quoted in Cowan 1994: 5–6)

Thus hate for our fallen lifeless times opens the path for the numinous: in hating we arrive at an emancipatory model for rhetorical protagonism and liberating self-creation where all contradictions run into harmony, the path of the child-Zeus: 'In this world only play, play as artists and children engage in it, exhibits coming-to-be and passing away, structuring and destroying, without any moral additive, in forever equal innocence' (Nietzsche 1871: 62).

Harrowing as such call to a militant innocence in hating current times might sound, its emotional background is illuminated by an 1872 manuscript, 'The Philosopher: Reflections on the Struggle between Art and Knowledge' (Nietzsche 1872b), where the pain-laden fall into abysmal spirits – in his words, into the loneliest loneliness – catapults a Promethean flight to self-creation:

> *87 – Oedipus – Soliloquy of the Last Philosopher* (A fragment from the history of posterity)

> I call myself the last philosopher, because I am the last man. No one speaks to me but myself, and my voice comes to me like the voice of a dying man! Let me associate for but one hour more with you, dear voice, with you, the last trace of the memory of all human happiness. With you I escape through self-delusion and lie myself into multiplicity and love. For my heart resists the belief that love is dead. I cannot bear the shudder of the loneliest loneliness, and so it forces me to speak as if I were two persons.
>
> Do I still hear you, my voice? Are you whispering as you curse? And yet your curses should cause the bowels of this earth to burst open! But the world continues to live and only stares at me even more glitteringly and coldly with its pitiless stars. It continues to live as dumbly and blindly as ever, and only *one thing* dies – man. And yet, I still hear you, dear voice! *Something* else dies, something other than me, the last man

in this universe. The last sigh, *your* sigh, dies with me. The drawn-out 'alas! alas!' sighed for me, Oedipus, the last miserable man.

(Nietzsche 1872b: 33)

Pain begets joy. As he jots in 1884: 'pain conceived as a tool, as the father of pleasure' (Nietzsche 1901: 546); a pain suffused by despair at the unbearable injustice of life. Of his twin *Soliloquy* voices, the forlorn sigh of the last living man and the wrathful curse ripping open the bowels of the earth, this last leads to idealize cruelty as indispensable for the vigor of life:

Refraining mutually from injury, violence and exploitation and placing one's will on a par with that of someone else . . . immediately proves to be what it really is – a will to the *denial* of life . . . life itself is *essentially* appropriation, injury, overpowering of what is alien and weaker . . . at least, at its mildest, exploitation.

(Nietzsche 1886a: 393)

And again in *The Will to Power*: 'Prevention of reduction to mediocrity. Rather destruction!' (1901: 544). Earlier on he had deemed cruelty to be the greatest of pleasures (Nietzsche 1881: 17) and he chillingly stated in 'The Genealogy of Morals':

To see others suffer does one good, to make others suffer even more . . . Without cruelty there is no festival: thus the longest and most ancient part of human history teaches – and in punishment there is so much that is *festive*.

(Nietzsche 1887: 503)

Cruelty is antidotal to mediocrity and constitutive of pleasure and celebration. However, to the two voices in the *Soliloquy*, the desolate forlorn voice and the wrathful cursing one, a third voice, an elegiac, laughing and mocking divine voice, is to be added. Pain at the break-up point as springboard to elegiac joy and divinity traverses as an Ariadne's thread Nietzsche's life and work, instructing us on the need to seek the rightful limits to the work of art.

Artistic creative activity, highlights the philosopher of art Richard Wollheim, is a process of self-knowledge only when it reflects precisely enough some complex constellation of inner states which the artist seeks to externalize: otherwise the artist fails to acquire self-knowledge and he strenuously attains to self-error. In such case the surface endowing the work of art presents an idealized version of the psyche, struggling to acquire a picture of himself which by many indications he has already shown himself not to be true (Wollheim 1993: 11).

A hugely idealized psychic state in the passage from pain to celebration shines in an aphorism that Georges Bataille pinpoints in *The Will to Power*: 'To see tragic natures founder and *be able to laugh* despite feelings of profound understanding, emotion, and sympathy, which are also felt: this is divine' (Bataille 1945: 175). With those numinous names, Dionysos and the Crucified – and also as Nietzsche Caesar – he signed the last letters sent before his collapse: according to his scholarly admirer Pierre Klossowsky his delight in the enormity of those simulations, where putting himself up as the triumphant Dionysos he erected a counter-reality making of the earth a festival where his own identity dissolved, is at the root of Nietzsche's lapse into madness (Klossowski 1969: 234, 248).

Relevantly, given Nietzsche's impact on academic postmodernism, while his forlorn sighing voice doubtlessly prompts the human, all-too human reader to identify with his pain and his enterprise, it is the divine Dionysian voice – paving the road for the yet-to-be-advened breed of the *Übermenschen* – the one that mightily resounds in academic circles beyond truth and falsity, beyond good and evil.

To Pierre-André Taguieff (1991) Nietzsche's current influence is mostly a style of protagonism: the radicality of negations, the absoluteness of affirmations, the contemptuous tone, the unconditionality of commitments, and the heroic to-the-bitter-end attitude in action. Small wonder that he was misused politically by extremisms on right and left: he fits into what in a perceptive article on the background to Nazism the philosopher Bernard Williams (2000) held against Wagner: his raising an aetheticist hope of a world construed on a higher, transcendental politics of pure heroic action.

Praising over half a century ago the lyric magnificence of Nietzschean poetry, the French philosopher Henri Lefèbvre pointed that in its seamless coupling to the literary his philosophy misses elemental precautions, and that in its evoking the Superhuman beyond Zarathustra, and Dionysos beyond the Superhuman absorbing the individual in the cosmic, Nietzsche elevates Greek tragedy to a cosmic tragedy where alone amid the cosmos he identifies ecstatically with the eternalities of becoming (Lefèbvre 1946: 129). As he puts it in 'Ecce Homo': 'far beyond all terror and pity, to be the eternal joy of Becoming itself -that joy which also involves the joy of destruction' (Nietzsche 1888: 868).

Such redemptory dream unfolding in future tense enacts the alluring role of the overall liberator in a style that uses ignorance as a zero point, putting to action the pleasures of unbound mocking playfulness whereby parody and pastiche pass for honest thinking. Here sociocultural postmodernity and academic postmodernism meet: to Fredric Jameson, a main author of the US academic left, we arrive at postmodernity when the processes of modernization meet no obstacles and implant their autonomous logic the parameters of which change from moment to moment (Jameson 1991: 366). In the ensuing social context of seriality personal futures become phantasmal because, to give an example, one's best efforts do not manage to sustain one's position in a job: we assist out of a feeling of terror of imminent anonymity leading in turn to deliberate distraction where what happens is reformatted or ejected into oblivion.

If it is valid that ethnographers can teach us that almost no culture misses some variant of the Babel-motif, the remembrance of a primal severance, of a brutal weaning, as Steiner (1997: 97) argues, what comes from the clinic in adults and children about the issues of trauma and weaning provides lived prototypes for the exile from Eden, while the dynamics of narcissistic identification shed light on a postmodern trademark in and out of the academy, the reversal of trauma and plain ignorance into parody and celebration.

CONSUMPTION AS A CURRENT PARADIGM OF NUMINOSITY

A Romantic mark, the shift of numinosity from the cosmos to the self, meaning to self-expression, met along the twentieth century with the overall link to objects and persons under the mode of consumption. That the joyous spontaneity of the postmodern emancipatory enterprise goes together with the dynamics of consumerism did not escape Lipovetzky (1986) who, taking as his example the events of May 1968, volunteers that they challenged everything in the established order and proposed nothing in its place, the paradox being that the movement was molded on the euphoria of the consumer age that it purported to denounce. To Godignon and Thiriet (1989) the pleasure of fleeting consumption expresses the subject's freedom: attachment to an object would attribute a definite value to it, thereby limiting and denying one's freedom; consumption negates an object that is a mere opportunity for self-affirmation, a pretext for the self. The external world is thereby wantonly drained of its meaning: reality loses its significance, while concerns for truth are cancelled.

That in postmodernity self-expression as consumption is at the core of identity impinges noticeably on personal links. Appropriation and seizing replace felt acknowledgement of receiving: gratitude, being a threat to the self's primacy, turns unsustainable, while a suspicion of genuine links surges from entrapment in the requisite trust. Grief, guilt and disappointment undermine the celebration, and given that contact with the emotionality of affective dependence entraps us, personal links are banalized: as forwarded by a transvestite in an Almodóvar film, *if you don't like it you take it off . . .*

Which fits what Lipovetzky (1987) notes in the neo-narcissism of contemporary personalities, where equality leads to indeterminacy and to a blurring of sex roles and identities in favor of a vast unisex tide of autonomy and attention to self, in the frame of shifting inequalities run by the primacy of seduction. The whirlwinds of enacted appearances pop up as counter-realities and counter-memories in a context where the self is but its own definition through action, and where freedom consists in ceaseless self-surpassing (Godignon and Thiriet 1990). Everyone feels *entitled not-to-need*, i.e., having a right not-to-depend (Ahumada 2002).

THE NUMINOSITIES OF 'THEORY': CONTENT AND SELF-BEGETTING IN ACADEMIA

What about Academy after the disenchantment of the world, after the death of evidences and after that later variant of the death of evidences, the 'linguistic turn' unbinding language from extra-linguistic referents, meaning from real-life on-goings, a prime move in the postmodernist radicalization of rhetoric? This topic was sketched before (Ahumada 2004), but further comments may be in order.

Pseudo-cyclical time, the time of image-consumption in the Society of the Spectacle, injects in daily life the intemporality of the unconscious, and also signs the ludic consumption of ideas in the Academy of the Spectacle (Debord 1967: 153); there, as Jameson puts it in *The Political Unconscious* (1981), an inmixing of undecidable grafts moves on by the sole virtue of the postmodern Will to Power. Thus academic postmodernism transpires the essence of consumer society, media society or the society of the spectacle. Once the subject of knowledge is abolished the freedom of desire turns assertorical and rules over the festivals of emancipation. Only the play of effects is valid, because attempts at veracity or seriousness are taken to be malevolent attacks targeted at the sovereignty of *collage/montage* and the innocence of playful myth-making.

In the context of undecidable repetition, *participation* turns hegemonic. The privileged link is to an idealized part of oneself as it reflects in the Mirror Arcades: it then becomes fully legitimate that stylish protagonism turn parasitic on content. As pointed out by Jameson, we assist in post-modernism to a quantum leap in the aesthetization of reality, whereby under the sign of amusement our 'representations' of things bring up an enthusiasm not necessarily sustained by the things themselves: 'theory' becomes a new discursive genre that might be called 'postmodernist theory', mostly parasitic on systems deriving from modernism. Beyond the euphoria of its apologists, an euphoria which in itself is a peculiar historical sign, the idea seems to be that the residual traces and the values and attitudes unconsciously reproduced are precious indexes of the obstruction to the advent of a new cultural reality. There results the serial production of 'lexical neo-events' where a multiplicity of neologisms re-catalogs and metamorphoses all that exists, proposing changes and new ideas under the promise of ending up whatever is felt as restrictive, unsatisfactory or boring: in such prodigious operation of rewriting everything is grist for the postmodernist mills (Jameson 1991: xiii–xiv). In the field of psychoanalysis, the discursive end result follows 'the dream of the analyst philosopher: a psychoanalysis without the clinic', as André Green (1998: 286) has quite aptly put it.

In a like vein, the poet laureate Czeslaw Milosz (1998) warns that nihilistic abjuration of judgment opens the field to all the treasons, voraciousnesses and cowardices, and it happens now that it has become so prevalent to think of oneself as a god in the mode of Nietzsche that courage is needed in order to raise a discrepancy; whereby in the academy as Mirror Arcade the numinosities of discursive self-begetting will rightfully substitute for the aridities of honest enquiry.

Symptomatically a foremost exponent of hermeneutics, Jürgen Habermas, recently questioned what has transpired out of the 'linguistic turn', saying that our everyday practices need to keep to a basic realism; on this basis we must sustain a distinction between belief and knowledge, because at any time our interpretations may lead us into error: such realism finds no place in the discursive practices unfolding in academia (Habermas 2000: 49). In such a way postmodernist discourses share the spell of the Romantic spite for realism shining up in aphorism 229 of 'Beyond Good and Evil': 'any insistence on profundity and thoroughness is a violation, a desire to hurt the basic will of the spirit which unceasingly strives for the apparent and superficial' (Nietzsche 1886: 349).

Now, will the aestheticist rivalry of seductions seeking primacy in the free-for-all of a histrionics of mirroring mark the fate of common-sense, and of psychoanalysis, in the age of Image?

AFFECT AND EMOTION AS IMMANENT NUMINOSITY

May one join Steiner's core postulate, that just two experiences enable human beings to participate in the truth-fiction, in the pragmatic metaphor of eternity, of liberation from the eradicating dictates of biological-historical time, which is to say: death? These two experiences are – in his view – authentic religious beliefs for those open to them, and the experiences of the aesthetic enabling us to escape the logic of madness and despair, which allow us to share in the experiences of time unbounded, in a *poiesis* authorizing the unreason of hope (Steiner 2001: 214–15). In other words, should one agree that it is a must to raise up a truth-fiction in front of passing time and incoming death?

During his final days Freud soberly pondered in 'Analysis Terminable and Interminable' on the limits and scope of his method (Freud 1940). The

German title *Die endliche und die unendliche Analyse* opens, however, further expansions on the immanent, earthly enough numinosities of lived affect and emotion which are well within reach of psychoanalysis. The creative *Geist*, avows Steiner, is boundless – *unendliche*; and it is precisely in terms of the making present, the making contemporary of the unbounded (*die Vergegenwärtung des Unendlichen*) that Hölderlin defines the function and aim of art (Steiner 2001: 102).

The everyday as numinous appears in the course of psychoanalyses as fleeting, momentary islets where serenity and joy find a place. These will conjoin mainly in the final stages of analyses, at a time when the roughest share of the unconscious anxieties and turmoils bringing the analyzand into treatment has been recognized and traversed.

Let us take as example a woman, Mrs M, who started treatment at age 50 after the devastating rupture of a 30-year-long first marriage, which happened when she uncovered that her husband led a double life. She threw him out in fury, but thereafter she collapsed: on coming into treatment she felt – in her words – 'run over by a garbage truck', which marks the huge self-demeaning brought out by the loss of her marriage. Self-demeaning had a variety of roots, ranging from conscious feelings that she had destroyed her family to obvious unconscious anchorings in a highly ideal primal scene: thus, she would stand transfixed fronting the apartment her husband had set up for his lover, to whom my patient attributed the feminine abilities of the Queen of Sheba while she herself felt as nothing at all. To cut an involved analytic course short, suffice to say that in due time sub-missiveness left place to episodes of fury: in one of those she physically battered her ex-husband who withstood, impassive, the assault! Anyway, evolution came mostly from analytic reviewing of her marital relationship to an, at some unconscious level, highly idealized husband, and of her own self-idealizing, manifestly submissive, possessive link to him; an under-standing which step-by-step permitted her forsaking the idealization, and then the link as such.

Concomitantly, she gained closer contact with the self-idealization pro-pelling her devoted generosity – in line with what I have called 'delusional goodness' (Ahumada 1982) – which had sustained her through her mar-riage but got her into all sorts of trouble, such as taking up impossible tasks beyond her competence or power, especially in relation to her sons and daughters, which led to conflicts or to her driving herself to exhaustion. Gradual acknowledgement, and then relinquishment, of her possessive devotion allowed her to handle herself and then gain a valid role as emo-tional administrator of the growth process in the family she had up to then felt as broken to pieces by the divorce; in such vein she took to managing her relationship to her ex-husband so that they both kept close affective roles toward the children. Also, she gained an understanding that her post-adolescent children's troubles did not derive solely from the trauma of the divorce – conflicting as divorce had been for them – but resulted in good measure from their own whooping resistance to arrive at adulthood, and thus her devoted anticipation of their problems or needs led mostly to further spoiling. She grasped that, as the saying goes, the road to hell is oft paved with good intentions and gradually, having become more resilient to mishaps, she came to enjoy the often complex on-goings, encouraged and joyful at the steps toward an evolving maturity that she came to perceive in those closest to her. Later on, when grandchildren started arriving, she thoroughly enjoyed their built-in numinosity. To be fair, such joy cannot be attributed solely, nor perhaps mainly, to the work of analysis, as decades earlier she had much enjoyed her baby children; however, her newfangled admiration at the intermingling there of a *poiesis* of play, affect and psychic growth on the part of both the baby and herself can fairly said to be an outcome of the psychoanalytic process.

To end, two questions to George Steiner. First, is it tenable to hold, as he steadily does, that a fundamental boredom and desperation marks the majority of lives, empowering with an irrefutable realism the archaic Greek postulate that 'it is best not to be born and next best to die young' (Steiner 1997: 94)? Second, and fundamentally, is it tenable that 'it is the instrumentalities of the imaginary, of the unverifiable (the poetic), it is the potentialities of fiction (lies) and syntax-leaps into tomorrows without end' (Steiner 1997: 95–6) in rebellion against death, that provides most of us with the road out of the ostracism from Eden and toward a dynamics of hope? That *poiesis* lays claim to primary making and the artist is indeed god-like to himself and to his public (Steiner 2001: 144) does not help matters. Even less, his enthusiastically endorsing that having fathered Natasha and Anna Karenina, Tolstoy came to doubt his own mortality (Steiner 2001: 144).

It stands in my view that the psychoanalyst is not a prophet or a *Dichter*, and offers no ready consolation. However, upon Mrs M's course and that of myriad other analyzands we can trust that despite our immanent finiteness, becoming finds commonplace outlets: fuller contact with affects and emotions in our daily lives provides plentiful uplifting and hope. Antipodially to rebellious appropriations and self-begettings casting oneself as an *antitheos* fighting the gods, such emotions require a relinquishing of possessivenesses on the side of the self, vehicling an awareness of, and a respect for, the unsurmountable otherness of others, and they are proof that we tread the terrain of the rightful end of analysis.

References

Ahumada, J.L. (1982) 'The Unconscious Delusion of "Goodness"', in *The Logics of the Mind: A Clinical View* (2002), pp. 65–82, London: Karnac.

Ahumada, J.L. (2002) 'A Short Comment on Jim Rose's Paper, "The Presence of

Absence in the Transference"', *Bulletin of the British Psycho-Analytical Society* 38(3): 26–7.

Ahumada, J.L. (2004) 'From Insight to Self-Begetting: On the Postmodern Vicissitudes of Psychoanalytic Ownership', in *Who Owns Psychoanalysis?*, ed. A. Casement, London: Karnac.

Bataille, G. (1945) *On Nietzsche* (1944), St Paul, MN: Paragon.

Berlin, I. (1975) 'The Apotheosis of the Romantic Will', in *The Crooked Timber of Humanity* (1990), pp. 207–37, Princeton NJ: Princeton University Press.

Collingwood, R.G. (1946) *The Idea of History* (1993), Oxford: Oxford University Press.

Cowan, M. (1994) Introduction, in F. Nietzsche, *Philosophy in the Tragic Age of the Greeks*, pp. 1–21, Washington, DC: Gateway.

Debord, G. (1967) *The Society of the Spectacle* (1985), New York: Zone Books.

Freud, S. (1927) 'The Future of an Illusion', *Standard Edition SE, 21*.

Freud, S. (1930) 'Civilisation and its Discontents', *SE, 21*.

Freud, S. (1940) 'Analysis Terminable and Interminable', *SE, 23*.

Godignon, A. and Thiriet, J.L. (1989) 'The End of Alienation?', in *New French Thought: Political Philosophy* (1994), ed. M. Lilla, pp. 220–5, Princeton NJ: Princeton University Press.

Godignon, A. and Thiriet, J.L. (1990) 'The Rebirth of Voluntary Servitude', in *New French Thought: Political Philosophy* (1994), ed. M. Lilla, pp. 226–31, Princeton NJ: Princeton University Press.

Green, A. (1998) 'Le déchainement du signifiant énigmatique désignifié dans le processus traductif-détraductif autothéorisant: De l'interêt à bien lire Jean Laplanche', *Revue Français Psychanalyse* 62: 263–87.

Habermas, J. (2000) 'Richard Rorty's Pragmatic Turn', in *Rorty and his Critics*, ed. R.B. Brandom, pp. 31–64, Malden, MA and Oxford: Blackwell.

Jameson, F. (1981) *The Political Unconscious: Narrative as a Socially Symbolic Act*, Ithaca, NY: Cornell University Press.

Jameson, F. (1991) *Postmodernism or, The Cultural Logic of Late Capitalism* (1999), Durham, NC: Duke University Press.

Jones, E. (1955) *The Life and Work of Sigmund Freud, Vol. 2*, New York, NY: Basic Books.

Klossowski, P. (1969) *Nietzsche and the Vicious Circle* (1997), Chicago: University of Chicago Press.

Lefèbvre, H. (1946) *El Existencialismo* (1954), Buenos Aires: Capricornio.

Lipovetzky, G. (1986) 'May 68, or the Rise of Transpolitical Individualism', in *New French Thought: Political Philosophy*, ed. M. Lilla, pp. 212–19, Princeton, NJ: Princeton University Press.

Lipovetzky, G. (1987) *The Empire of Fashion: Dressing Modern Democracy* (1994), Princeton, NJ: Princeton University Press.

Marí, A. (1998) 'Prólogo', in *El entusiasmo y la quietud: Antología del romanticismo alemán*, ed. A. Marí, 2nd. rev. ed., pp. 11–29, Barcelona: Tusquets.

Milosz, C. (1998) 'Discreet Charm of Nihilism', *The New York Review of Books* (November 19), p. 17.

Nietzsche, F. (1871) *Philosophy in the Tragic Age of the Greeks* (1994), Washington, DC: Gateway.

Nietzsche, F. (1872a) 'The Birth of Tragedy from the Spirit of Music', in *The*

Philosophy of Nietzsche (1927), trans. C.P. Fadiman, pp. 949–1088, New York, NY: Modern Library.

Nietzsche, F. (1872b) 'The Philosopher: Reflections on the Struggle between Art and Knowledge', in *Philosophy and Truth: Selections from Nietzsche's Notebooks of the early 1870's* (1999), pp. 3–58, Amherst, NY: Humanity Books.

Nietzsche, F. (1881) *Daybreak: Thoughts on the Prejudices of Morality* (1997), ed. M. Clark and B. Leiter, Cambridge: Cambridge University Press.

Nietzsche, F. (1882) *The Gay Science* (1974), ed. W. Kaufmann, New York, NY: Vintage.

Nietzsche, F. (1886) 'Beyond Good and Evil', in *Basic Writings of Nietzsche* (1992), trans. and ed. W. Kaufmann, pp. 191–435, New York: The Modern Library.

Nietzsche, F. (1887) 'The Genealogy of Morals', in *Basic Writings of Nietzsche* (1992), trans. and ed. W. Kaufmann, pp. 449–599, New York: Modern Library.

Nietzsche, F. (1888) 'Ecce Homo', in *The Philosophy of Nietzsche* (1927), trans. C.P. Fadiman, pp. 809–946, New York: Modern Library.

Nietzsche, F. (1901) *The Will to Power* (1968), ed. W. Kaufmann, New York: Vintage.

Steiner, G. (1975) *After Babel: Aspects of Language and Translation* (1998), Oxford and New York: Oxford University Press.

Steiner, G. (1986) 'A Reading against Shakespeare', in *No Passion Spent: Essays 1975–1995* (1996), pp. 108–28, New Haven, CT and London: Yale University Press.

Steiner, G. (1997) *Errata: An Examined Life*, New Haven, CT and London: Yale University Press.

Steiner, G. (2001) *Grammars of Creation* (2002), London: Faber & Faber.

Taguieff, P.-A. (1991) 'The Traditionalist Paradigm-Horror of Modernity and Antiliberalism: Nietzsche in Reactionary Rhetoric', in *Why We Are Not Nietzscheans* (1997), ed. L. Ferry and A. Renaut, pp. 158–224, Chicago and London: University of Chicago Press.

Williams, B. (2000) 'Wagner and Politics', *The New York Review of Books* 47(17), 2 November: 36–43.

Wollheim, R. (1993) *The Mind and its Depths*, Cambridge, MA and London: Harvard University Press.

Chapter 7

Jung and Derrida: the numinous, deconstruction and myth

Susan Rowland

The *numinosum* is either a quality belonging to a visible object or the influence of an invisible presence that causes a peculiar alteration of consciousness.

(Jung 1938/1940: 6)[1]

A great many ritualistic performances are carried out for the sole purpose of producing at will the effect of the *numinosum* . . . But a religious belief in an external and objective divine cause is always prior to any such performance.

(Jung 1938/1940: 7)

[I]f the image is charged with numinosity, that is, with psychic energy, then it becomes dynamic and will produce consequences . . . the archetype is living matter.

(Jung 1961: 589)

[O]ur consciousness has deprived itself of the organs by which the auxiliary contributions of the instincts and the unconscious could be assimilated. These organs were the numinous symbols, held holy by common consent.

(Jung 1961: 583)

Introduction

The idea of the numinous haunts Jung's psyche. When used synonymously for psychic energy (in the fourth quotation above), it opens the ground of Jungian psychology to the discipline's ancestry in theology and philosophy. In itself, Jung's numinous proves liminal, a quality denoting disputed regions between consciousness and unconsciousness, the conceivable and the unknowable, the 'inside' psyche and the 'exterior' cosmos, of the distinction between form and matter.

For example, is the numinous a gift from outside the individual, the grace of God, as construed by monotheistic religions? Or, is it a psychic creation of the deep interior? This question is yet another version of the Cartesian split between self and world. As a founding structure of modernity, it is now a commonplace to assume a separation of conscious rational mind from unconsciousness, body, matter and cosmos. Jung's treatment of the numinous, then, is first of all to trouble such an assumption. For in the quotations above, the numinous is the influence of a presence that cannot be securely consigned to either 'outside' or 'inside' the psyche. Carried by the religious symbolism of a culture, the numinous is the psychic matter that *matters*. It will prove integral to Jung's urgent attempt to heal the modern psyche, now dwelling in alien territory because it has lost the connection to its *vitally* charged symbols.

So Jung's numinous is at the heart of his cultural criticism. To him the modern world is sick because it has exalted rationality and the knowledge created by it, so far above unconscious sources of being that the resulting neglect of the whole psyche has turned it dark. When rationality is entirely divorced from its irrational roots it proves fragile. It is dangerously liable to being swallowed up by unconscious powers. These powers have turned demonic through being ignored too long.[2] Jung, always concerned with the relation of the individual to the collective (unconscious and culture), argues that the cultural numinous is not extinguished. Rather, when traditional religious symbols lose their potency to regulate the psyche, the collective turns to other icons. What Jung liked to call the devilish 'isms' exert a hypnotic fascination as the psyche succumbs to fanaticism.

Fortunately, Jung takes his cultural criticism in two directions that ultimately will provide tools for social-psychic reconstruction: that of myth, and of an essentially aesthetic re-ordering of science. For if the problem of modernity is the privileging of reason above all other modes of the psyche, then one prominent example is the construction of modern science. The Enlightenment belief that science is built upon objective observations of a reality exterior to the observing process is not only questioned by twentieth-century particle physics, it is also a logical contradiction for psychology. Since there is no exterior point outside the psyche from which to observe it, psychology is necessarily a 'science' from within. Consequently, as Jung was well aware, phenomena that alter consciousness, such as the numinous, can never be definitively attributed to either 'inside' or 'outside' realms.

After the critique of reason and 'objective' science, a third element of Jung's cultural criticism is his questioning of the hero myth as the major structure of western consciousness. The myth supplies the narrative model of the masculine hero who fights the monstrous (m)other of the uncon-scious, seizes the territory of the other, and wins union with the feminine as a prize. Such a powerful narrative is, as Jung noted, a close sponsor of the cultural triumph of reason and colonialism. Rationality as hero conquering the psyche and colonising its habitable, knowable domain, is an aspect of the mythical dimension of modern ills. So in order to comprehend Jung's numinous, it will be necessary to trace the deep myths of being that struc-ture psyche, culture and history.

THE MYTHICAL FRAME

To Jung, the 'objective' mode of modern scientific observations was closely related to theological error. He understood that modern scientific assumptions about the world are directly descended from Christian theology. His book, *Aion*, is an exploration of the legacy of this history (Jung 1951). With a model of God as transcendent of and separate from 'his' creation, theologians sought to understand the mind of God, the logos, by studying its secondary product, nature. Just as God is separate from his creation, nature and man, so man, conceived in the image of God, is similarly separate from, and indeed transcendent of, nature. God exists above man, is 'outside' and has given man dominion over nature, which man is similarly 'outside'. To Jung, the theological error derives from this regimented portrayal of reality. Transcendent God is defined as wholly good. To achieve such a structuring of good means splitting the supreme divine being off from evil and irrationality. Hence evil and irrationality become properties of matter.

So theologians continue to seek the good and rational mind of God as logos transcendent of creation. Eventually belief in this sacred in the sky declines and those theologians studying creation re-define themselves as scientists. They are still in pursuit of a logos: now science, knowledge and reason are regarded as transcendent, logocentric, and divisible from irrationality, the human psyche and matter. The Christian myth of transcendence produces the scientific myth of objectivity.

Significantly, the myth of transcendence is also highly gendered. With Christianity's male actors of Father and Son, reason and logos become associated with masculinity, while irrationality and matter are gendered feminine. Much of Jung's writing is marked with a struggle to both resist and recuperate this not-so-hidden gender politics of modernity. For example, he posits a psychic binary of logos and eros as factors in the psyche. In the first instance these appear to be more an expression of the triumph of masculine logos than its amelioration. For Jung's logos connotes rational consciousness and spirit, regarded as masculine and proper to the male conscious psyche. Eros is connectedness and feeling, said to be more characteristic of the female psyche.

Here, as elsewhere in Jung's work, a potentially radical feminine is introduced, only to serve as a support to the fragile nature of masculine reason in modernity. Jung is a conservative with revolutionary ideas. He wants to save the modern world more than he wants to transform it. Nevertheless his healing project has subversive implications that bring him close to a later attempt to re-make culture and meaning: that of Jacques Derrida's deconstruction.[3] For, taken mythically, what both thinkers are doing is realigning the two great myths of creation shaping cultural signifying: the Sky-Father logos and the Earth-Mother eros.

TWO CREATION MYTHS AND THE RELATIVITY OF FORM AND MATTER

The Judaeo-Christian creation myth appears to be a straightforward version of a Sky-Father. This is a mythical form that gained ascendancy over earlier religions in the ancient world when nomadic tribes took over formerly agrarian societies (Baring and Cashford 1991: 666). 'He' creates the worlds as separate from himself and so remains the logos, transcendent of it. 'He' needs no feminine consort. Such a narrative becomes the founding structure of logocentrism. It shapes basic assumptions such as distinctions between inside and outside, and form and matter. In the myth of the logos, transcendent mind is a 'masculine' creative principle working on inert 'feminine' matter. Typically, Jung seems to accept the distinction while problematising it.

> [I]t makes no substantial difference whether you call the world principle male and a father (spirit), or female and a mother (matter). Essentially we know as little of the one as of the other.
>
> (Jung 1961: 582)

Derrida is equally very conscious that his life-long critique of the apparently obvious nature of basic distinctions such as form and matter, is, at root, a challenge to the Sky-Father creation myth.

> In any case, Christian creationism would . . . have brought with it . . . a supplementary motivation for considering the form-matter complex as the structure of every entity, the *ens creatum* as the unity of *forma* and *materia*. Though faith has disappeared, the schemas of Christian philosophy remain effective.
>
> (Derrida 1987: 66)

Jung's analysis reminds us of another creation myth, this time gendered feminine. In the Earth-Mother story, the Earth herself is sacred and generative of all reality in a great web of being. Here the sacred is not transcendent. Rather it is immanent within her fertile materiality. Matter and spirit are one rather than entirely separate. The Earth-Mother gives birth to a divine son, who becomes her lover. He suffers a fall in death, only to be reborn again with the aid of the feminine principle.

Such a founding story of Earth-Mother with her son-lover is the core of the myths of Osiris and Attis. More controversially, it is still perceptible in Christianity. Within the Sky-Father's impregnation of a virgin, is the pagan story of a divine son of Virgin Mother Earth who dies only to be resurrected. Much iconography of the Christian Virgin Mary portrays her in the garb of the Mother Goddess. She clasps her dying son much as the Great

Mother embraced her son-lover. So entwined, yet barely visible in Christian myth, is an earlier myth of the immanent Goddess giving birth out of the sacredness of matter.

Indeed, the word 'matter' is derived from 'mater', mother. Where the logocentric perspective of separation has feminine matter as the evil 'other' of transcendent rational good, Earth-Mother sponsors a theology of the connectedness of all the cosmos. 'She' has no form/matter distinction. Matter and spirit, humanity and nature, are all part of an unimaginable whole; a whole whose plurality cannot be contained in a single image. In fact such a 'whole' cannot be represented, because we cannot get 'outside' her embrace to see this sacred reality as separate from ourselves.

Here we can see Jung's principles of logos and eros are simultaneously Sky-Father spirit and Earth-Mother connectedness. By bringing them together in the psyche he is attempting to reconcile two gendered myths of creation. His point that neither is self-evidently 'the truth' (because we cannot get outside psyche and world to know it rationally) will prove to be an opening to his profound evocation of the numinous.

So although Christianity is predominantly a Sky-Father logos oriented myth, it retains significant Earth-Mother elements. In addition to the bodily incarnation of the son-lover, the story of creation in a garden, the moulding of human beings out of clay, and the presence of that 'other' to God's commands, the serpent (ancient image of the Mother Goddess), all include the substance of the earlier myth.

In fact, Christianity's constitution as an entwinement of two myths, one dominant, one virtually invisible to Christian culture, suggests that the mythical frame of consciousness may necessarily be plural. The psyche requires more than one myth. While the two gendered myths of creation each beget other generations of mythical stories of the gods and goddesses, perhaps, as Jung hints, proper psychic health requires a better balance between the two contrasting frames. So how, precisely, might the Earth-Mother be rescued – in a world in which the Sky-Father of rational consciousness is dying of loneliness?

THE MOTHER GODDESS AND MODERNITY

To call the Sky-Father logocentric is to recognise that his form-matter narrative structures all kinds of oppositions that make up the tacit assumptions of modernity: that between good and evil, inside and outside, above and below, masculine and feminine, matter and spirit. By contrast, Earth-Mother eros is to be found in all the cultural challenges to such 'natural' oppositions, including the environmental movement that seeks to overcome the notion that man is inherently transcendent of nature. Eco-logically, human beings are immanent *in* nature and need to respect rather than obliterate 'her' nurturing properties. Culture needs to reawaken its ancient form in *cultivation*.

Many non-monotheistic religions similarly place human beings in a vital relationship to non-human nature. For example, animism, which is the belief that the non-human is alive, and in some sense could open a dialogue with human beings, has a three-fold presence on the margins of mono-theism: in a pagan past not wholly eradicated by cutting down the sacred groves, in non-western religions, and in New Age rituals.

Something so potently marginal is, of course, likely to be textual in the material sense of writing, as well as in the larger sense of cultural systems of meaning. I have already pointed out some of the traces of the Earth-Mother in the Christian bible, with her material plurality and immanence challenging the one God, one truth, logos of the Sky-Father. Yet any examination of Christian history would similarly detect traces of an ani-mistic conception of nature. Sometimes it is literally visible in the margins of medieval manuscripts. Sometimes it is uneasily debated in those practices liminal (so marginal) to Christianity such as alchemy.

What has been less recognised is the way that the tension between logos and eros has been played out in practices of reading. As Christopher Manes has pointed out, medieval Christian theologians were largely responsible for *producing* the Sky-Father as logos by their method of reading biblical texts for a singular transcendent truth. Through their exegesis, the material world of the Sky-Father's creation becomes the symbol of a 'higher' truth, rather than a sacred entity in itself.

> Exegesis established God as a transcendental subject speaking through natural entities, which, like words on a page, had a symbolic meaning, but no autonomous voice. It distilled the veneration of words and reason into a discourse that we still speak today.
>
> (Manes 1996: 20)

In effect, animism, the many voices of nature and of the plural immanent sacred, was removed to the one voice of the logos speaking through the text. Animism of nature became textual logos. Indeed, modernity's rela-tionship to texts is deeply animistic. Long ago, nature spoke to us, now texts do. Casually we assert: 'the book says . . .'. In particular, the medieval theological practice of reading texts for logos, truth transcendent of matter (including textual matter), is bequeathed to the Enlightenment and science as the textual practice for producing 'objective' knowledge. It sought a singular, monotheistic logocentric voice from texts. On the other hand, the inherent plurality of pagan animism also found a textual home in the arts and literature in particular. Here I could speculate on a link between the simultaneous intensification in medieval exegesis for the 'one truth' and the eros-sponsored plurality of voices of authors such as Chaucer.

I am going to suggest that Jung and Derrida are both aware of the need to realign Sky-Father and Earth-Mother relations at a textual, mythical and conceptual level. For Jung, this project hinges upon his idea of synchronicity (the conceptual), the myth of the trickster, and crucially, the textuality of the numinous as the creative undoing of the rule of the Sky-Father over texts in the widest sense of cultural signifying.

Through introducing logos and eros as key principles in the psyche, Jung urges a negotiation and exchange between them. His conservative weighting of these two creation myths is apparent in regarding each principle as more identified with one gender. Without such a traditional pinning down, Jung's idea of individuation would be seen to contain a radical deconstruction of Sky-Father dominance over Earth-Mother immanence.

'Synchronicity' is Jung's version of individuation for culture. He is explicit that it is designed to give Earth-Mother or 'Nature' space to 'be' in the ambit of modern logos science.

> For [experimental science] . . . [t]he workings of Nature in her unrestricted wholeness are completely excluded . . . [W]e need a method of enquiry which . . . leaves Nature to answer out of her fullness.
>
> (Jung 1952a: 864)

For the purposes of this chapter I will simply define Jung's concept of synchronicity as a way of regarding events (psychic and extra-psychic) that are not causally linked, as capable of being connected by meaning. Synchronicity recognises coincidences of psyche and outer world as meaningful. It takes reality seriously outside the mechanisms of cause and effect. The cosmos is a web connected by more than the inert mechanistic characterisation of it. Suggestively, Jung refers to synchronous events as, '*acts of creation in time*', the on-going generative powers of nature, the Earth-Mother (Jung 1952a: 965).

Of course, the extent to which Jung sought scientific credibility for his concept of synchronicity is a measure of his desire to privilege the masculine logos. On the other hand, his writing about the new science of particle physics draws upon its apparently 'irrational' and immanent qualities; its need to regard (feminine) matter as dynamic and animate.

Jung's second way of cultural individuation lies in his treatment of myth in general and of the trickster in particular. My argument here is that the trickster, in all his protean animality and fertility, is the Mother-Goddess in a guise suitable for Jung's underlying gender politics. For example, he is erotic in being a god(dess) out of whose *body* the world was created (Jung 1954: 472). Moreover, it is indicative that in his characteristically 'tricky' essay on the trickster, Jung is able to locate 'him' both in non-western religions and in medieval Christianity. The latter, at a popular level, gives space to the trickster by absorbing many pagan animistic practices such as an ass festival, when the animal was worshipped in church (Jung 1954: 461–3).

For modernity, the trickster as mythical *narrative* has been de-natured into the thinner, and altogether blacker *image* of the shadow, Jung says. Such a move is both a symptom of modernity's psychic sickness and Jung's opportunity to revise its symbolism upon traditional lines. It is a symptom in that the loss of the trickster narrative means that 'he' no longer embodies the same degree of psychic *animation*. 'He' can no longer effect the vital social function of making visible the unconsciousness of the collective, so subjecting it to conscious and ethical criticism. Without such a dynamic internal resource, collective errors are ignored, because invisible to a logos-dominated psyche that only recognises consciousness. Disregarded and despised, unconsciousness turns black and evil, resulting in what Jung sees as a typical product of modernity: the soldier who blindly obeys orders with no capacity for his own ethical judgement (Jung 1954: 479).

Ultimately, the trickster reveals the ethical function of the Earth-Mother, in enabling collective self-examination. She (as trickster here) is necessary to forge a negotiation between logos-oriented modern consciousness and unconscious psyche, especially when that unconsciousness is projected onto others. Ethics means Earth-Mother and Sky-Father in a dynamic relationship.

So if the trickster has given way to the shadow image, then modernity has lost a valuable psychic resource for its ethical being. That, at any rate, is Jung's diagnosis. Fortunately his diagnosis is his opportunity to add the trickster image to his other collection of archetypal images: those of anima, wise old man and self (Jung 1954: 485). Therefore engagement with the unconscious shadow is but a prelude to 'higher' or deeper challenges leading to the self image as saviour.

> [T]he recognition and integration of the shadow create such a harrowing situation that nobody but a saviour can undo the tangled web of fate.
>
> (Jung 1954: 487)

Crucially, substituting trickster-*narrative* with Jung's own favourite individuation collection of *images* means that the trickster-goddess can be slotted into a subordinate role in Jung's essentially Christian model for the individuating psyche. The Sky-Father triumphs again over the largely obscured Earth-Mother trickster. Feminine signifying is still wrenched into the position of shoring up traditional masculine signifying. After demonstrating such doubts with the hero myth, Jung allows him to re-emerge as the chief mythical structure of consciousness.

On the other hand, the oscillation in Jung's psyche between images pointing to Christian logos and mythical narrative incarnating eros-relationship suggests Jung's inability to leave narrative behind. It is innate in the on-going dynamism of individuation and is an incarnation of the numinous presence of the Earth-Mother in his psychology. I use the word 'incarnation' here advisedly, because the myth-making quality of the psyche is a weaving together of body, consciousness and unconsciousness. Narrative and its numinous psychic enactment in myth is the way Jung's writing goes beyond psyche-logos into psyche-logos *and* eros-mythos. Narrative drives synchronicity as making meaning by incorporating irrational connections, *telling stories* that in the act of telling put the human psyche as immanent in nature and cosmos. So Jung's numinous has an aesthetic component. It is reading reality aesthetically: the numinous tells a story about the Earth-Mother and Sky-Father *together*.

For more on reading we need to turn to that other architect of mythical re-individuation: Jacques Derrida.

THE MYTH OF DECONSTRUCTION

If the modern world's relationship with texts is animistic in hearing them 'speak' to us, then deconstruction intensifies that animism to an almost chaotic degree. For deconstruction a text is a web of voices, a plurality that is unable to maintain a singular logos or a one truth. In deconstruction, 'truth' in a text is immanent, so not abstractable as objective, singular or coherent. Deconstruction thinks texts from within the realm of the Earth-Mother.

However, just as the most devoted work of the logos Sky-Father builders of modernity could not entirely eradicate animism and the Earth-Mother, no more can deconstruction wholly abandon the logos. Like Jung, Derrida wants to realign the creation myths. Unlike Jung, he is no social conservative. So his recognition of the impossibility, and even undesirability, of living in just one myth is differently oriented to Jung's.

On the one hand, deconstruction's critique of 'presence' is actually a critique of the Sky-Father's logos claim to stand supreme, eliminating all others. For if meaning is to be fully present in a sign, there is required to be a metaphysical source, exterior to the system of meaning-making itself, which would guarantee such 'presence'. Such a logos (exterior 'sky' source), is necessary for language to signify, yet deconstruction argues that it is itself a product of that necessity. It is metaphysical in its unprovable exterior status. So the perspective that deconstruction has of language is of a web of signifying with no intrinsic 'outside', that has to give *birth* to something posited as 'outside' in order to work – the Earth-Mother myth of sexuality is in the textuality. Deconstruction/Earth-Mother's perspective on the logos is that it is a divine son who has 'forgotten' or 'repressed' his sacred origin.

On the other hand, modernity cannot simply discard logocentrism and switch over entirely to Earth-Mother plurality and generativity. Although the distinctions that structure rationality, such as that between form and matter, are not as absolute as the logos pretends they are, deconstruction does not do away with them. Rather meaning is shown to be disseminated as the signified of a signifier proves to be another signifier, and so on. While deconstruction offers a glimpse of a potentially endless dissemination where the fertility of the Mother-Goddess is enacted in the animistic plurality of matter in textual mode, the Sky-Father can still be detected in the impossibility of completely undoing the signifier–signified relationship. Nevertheless, deconstruction reading texts (deconstruction as an activity), which undoes the supposed unity of the reader, enters the body of the Earth-Mother as her multiple 'acts of creation in time' make and unmake meaning.

So deconstruction also contains the realisation that culture needs more than one myth. Logocentrism can be displaced as centre, but not wholly replaced, in Derrida's realisation that, like Jung, both Sky-Father logos and Earth-Mother eros are necessary for psyche and the collective. Indeed, deconstruction embraces Jung's mythical thinking of the two creation stories at the level of 'play'.

> Derrida argues that we can never get 'outside' metaphysics in order to undo it. Nevertheless it is utterly crucial to see that this statement conceives of metaphysics as always open and dynamic. There is always some play within any metaphysical concept . . . Play in general is the condition of metaphysics.
>
> (Lucy 1997: 102)

Play here is a kind of 'give' as in play of a rope within the rigidities of the logos ideal. If it is not possible to do without logos, it is possible to deconstruct, to exploit the playful trickiness of language as immanence in the textual body. It seems to me that Derrida's call to think the structurality of structure is answered by Jung's treatment of myth as the 'play' of psychic energy; the engine of the numinous. Deconstruction's myth is Jung's trickster.

JUNG FROM THE PERSPECTIVE OF DERRIDA

At this point it is useful to return to Jung's stated position on the two creation myths.

> [I]t makes no substantial difference whether you call the world principle male and a father (spirit), or female and a mother (matter). Essentially we know as little of one as of the other.
>
> (Jung 1961: 582)

Here Jung appears to be accepting the form/matter distinction and its logocentric interpretation of Sky-Father forming inert feminine matter. Yet at the same time these words offer the interpretation that the 'world principle' is matter as mater, the Earth-Mother. What is indicative of his whole attitude to the psyche, however, is his emphasis on the *unknowable* dimensions of these creation stories. To Jung, *his* founding principle was the unknowable nature of the unconscious psyche and its consequences for claims to knowledge. If Jungian psychology has a metaphysical entity, from the perspective of deconstruction, it is the dynamic function of the unknown and unknowable. Such an epistemological base means that all human knowledge, language and culture is relative to an unknown degree. In effect, Jung's founding *presence* is a founding *absence*.

So far in this chapter I have concentrated on Jung, and then on Derrida, from the position of Jung's treatment of myth as the structuring of the liminal realm between form and matter. To turn around the angle of vision and see Jung through Derrida is revealing. For deconstruction's reaction to Jung's hypnotic metaphysical unconscious is two-fold. I am indebted to the philosopher, Christian Kerslake, for help with the next part of this argument. On the one hand, it could be argued that the Jungian unconscious represents an example of an undeconstructable logos. It is a metaphysical 'outside' that in its dynamism and unknowability enfolds the deconstructive project itself. Such a version of Jung positions his metaphysical unconscious as logos, as the forming principle itself, a cosmic Sky-Father. Or, as Christian Kerslake puts it:

> On this alternative, deconstruction itself would be superseded by the Jungian insistence on the inherent ungraspability of the unconscious (revealing a metaphysical residue that delimits deconstruction, or an ultimately undeconstructable moment).
>
> (Kerslake 2004: private e-mail)

But on the other hand, it could of course be argued that by virtue of it remaining a metaphysical notion, the Jungian unconscious is eminently deconstructable as Kerslake also points out (Kerslake 2004: private e-mail). However, perhaps we can see that these alternatives are interconnected aspects of a wider Jung–Derrida relationship (that a possibility beyond either/or alternatives is to understand them as connected). For if Derrida admits that deconstruction does not wholly banish the logos Sky-Father, then, by admitting that the Earth-Mother trickster makes a web out of the claims of the unconscious to transcendence, Jung also implicitly surrenders the 'transcendent' nature of his claims to deconstruction. The deeper, underlying connection lies, I believe, in narrative, which, as myth, for Jung is his equivalent of Derrida's dissemination.

For Derrida, meaning is subject to slippage as signifiers lead to other signifiers in a potentially endless sequence of deferral of a final fixed meaning (which can only be bestowed by the logos). This is the trickster at play in the body of the Earth-Mother where logocentrism cannot be entirely rooted out. It is what Derrida means by not being entirely able to think outside metaphysical oppositions such as form and matter.

For Jung it is myth that disseminates. Myth brings together Jung's metaphysical unknowable unconscious with psychic signifying in images. When Jung is in his more logocentric mood, desiring to shore up masculine signifying of the Sky-Father, he has to extract images, such as shadow, from mythical narrative such as trickster. Only such a move will enable him to privilege Christian logos in his project of restoration.

A useful example in Jung's writing is his book, *Answer to Job*, which weaves a mythical narrative deconstructing Christian transcendence while not eradicating it (Jung 1952b: 553–758). In this fantastical biography of the Judaeo-Christian God, Jung describes successive attempts at divine–human relations as highly problematic. Finally, after the sacrifice of the son, the immanent qualities of the divine remain neglected (Earth-Mother eros too much obscured), and so turn demonic. An ignored immanent irrationality takes on even more terrible material form in weapons of mass destruction. Now the onus is on the human psyche to embrace eros, learn the ways of the Earth-Mother, so that the irrational may be incorporated into the body of the whole. No longer should the 'other' to rational modernity be cast into darkness where Christian logos will construct the daimonic as demonic.

God's irrational proclivities find their home in the creative unconscious, and the insistence on unknowability and the subjective structuring of this myth mean that god and goddess mutually define as well as challenge each other. Myth is Jung's mediation between the realm of Sky-Father and the generative properties of the Earth-Mother. Myth is the psyche as potentially endless storytelling (Earth-Mother) and so stories yielding images capable of bearing logos signification (Sky-Father). Without the images, myth could have no meaning, no psychic signifying. Yet without the narrative, myth would become iconic and allegorical producing static, logocentric 'truths' that repress the other or (m)other. So Jung's myth is the liminal dance of the Sky-Father and Earth-Mother in the human psyche.

THE FRAME, THE TEXT AND THE SUBLIME

To continue my argument about the re-framing of god and goddess relations for modernity, I come to the numinous and that element linking both myths: the son of the god(dess).

First of all, I would like to suggest that further understanding of Jung's use of myth is available through comparison to Derrida's analysis of the 'frame'. For the frame, such as the border of a work of art on a wall, is surely vital to the assumed opposition of form and matter. A frame borders the inside and the outside of a work of art. It marks the limit of the art and where the 'world' beyond it begins. But what of the frame itself? Is the frame inside or outside? The assumption that a frame is unproblematic, that inside and outside are self-evident logical distinctions, is part of the form/matter distinction in Christian theology.

> And the formality effect is always tied to the possibility of a framing system that is both imposed and erased.
>
> (Derrida 1987: 67)

In deconstructing the erasure of the frame, Derrida demonstrates the possibility of seeing art as not marked off from the world. In that sense again, there is no representation. Signs do not simply portray a reality 'out there', for there is no unproblematic frame delineating representative sign from represented world. Rather reality itself becomes textual: there is no representation, there is only the weaving of texts against and within each other. So rather than the art work regarded as transcendent of the world it represents (by virtue of the frame), it is immanent in its burgeoning textuality. Again, the animation and animism of textuality manifests the Earth-Mother. And the notion of animism helps us understand that textuality does not simply denote words. A greater mythical sense in deconstruction would help its adherents perceive that linguistic animation is an aspect of nature's animism, and vice versa. For example, the ecocritic Gary Snyder argues that language itself is rooted in nature once humans are regarded immanently rather than transcendent of natural processes (Snyder 2000: 127–31).

Again, this vision of the Earth-Mother in the deconstruction of the frame does not mean that framing as an activity is entirely depleted. Indeed, it is in the very problematics of the frame, not its discarding, that what Derrida calls the sublime (after Kant) is to be found. If the frame marks off the aesthetic from the extra-aesthetic such as theory or politics, thereby creating that very division, then the sublime inheres in the frame as *work*, as activity of separating and re-situating. The sublime is produced by the frame as deconstruction (Lucy 1997: 181). To put it another way, the sublime is in the negotiation between logos-oriented constructions of reality, such as history and society as separate from art, and the eros counter to that separation, in the textual negotiations of god and goddess that make up culture (in all senses).

So I suggest that what is from the perspective of Derridean deconstruction, sublime, the frame as *work* between goddess and god, is from the point of view of Jung termed, 'the numinous', that *produced* by the framing activity of myth as it engages the passions of its logos god and eros goddess. Jung's numinous cannot be assigned to either the gift of the transcendent god or the pure product of the immanent psyche within. It is a 'presence' and a quality, yet sometimes synonymous with psychic energy. It is made visible by myth acting as a frame. The numinous is framed by myth as a co-producer of its consciousness altering effects, as an aspect of the endless generativity of the creative unconscious.

Myth makes elements of the textuality of the psyche into the equivalent of sublime works of art: pregnant with meaning that can never be wholly absorbed into logocentric rational knowledge, yet neither wholly dissipated in the dissemination of psychic signifiers. Where Derrida, emphasising the goddess, offers the sublime, Jung, so often veering towards Christian logos, welcomes the numinous.

And in this *product*, this emanation of *work*, in the antagonistic yet mutually defining and sustaining embrace of two myths, the sublime/numinous, is the absence/presence of the divine son.

THE TEXT AND THE MESSIAH

In order to look at the son-lover of deconstruction, its entire attitude to history needs some examination. By problematising the convention of the frame, deconstruction brings into question the assumed dichotomy of inside and outside. The infamous aphorism that 'there is nothing outside the text', is more properly that 'there is no outside text' since 'outside' is regarded as an *effect* of textuality, not its precondition. So for Derrida, a text is not an imitation of a presence, rather presence is an effect of textuality. (In mythical terms, 'presence' and 'outside' are products of the abrasive yet constructive dialogue of goddess and god, eros and logos.)

Such a position as Derrida's tries to keep the sheer immanence of textuality within the frame of writing and thinking that is inevitably structured through the logos; hence Derrida's increased attention to textuality as *texture*, as weaving, textiles, cloth used in religious practices that incarnate something of the *body* of the trickster.

> You're dreaming of taking on a braid of a weave, a warp or a woof, but without being sure of the textile to come, if there is one, if any remains and without knowing if what remains to come will still deserve the name of text, especially of the text in the figure of a textile.
>
> (Derrida 2002: 313)

Here, in 'A Silkworm of One's Own', Derrida meditates on the textuality of the veil, with its long metaphysical history of veiling and unveiling truth

(Derrida 2002: 309–55). This logos-oriented drapery is contrasted to the Jewish prayer shawl, the tallith, in an attempt to think of another kind of religious history. The textuality Derrida summons also undoes, deconstructs or makes playful the logos separation between humans and nature for it embraces 'the culture of the silkworm, and the quite incomparable patience it demands from . . . the sericultivator' (Derrida 2002: 317). Humans need to learn the *culture* of the silkworm.

No longer simply nature in opposition to culture, the silkworm teaches a patience beyond that required for the spinning of its thread. Or rather, the spinning of the silkworm is a natural practice that humans can guide, yet not control. It therefore becomes 'culture' in which a text grows immanently – through the bonding of humans with nature. This text is nature-culture in playful deconstruction and so embodies a different relationship to metaphysical logos notions of 'history', 'future' and 'events'.

> Patience, yes, the culture of the silkworm, and the quite incomparable patience it demands from . . . the sericultivator. Where we're going . . . at the end of this time that is like no other, nor even like the end of time, another figure perhaps upsets the whole of history from top to bottom, and upsets even the meaning of the word 'history' neither the history of a veil, a veil to be lifted or torn . . . nor a theorem wrapped up in a shroud . . .
>
> (Derrida 2002: 317)

To follow the deconstruction of history here it is necessary to bear in mind the immanent relationships posited between text and world. The idea of 'events' as a reality 'outside' textuality, as something that is then re-presented, belongs to the logos with its dependence upon framing as unproblematic. According to logocentrism, events and therefore (metaphysical) history itself, happen outside the text as a reality independent of representation. The past and future are equally assumed to have a reality, even a possible 'truth', prior to textual being.

However, the reality of past and future proves as troubling as that of the frame. For surely the past is not 'real' in the sense of being materially present, yet it is not wholly unreal either. Derrida gave the name 'spectrality' to the non-opposition of real and unreal, for he perceived that in the cultural preoccupation with ghosts lay a practice of accommodating the inherent problems in opposing real and unreal. Perhaps the deconstructive logic of the spectre (neither real as a person yet not without an *effect*), enables the binary real/unreal to be produced and maintained.

Returning to Derrida's silkworm teaching humanity a textual patience provides a glimpse of the special nature of that patience. For the worm waits, might enable humans to wait, for something that would not constitute a transcendent object.

[B]ut another unfigurable figure . . . who comes to strike dumb the order of knowledge: neither Known nor unknown, too well-known but a strange form head to foot, yet to be born.

(Derrida 2002: 317)

The unfigurable figure is what Derrida calls the Messiah. Of course this is not the transcendent Messiah of a proper name, a particular person, or even a particular idea or theory. This is the Messiah of textuality with no outside, no absolute truth to dwarf its generative plurality. This Messiah must be waited for without the preconditions and assumed truths that accompany waiting for the birth of a god in logos myths. Such a Messiah will not 'unveil' truth or penetrate it like a hymen. Spectral Messiah is a patient, participatory attention to the possibilities for a better future.

[Y]ou have to wait for the Messiah as for the imminence of a verdict which unveils nothing consistent, which tears no veil.

(Derrida 2002: 314)

This saviour son will be what is known and unknown about the future: 'he' will be incorporate in textuality so he will be the child and lover of the goddess. In his deconstruction of the alive/dead binary, he will die and be resurrected. The silkworm spinner from nature as co-creator of culture is also a figure of the unfigurable (what humans can never finally 'know' logocentrically), *whole* of textuality itself; a textual web in which all puny human signifying is caught. The silkworm, serpent worm from the Garden of Eden, is yet another image of the goddess. Evil serpent denying the unchallenged rule of the transcendent god is the logos understanding of the goddess. Derrida, by contrast, tries to angle his vision from within her generative ever-weaving textuality – so offers up the silkworm.

The serpent first appears as a serpent mother goddess in the neolithic era . . . As the male aspect of the goddess was differentiated, the serpent became the fertilising phallus, image of the god who was her son and consort, born from her, married with her and dying back into her for rebirth in unending cycle.

(Baring and Cashford 1991: 499)

Derrida's text-generating silkworm is a vibrant deconstruction of the goddess as serpent 'other' to logos Christianity. Unable to go completely 'outside' the metaphysical thinking sponsored by the form/matter opposition of the Sky-Father, the patience of the silkworm is nevertheless an inside *and* outside vision of the goddess. Keeping textuality immanent and so keeping human beings as immanent within textuality, within the frame,

Derrida reinscribes the goddess myth of creation. Deconstruction pivots its textual *matter* to wait without waiting for a Messiah-saviour, who will not tear open the body of the goddess. It seeks a textual embrace rather than a rupture. Such a son-lover is the messianic as hospitality, one which would 'open itself to an other that is not mine . . . my other, not even my neighbour or my brother' (Derrida 2002: 363). For the goddess embracing the son-lover, there can be no framing off of the other, no 'outside' text.

CONCLUSION: THE DIVINE CHILD

What Jung calls 'the numinous' and Derrida the 'sublime', inheres in texts (of all kinds) produced by the struggle between the logos god and eros goddess. Each structures the other in an encounter in the human psyche that is both annihilating and generative. Since neither is able to finally banish the other, it has been argued that both myths must be necessary for consciousness (Baring and Cashford 1991: 669–70). Unfortunately, their imbalance has resulted in the fragility of the modern psyche.

Jung and Derrida approach the same problem from different political, cultural and disciplinary positions. Jung the conservative tries to smuggle the goddess into modernity and believes in shoring up traditional masculine symbolism. Derrida the radical aims to go as far as possible in rethinking modernity from the perspective of the immanent goddess. Jung uses myth as a language for deconstructing congealed oppositions and (somewhat) liberating the irrational psyche. Derrida uses language more directly, yet is also rooted in narrative (the spectral as ghost stories) and myth (the Messiah as son-lover).

In this chapter I have not sought a so-called 'neutral' language to contrast the two thinkers. Rather I have tried to regard both as contrasting perspectives able to look at each other. After all the numinous/sublime means being within as well as without the textual or representative system being used. For example, Jung too has his spectrality. He concentrated on the psyche as that immediate realm of the neither real nor unreal, and similarly regarded the spectre as its key denotation (Jung 1940: 267). In Jung's psyche the opposites born of the transcendent logos are deconstructed in individuation. He powerfully imagines the two creation myths as immanent powers within, connecting to realities/texts beyond. And synchronicity is how Jung portrays god and goddess deconstructing the frame of inside/outside the psyche. Within such deconstruction/individuation, the child (framed by both myths) is the numinous harbinger of the future.

> Since, however, the solution of the conflict through the union of opposites . . . is moreover the very thing that the conscious mind is looking for, some inkling of the creative act, and of the significance of

it, nevertheless gets through. From this comes the numinous character of the 'child'.

(Jung 1940: 285)

Crucially, Jung's numinous child is the offspring of the goddess as Mother Nature (Jung 1940: 286). This child is the goddess's son-lover in that 'he' is driven by the need for realisation, driven to become a 'hero' (Jung 1940: 289). Hence 'he' enters the realm of the Sky-Father and risks losing contact with his Earth-Mother in nature. Jung's numinous is a reminder that both myths must be respected in the psyche, lest modernity's love of oppositions be 'realised' in terrible violence.

Both Derrida and Jung rethink god and goddess relations for modernity. They differ. Where Derrida tries to remain within the immanent text of the goddess, he has to acknowledge that the logos god remains *present*. So 'there is nothing outside the text' is a momentary vision of humanity immanent in the body of the goddess, as her web makes and remakes reality. The sublime is produced by the struggle between logos thinking and eros being in the endless re-framing of the text.

Jung likewise manifests both god and goddess perspectives, emphasising the former. His logos is his 'outside' to the goddess weaving texts of culture, but it is a logos of the unknowable unconscious. Myth (such as the trickster), synchronicity and the numinous are traces of the creative union of god and goddess in the human psyche. If we try to think of Jungian psychology largely from the perspective of the goddess (wholly not being possible), we see another weave of immanent textuality. From the point of view of the god we see an exterior metaphysical and undeconstructable logos of Jung's unconscious, an undeconstructable residue, so superseding deconstruction and the goddess.

However, Jung did not regard his psychology as belonging to either god or goddess. Ultimately, his prime language was myth, and myth connected to unknowable potential structures in the mind, archetypes. In positing a biological causal connection, Jung refuses to surrender all logocentrism. Yet in regarding his *psychology, and modern science as a whole*, as yet another manifestation of those mythic structures that have shaped human history, structures, moreover, rooted in what can never be definitively known, Jung places his writing as *also* inside the textual web of the goddess.

Psychology . . . operates with ideas which in their turn are derived from archetypal structures and thus generate a somewhat more abstract kind of myth. Psychology therefore translates the archaic speech of myth into a modern mythologem . . . which constitutes one element of the myth 'science'.

(Jung 1940: 302)

Jung knows, like Derrida, the patient cultivation of the worm. Both thinkers, in the numinous and the sublime, reimagine the goddess and god wrestling for the soul of modernity.

Notes

1 All references to Jung are to *The Collected Works of C.G. Jung* (1953–91). Edited by Sir Herbert Read, Dr Michael Fordham and Dr Gerhard Adler, translated by R.F.C. Hull, London: Routledge, Princeton, NJ: Princeton University Press, and to paragraph numbers.
2 Rachael Steel (2004) has observed that Jung is concerned to separate out the daimonic from the demonic.
3 I would like to pay tribute to the ground-breaking work of Michael Vannoy Adams on Jung and deconstruction that has made this chapter possible.

References

Adams, M.V. (1985) 'Deconstructive Philosophy and Imaginal Psychology: Comparative Perspectives on Jacques Derrida and James Hillman', *Journal of Literary Criticism* 2(1) (June): 23–39.

Baring, A. and Cashford, J. (1991) *The Myth of the Goddess: Evolution of an Image*, London and New York: Penguin Arkana.

Derrida, J. (1987) *The Truth in Painting*, trans. Geoff Bennington and Ian McLeod, Chicago and London: University of Chicago Press.

Derrida, J. (2002) *Acts of Religion*, ed. and intro. G. Anidjar, New York and London: Routledge.

Jung, C.G. (1953–91) *The Collected Works of C.G. Jung* (ed. Sir H. Read, M. Fordham, G. Adler and W. McGuire), 20 vols, London: Routledge & Kegan Paul.

Jung, C.G. (1938/1940) 'Psychology and Religion (The Terry Lectures)', *CW* 11, 1958.

Jung, C.G. (1940) 'The Psychology of the Child Archetype', *CW* 9i, 1959.

Jung, C.G. (1951) *Aion: Researches into the Phenomenology of the Self*, *CW* 9ii.

Jung, C.G. (1952a) 'Synchronicity: An Acausal Connecting Principle', *CW* 8, 1960.

Jung, C.G. (1952b) 'Answer to Job', *CW* 11, 1958.

Jung, C.G. (1954) 'On the Psychology of the Trickster-Figure', *CW* 9i, 1959.

Jung, C.G. (1961) 'Symbols and the Interpretation of Dreams', *CW* 18, 1977.

Kerslake, C. (2004) 'Jung and Derrida'. E-mail (12 November).

Lucy, N. (1997) *Postmodern Literary Theory: An Introduction*, Oxford, UK and Massachusetts, USA: Blackwell.

Manes, C. (1996) 'Nature and Silence', in *The Ecocriticism Reader*, ed. C. Glotfelty and H. Fromm, Athens, GA and London: University of Georgia Press.

Steel, R. (2004) 'Jungian Artists: The Golden Gleam of Sexuality in the Art of C.G. Jung', paper given at Greenwich Jung Research Forum, 11 October.

Snyder, G. (2000) 'Language Goes Two Ways', in *The Green Studies Reader*, ed. L. Coupe, London and New York: Routledge.

Chapter 8

The idea of the numinous in Goethe and Jung

Paul Bishop

Although the context of the discussion by Rudolf Otto (1869–1937) in *The Idea of the Holy* (1917) of the various aspects of the numinous and the sacred – the sense of Terror (*tremendum*), the All-Powerful (*majestas*), the Sublime (*augustum*), and Fascination (*fascinans*), as well as the Uncanny, the Void, and the Wholly Other – was clearly a theological one, he chose as the prooemium to his book a quotation, not from a religious, but from a secular text – Goethe's *Faust: Part Two*. He cited this same passage in the pages devoted to his discussion of the sense of Immensity. According to Otto, what he called the Numinous is precisely named by the term *das Ungeheure* as it is used by Goethe in the famous scene from *Part Two* where Faust visits the Mothers:

> Our sense of awe's what keeps us most alive.
> The world chokes human feeling more and more,
> But deep dread still can move us to the core.

> *Das Schaudern ist der Menschheit bestes Teil.*
> *Wie auch die Welt ihm das Gefühl verteuere,*
> *Ergriffen fühlt er tief das Ungeheure.*[1]

In his attempt to define and describe the Numinous Otto also highlighted four other passages in Goethe's writings.[2] First, with reference to the sense of immensity experienced by someone looking at the night sky, a feeling that moved Kant to claim it was equal to the 'wonderment and fear' inspired by contemplation of the moral law,[3] Otto cited the passage in *Wilhelm Meister's Years of Wandering* which tells of Wilhelm's reaction when he is led by the astronomer up to the observatory in Makarie's house: 'Overwhelmed and amazed, he covered both eyes. The colossal [*Das Ungeheuere*] ceases to be sublime; it exceeds our power to understand, it threatens to annihilate us.'[4] Second, in the novel *Elective Affinities* Goethe's narrator uses the word, Otto claims, in the sense of the Immense-Uncanny-Terrible (*das Ungeheuerlich-unheimlich-entsetzliche*): 'A house or city where a monstrous deed [*eine ungeheure Tat*] has taken place remains terrifying to anyone who enters it. The light of day is not so bright there, and the stars seem to lose their shine.'[5] Third, in the context of Goethe's description of his religious development as a child, Otto directs us to the following passage in *Poetry and Truth* where Goethe, speaking of himself in the third person, writes: 'He became increasingly convinced that it was better to divert his thoughts from vast and incomprehensible subjects [*den Gedanken von dem Ungeheuren, Unfaßlichen*].'[6] Finally, in connection with the unexpected and alienating aspects of the Numinous, Otto cites the following lines from *Torquato Tasso*: 'Unhappy man, I scarcely yet can speak. / When something quite unheard-of has occurred, / When our own eyes have glimpsed a monstrous act [*Wenn unser Blick was Ungeheures sieht*], / Then for a while our very minds are halted: / All measure fails then, all comparison.'[7]

Close attention to some other passages, however, where Goethe talks about the Numinous, in the sense of the Monstrous (*das Ungeheure*), and to accounts of analogous experiences in the case of C.G. Jung, allows us to read Jung's notion of the Numinous afresh, revealing him to be, like Goethe, a participant in the tradition of a tragic aesthetic.

In his discussion of Goethe with reference to the Numinous, Rudolf Otto mentions the account given in *Poetry and Truth* of Strasbourg cathedral.[8] When he first saw the cathedral, Goethe regarded 'this marvel' (*dieses Wunderwerk*) as 'something monstrous and terrifying' (*ein Ungeheures*) – or he would have done, 'had it not at the same time seemed comprehensible in its disciplined order and even pleasant in its planful execution'.[9] On closer inspection, the cathedral – a true *fascinans* for Goethe – revealed to him more of its terrible, yet also beautiful, nature:

> The more I contemplated its façade, the more my first impression was confirmed and expanded, namely, that here sublimity and amenity [*das Erhabene mit dem Gefälligen*] had entered into a covenant. If enormousness [*das Ungeheuere*], encountering us as a mass, is not to frighten and confuse us as we attempt to investigate its details, then it must accept an unnatural, seemingly impossible, combination: it must be joined with the pleasant [*das Angenehme*]. [. . .] If we approach [the façade] at dusk, or in moonlight, or on a starry night, when its parts grow more or less indistinct and finally are indistinguishable, then all we see is a colossal wall, the height of which is in pleasing proportion to the width. If we contemplate it by day and exert our minds to abstract the whole from the details, then we perceive a front which not only closes off the inner spaces of the building but also covers much that is adjacent to them. [. . .] It cannot be denied that the whole mass has a

beautiful proportion of height to breadth, and thanks to these pillars and the slender sections between them its details acquire a uniformly light quality.

(GE 4: 284)

Goethe's reaction to the cathedral is also deserving of close attention for another reason. In Book Nine of Part Two, which recounts his years as a law student in Strasbourg, Goethe records how he felt 'locked in combat with myself, with objects, nay, with the elements', suffering from 'a certain hypersensitivity': 'I detested loud noises, and morbid objects aroused my disgust and horror. But I was especially uneasy about the dizziness that always attacked me when I looked down from a height' (GE 4: 277–8). To combat his hypersensitivity Goethe forced himself to listen to the roll of the drums when the evening tattoo was being played, and to combat his dizziness, he forced himself to climb the tower of the cathedral, precisely the object whose aspect he had found so *ungeheuer*:

All alone, I climbed up to the highest part of the cathedral tower and sat in its so-called 'neck', under the knop or 'crown', as it is named, for a good quarter of an hour, until I dared to go back out in the open air and stand on a platform that is hardly a yard square and has hardly any handhold. From there one sees the infinite landscape before one's eyes, while the ornaments and other things round about hide the church and everything upon and above which one is standing. [. . .] I exposed myself to similar fears and torments often enough so that I became quite indifferent to the impression they made.

(GE 4: 278)

Similarly, attending medical courses in obstetrics allowed Goethe to 'liberate himself' (*sich befreien*) from 'all apprehensiveness about repulsive sights'. As becomes clear, however, Goethe imposed this 'aversion therapy' on himself not just to cure himself of the fear of physical objects or situations, but to enable him to confront the dark side of the Numinous:

I sought to steel myself not only against these physical impressions [*sinnliche Eindrücke*] but also against the assaults of fantasy [*die Anfechtungen der Einbildungskraft*]. I succeeded in becoming indifferent to the eerie and uncanny impressions [*die ahndungs- und schauervollen Eindrücke*] made by darkness, cemeteries, solitary places, churches and chapels at night, and everything of that nature; and in this, too, my progress was such that day and night and every locality were all the same to me.

(GE 4: 278)

Such was Goethe's success that he was unable, we are told, to feel 'those pleasant youthful shudders' (*die angenehmen Schauder der Jugend*) again in later life, even when he summoned up 'the weirdest and most frightful images' (*die seltsamsten und fürchterlichsten Bilder*) he could evoke.

There are clear parallels between Goethe and Jung in terms of their encounters with the Numinous, and in terms of the psychological strategy they developed, turning fears and weaknesses to creative account.[10] According-ing to *Memories, Dreams, Reflections* (1961),[11] we can find two examples from Jung's life. First, as a 12-year-old child, Jung was prone to fainting-fits, until he willed himself out of them. 'That was when I learned what a neurosis is', he tells us (*MDR*: 48). Second, during the breakdown following his move away from Freud, Jung deliberately subjected himself to those psychic experiences that enabled him to engage with the Unconscious. As he put it in one of the most well-known passages of his autobiography: 'I was sitting at my desk once more, thinking over my fears. Then I let myself drop' (*MDR*: 203). And so began his 'confrontation with the unconscious'.[12]

But Jung's childhood experiences as they are recounted in *Memories, Dreams, Reflections* also hint a continuity in the profound sense of the Numinous in his life. According to Rudolf Otto, the sense of 'the Wholly Other' is closely bound up with the sense of the Numinous, and the problem of God as something profoundly Other came to define Jung's religious development as a school child and then as a student in Basel. As a child, Jung had a dream of an underground temple containing a giant ritual phallus, which he called 'a subterranean god not to be named', through which he believed himself to have been initiated into 'the secrets of the earth' (*MDR*: 28 and 30).[13] If this dream of the ithyphallic god had been, in the words of *Memories, Dreams, Reflections*, Jung's 'first great secret', and his first encounter with the Numinous, then his second great secret, and his second encounter, was a small wooden mannikin, which he carved as a seven- or eight-year-old out of the end of a ruler, coloured black with ink, and placed, together with a special stone, in a pencil-case which he kept hidden under one of the roof-beams in the attic (*MDR*: 42 and 36).[14] For Jung, God seemed to be both divine and, in a terrible way, anything but divine: 'annihilating fire and an indescribable grace', 'on the one hand a bloody struggle, on the other supreme ecstasy' (*MDR*: 74 and 65). The creation of the mannikin, Jung recalled, coincided with a growth in his interest in plants, animals, and stones:

> I was constantly on the lookout for something mysterious. Con-sciously, I was religious in the Christian sense, though always with the reservation: 'But it is not so certain as all that!' or, 'What about that thing under the ground?' And when religious teachings were pumped into me and I was told, 'This is lovely and this is good', then I thought

to myself, 'Yes, but there is something secret and very Other [*es gibt noch etwas sehr geheimes Anderes*], and people don't know about it'.

(*MDR*: 38; translation modified)

This sense of a secret and, indeed, terrible aspect to God lies behind the vision that Jung had in 1886 and that also focused on a cathedral – not, as in Goethe's case, the one in Strasburg, but the cathedral in Basel. The essential content of this vision was of God as a deity that defecates. The account is now famous of how Jung, leaving school one sunny day and passing the cathedral in Basel with its glittering, multi-coloured roof, was 'overwhelmed by the beauty of the sight, and thought: "The world is beautiful, and the church is beautiful, and God made all this and sits above it far away in the blue sky on a golden throne and . . ." '. Here came, we read, 'a great hole' in his thoughts, and 'a choking sensation' (*MDR*: 52–3). Reluctant to think his vision through to its conclusion, Jung struggled, so this account tells us, to repress his thought for two days until, on the third night, he permitted himself to acknowledge the conclusion to the vision: 'God sits on His golden throne, high above the world – and from under the throne an enormous turd falls upon the sparkling new roof, shatters it, and breaks the walls of the cathedral asunder' (*MDR*: 56).[15] Jung describes his resultant sense of relief as 'an enormous relief [*eine ungeheure Erleichterung*] and an indescribable salvation', as a moment of 'grace' and as 'an unutterable bliss', and as though he had experienced 'an illumination [*Erleuchtung*]' (*MDR*: 56). For the acknowledgement that God could befoul his cathedral had brought with it 'the intuition [*die Ahnung*] that God could be something terrible', and Jung believed he had been vouchsafed nothing less than 'a terrible secret', 'a dark and worrying matter' (*MDR*: 57). The contemplation of such secrets apparently strengthened Jung in his sense of vocation (*MDR*: 65), but it made, not surprisingly, his experience of the church services he attended, and over which his father presided, extremely problematic (*MDR*: 63). In particular, Jung's own first communion turned out to be a bitterly disappointing event (*MDR*: 71–3); so much so, in fact, that it constituted, *Memories, Dreams, Reflections* tells us, 'the greatest defeat' of his life, for along with his 'religious outlook' had disappeared his 'sole meaningful relation with the universe'. For Jung, it might be true that 'God alone was real', but this God was a terrible God as well as a gracious one; it was 'annihilating fire and an indescribable grace'.

Jung's childhood encounters with the Numinous, particularly his vision of God and Basel cathedral, became transmuted into an interest in Gothic architecture. *Memories, Dreams, Reflections* draws a link between the natural world as the locus of ultimate meaning and Gothic cathedrals. For Jung, the woods were 'the place where one most closely feels the deepest meaning and awe-inspiring workings [*tiefsten Sinn und schauervolles Wirken*]' and trees 'the immediate representation of the incomprehensible meaning of life', an impression that was 'reinforced' when Jung became interested in Gothic cathedrals. 'But here the infinity of cosmos and chaos, of meaning and meaninglessness, of subjectless intentionality and mechanical law, was hidden in stone. It contained and at the same time was the groundless secret of being, the quintessence of spirit' (*MDR*: 86). Perhaps mindful of Goethe's interest in the Gothic as reflected in his essay 'On German Architecture' (1772) in Herder's *Concerning German Art and Manner* (1773), Jung associated Gothic architecture with another work by Goethe, the literary edifice of *Faust*, in his lecture 'On Psychological Understanding' (1914), published as a supplement to the second edition of *The Content of the Neuroses* (1908; 2nd edn, 1914). Here Jung articulated the difference between an 'analytic' approach (Freud's) and a 'synthetic' approach (his own) with reference to the appreciation of Gothic architecture and to the problem of interpreting *Faust*:

> Anyone who understands *Faust* 'objectively', from the causal standpoint, is – to take a drastic example – like a man who tries to understand a Gothic cathedral under its historical, technical, and finally its mineralogical aspect. But – where is the meaning of the marvellous edifice? [*Wo aber bleibt der* Sinn *des Wunderwerkes?*] Where is the answer to that all-important question: what goal of redemption did the Gothic man seek in his work, and how have we to understand his work subjectively, in and through ourselves?
>
> (*CW* 3: §396)

Throughout his life, Jung derived inspiration from painting pictures or sculpting stone (*MDR*: 199),[16] much as Goethe had attempted to master the skills of sketching and water-colour painting – with mixed results.[17] And, aside from their relationship to Gothic architecture, there is also a sense of the Numinous which can be detected in the works of sculpture and art associated with Goethe and with Jung.

On 6 April 1777 Goethe erected a sculpture in the garden of his garden-house, the 'Altar of Good Fortune', as he called it. This sculpture consists of 'a sphere, the emblem of mobility, supported by a cube, the emblem of what is stable'.[18] When his birthday was celebrated in Weimar in 1787 – Goethe himself at this time was away in Rome on his Italian journey – a firework display was held in the evening, illuminating the Altar of Good Fortune in the garden.[19] For his part, Jung built, as he explained to Hermann Graf Keyserling, 'a little house way out in the country near the mountains and carved an inscription on the wall': *Philemonis sacrum – Fausti poenitentia*, 'the Shrine of Philemon, the Repentance of Faust'.[20] The 'small house near the mountains' is Jung's Tower at Bollingen, the construction of which had begun in 1923, and to which various developments and additions were made in the 1950s.[21] The inscription *Philemonis sacrum*

– *Fausti poenitentia* was first placed above the gate of the Tower, and when the gate was walled up the inscription was then placed over the entrance to the second tower. The name 'Philemon' in this context recalls the figures of Philemon and Baucis, the old couple whom Faust has murdered in order to pursue his project of land reclamation in Act 5 of *Part Two*,[22] and whom *Memories, Dreams, Reflections* associates with the actions of Germany in the First World War (*MDR*: 261–2).[23]

For all the remarkable parallels between Goethe and Jung in respect of the Numinous, it is important to note that, even though Goethe's experiences were closely associated with the Numinous, they remained very much physical and psychological. The accounts given by Goethe could be said to 'de-transcendentalize' the Numinous. Nevertheless, there is evidence that Goethe retained a positive sense of the Numinous throughout his life which came to the fore during his later years. The name Goethe gave to the Numinous in these later texts was 'the daimonic', *das Dämonische*.[24] In Part Four, Book 20 of *Dichtung und Wahrheit* Goethe defined the daimonic as 'something in nature (whether living or lifeless, animate or inanimate) that manifested itself only in contradictions and therefore could not be expressed in any concept, much less any word':

> It was not divine, for it seemed irrational; not human, for it had no intelligence; not diabolical, for it was beneficent; and not angelic, for it often betrayed malice. It was like chance, for it lacked continuity, and like Providence, for it suggested context. Everything that limits us seemed penetrable by it, and it appeared to dispose at will over the elements necessary to our existence, to contract time and expand space. It seemed only to accept the impossible and scornfully to reject the possible. This essence, which appeared to infiltrate all the others, separating and combining them, I called daimonic, after the example of the ancients and others who had perceived something similar. I tried to save myself from this fearful thing by taking refuge, as usual, behind an image [*hinter ein Bild flüchtete*].
>
> (GE 5: 597)

And Goethe uses quasi-theological language when he says of the daimonic element that it has given rise to the saying *Nemo contra deum nisi deus ipse* ('no one opposes God except God himself') (GE 5: 598).

Dreams were one of the ways in which, for Goethe, the daimonic exercised its creative power. *Dichtung und Wahrheit* tells us how Goethe found a sure confirmation of his independence, even from the deity, in his own 'productive talent', of which dreams formed an important part: '[W]hat I perceived while awake in the daytime, often developed into orderly dreams at night, and when I opened my eyes I would see either an amazing new whole or a part for something already begun' (GE 4: 468).[25] Elsewhere, Goethe gave an example of the kind of hypnagogic images he was also capable of experiencing:

> I had the gift, when I closed my eyes and bent my head, of being able to conjure up in my mind's eye the imaginary picture of a flower. This flower did not retain its first shape for a single instant, but unfolded out of itself new flowers with coloured petals and green leaves. They were not natural flowers, but fantastic ones, and were as regular in shape as a sculptor's rosettes. It was impossible to fix the creative images that sprang up, yet they lasted as long as I desired them to last, neither weakening nor increasing in strength.[26]

For Jung, the term 'daimon', like *mana* and God, is just one of so many synonyms for the unconscious (*MDR*: 369), and the final pages of *Memories, Dreams, Reflections* are saturated with this and other Goethean echoes, as when we read the following fusion of the daimonic and *Faust II*: 'The man, therefore, who, driven by his daimon, steps beyond the limits of the intermediary stage, truly enters the "untrodden, untreadable regions" [ll. 6222–3], where there are no charted ways and no shelter spreads a projecting roof over his head' (*MDR*: 377). And the text brings the concept of the daimonic into relation with the idea of the Numinous when it states: 'It is important to have a secret, a premonition of things unknown. It fills life with something impersonal, a *numinosum*' (*MDR*: 389). In fact, Jung's entire intellectual and personal development is placed under the sign of the daimonic Numinous:

> I have had much trouble in living with my ideas. There was a daimon in me [*Es war ein Dämon in mir*], and in the end its presence proved decisive. It overpowered me, and if I was at times ruthless it was because I was in the grip of the daimon. [. . .] A creative person has little power over his own life. He is not free. He is captive and driven by his daimon.
>
> (*MDR*: 389–90)

Just as Goethe relied on his dreams and his hypnagogic intuitions, so throughout his life Jung experienced extraordinary dreams and visions – 'Visions as such are nothing unusual for me, for I frequently see extremely vivid hypnagogic images', *Memories, Dreams, Reflections* explains (*MDR*: 237). Jung trained himself in controlling his visions just as Goethe had controlled his anxiety, but using a method similar to the one proposed by St Ignatius Loyola (1491–1556) in his *Spiritual Exercises*, on which he gave a seminar in 1939.[27] And some passages in *Memories, Dreams, Reflections*, such as his accounts of viewing the Athai Plains in Kenya (*MDR*: 284), of the sunrise on Mount Elgon (*MDR*: 297–8), or of his participation in an indigenous people's dance on the way from Lake Albert to Rejâf in Sudan (*MDR*: 300), evince a phenomenological quality that has led Roger Brooke to describe them as nothing less than 'ontological visions'.[28]

The most startling example, however, of Goethe's numinous experiences is mentioned neither by Rudolf Otto nor, for that matter, by Jung. This passage occurs at the end of Part Three, Book 11 of *Dichtung und Wahrheit*, when Goethe tells of his final parting in 1771 from Sesenheim and from Friederike Brion (1752–1813), with whom he had had a love affair.[29] According to Goethe's extraordinary account, he had an intuition of his future return to Sesenheim as part of his second journey to Switzerland in 1779:

> When, from horseback, I gave her my hand for the last time, there were tears standing in her eyes, and I felt very bad. As I rode along the footpath to Drusenheim, I was seized by the strangest premonition, namely, I saw myself, not with the eyes of the body, but with those of the spirit [*nicht mit den Augen des Leibes, sondern des Geistes*], coming toward myself on horseback on the same path, and, to be sure, in clothing I had never worn: it was bluish grey with some gold trimming. As soon as I shook myself awake from this dream, the figure vanished. Yet it is curious that eight years later I found myself on the same path, coming to visit Friederike once more and dressed in the clothes I had dreamed about, which I was wearing not by choice but coincidence.
>
> (GE 4: 370)

For Jung, of course, it would have been no coincidence (*Zufall*) that he would, eight years later, be wearing the same clothes as he had seen in his vision; what we have here, it would seem, is an experience related to the kind that Jung described as 'synchronicities'. Speaking with Mircea Eliade in 1952, Jung identified synchronicity with the Numinous, claiming that 'religious experience is *numinous*, as Rudolf Otto calls it, and for me, as a psychologist, this experience differs from all others in the way it transcends the ordinary categories of space, time, and causality', adding that 'recently I have put a great deal of study into synchronicity (briefly, the "rupture of time"), and I have established that it closely resembles numinous experiences where space, time, and causality are abolished'.[30] Goethe's experience here clearly constitutes just such a 'rupture of time', yet in this passage, the expression 'eyes of the spirit' (*Augen des Geistes*) suggests that this experience, which might well be considered to be an example of the Numinous, provides us with an example of a kind of intuition which, far from being 'intellectual' in the sense of *intellektuelle Anschauung*, was, as far as Goethe was concerned, aesthetic.[31]

For the notion of the 'mind's eye', the *geistiges Auge*, occurs in several places in Goethe's writings, particularly his scientific ones. In *Zur Morph-ologie*, for example, he writes that 'we learn to see with the eyes of the spirit' (*wir lernen mit Augen des Geistes sehen*).[32] As Ernst Cassirer pointed out, Goethe was drawing attention to the role of the 'productive imagination' not just in scientifically determined or artistically formed intuition, but in simple empirical intuition as well.[33] And he draws a link between what Goethe called 'seeing with the eyes of the mind' (*sehen mit Geistes Augen*) and the *saper vedere*, 'the perfection of seeing', of which Leonardo da Vinci had spoken.[34] Elsewhere, in one of his drafts (1805) for the introduction to his *Doctrine of Colour* (*Farbenlehre*), Goethe emphasized the uniqueness of the organ of sight in his conclusion that 'the totality of the inner and outer is completed by the eye' (*Die Totalität des Innern und Äußern wird durchs Auge vollendet*).[35] In the course of the *Farbenlehre* (1810), however, it becomes apparent that Goethe is thinking, not just of physical sight, but of a particular kind of *schauen* or contemplation, which could be termed 'aesthetic perception'. In the aesthetic theory of Goethe's teacher, Herder, (aesthetic) seeing is the end-product of all the senses working in concert – 'the eye is merely the signpost, merely the reason of the hand; only the hand provides the *forms*, concepts of what they *mean*, what *dwells* within them'.[36]

Now, in 'A Few Remarks' (1817) on the botanical theories of Caspar Friedrich Wolff, Goethe draws on Herder's emphasis here on the 'haptic sense', the sense of touch, contrasting the 'eyes of the body' (*Augen des Leibes*) with what he called 'spirit-eyes' (*Geistes-Augen*). These 'spirit-eyes', he writes in 'On the Spiral Tendency in Vegetation' (1831), enable the spectator to gain access to 'an inner perception' (*ein inneres Anschauen*).[37] In his writings on morphology, Goethe speaks of the necessity of seeing science in terms of art: 'Because, in knowledge just as in reflection, no totality can be brought together, because the former lacks what is internal and the latter what is external, we must necessarily conceive of science as art, if we are to expect any kind of totality from it.'[38] In the historical section of the *Farbenlehre* Goethe speaks of the need to understand any given moment of time within an aesthetic framework:

> The abysses of intuition, a certain perception of the present, mathematical depth, physical precision, heights of reason, acuity of understanding, flexible, desiring fantasy, loving delight in the sensuous, nothing can be neglected in the living, fruitful seizing of the moment, through which a work of art, whatever its content, can be created.[39]

In his essay 'Perceptive Judgment' (1820; *Anschauende Urteilskraft*) Goethe sought to align this 'judgment through intuitive perception' with Kantian epistemology. The term *Anschauung* can be found in many places in Goethe's *œuvre*, as in, for example, his maxim 'thinking is more interesting than knowing, but not more than intuition' (*Denken ist interessanter als Wissen aber nicht als Anschaun*).[40] And such an *Anschauung* is thematized, too, in many of Goethe's poetic texts, the best-known example perhaps being the affirmation in the conclusion of his 'Metamorphosis of Animals' (1820) of 'the delightful utter certainty' that we can *see*, not just fantasize.

In this respect, Goethe, and, by the same token, Jung, are participants in an intellectual tradition that goes back at least as far as the neo-Platonic philosopher Plotinus (204–70). In the paralipomena to *Dichtung und Wahrheit*, Goethe recalled how, in 1764, he became fascinated with Plotinus,[41] returning to him at the encouragement of F.A. Wolf in 1805,[42] and citing the famous lines *neque vero oculus unquam videret solem, nisi factus solaris esset* from the sixth tractate of the first *Ennead* in the preface to his *Farbenlehre*.[43] In that *Ennead* Plotinus describes the kind of vision, 'the simplicity of looking',[44] towards which his philosophy strove and which it sought to cultivate. For Plotinus, the same insight had been vouchsafed to the participants of the great Mystery Religions, hence the injunction to their followers not to divulge information about what had been revealed to the uninitiated:

> Caught away, filled with God, [the beholder] has in perfect stillness attained isolation; all the being calmed, he turns neither to this side nor to that, not even inwards to himself; utterly resting he has become very rest. He belongs no longer to the order of the beautiful; he has risen beyond beauty; he has overpassed even the choir of the virtues; he is like one who, having penetrated the inner sanctuary, leaves the temple images behind him.[45]

Now the intellectual historian Pierre Hadot has suggested that the neo-Platonic conception of form as expounded by Plotinus is assimilable to the conception of the *Urphänomen* or 'primordial phenomenon' proposed by Goethe.[46] After all, in his philosophy Plotinus assigned an important place to the Beautiful (First Ennead, Sixth Tractate, §1), to which only the Good is superior (Fifth Ennead, Fifth Tractate, §12), just as Goethe described the Beautiful as an *Urphänomen*.[47]

Yet it is important to differentiate here. For Goethe it is not possible to 'rise beyond beauty', to 'penetrate the inner sanctuary'; in his introduction to the journal *Propylaea* (1798), named after the architectural threshold to a temple, Goethe makes this explicit: 'A young man who feels attracted to nature and art expects, by striving vigorously, to gain immediate entrance to the inner sanctum. As an adult he discovers that after a long and arduous pilgrimage he is still in the vestibule.'[48] Equally, one of the aphorisms in 'From Makaria's Archive' in *Wilhelm Meister* amounts to nothing less than an 'outright refutation' of Plotinus' doctrine: 'A form in the mind suffers no loss when it is made manifest; on the contrary, if its manifestation is a true begetting, a fruit of the marriage between mind and medium, then the product may well surpass either parent.'[49]

Nevertheless, the visionary intuition of the moment espoused by Plotinus confers on it a numinous quality that underpins the ethics of the even earlier, ancient philosophies of Epicureanism and Stoicism. And as Hadot points out, Goethe developed a position that could well be described, to use the phrase he coined in conversation with J.D. Falk, as 'half-Stoic, half-Epicurean' (*halb Stoiker und halb Epikuräer*).[50] On the Epicurean side, the insight into the nature of the moment becomes an injunction to live life to the full, in the now, to 'receive each added moment of time, recognizing its value', as Philodemus of Gadara put it, 'as if it arrived by an incredible chance'.[51] For such Stoics as Marcus Aurelius, 'he who has seen the present has seen everything, all that from eternity has come to pass, and all that will come to be in infinite time'.[52] Or in the inspired words of William Blake, we should learn '[t]o see a World in a Grain of Sand / And a Heaven in a Wild Flower / Hold Infinity in the palm of your hand / And Eternity in an hour'. For, as Blake noted in his manuscript note-book, 'He who bends to himself a joy / Doth the winged life destroy / But he who kisses the joy as it flies / Lives in eternity's sun rise.'[53]

According to Freud in *Leonardo da Vinci and a Memory of His Childhood* (1910), Leonardo has been called the Italian Faust – and rightly so, 'because of his insatiable and indefatigable thirst for knowledge'. For Freud, what was 'fundamental' in the tragedy of Faust was 'the possible transformation of the instinct to investigate back into an enjoyment of life' (*die mögliche Rückverwandlung des Forschertriebs in Lebenslust*),[54] thereby articulating one of the central themes of Goethe's dramatic poem. For in *Part One* of *Faust*, the problem of knowledge and of its existential relevance constitutes the subject of the opening lines of the verse drama, particularly the problem of transitoriness, as expressed in the elderly academic's ironic challenge to the devil: 'Show me the fruit that rots before it's plucked', and in the detail of the wager itself, if he expresses the desire to stop time.[55] In *Part Two*, the problem of the transient nature of beauty is allegorized in the encounter between Faust and Helena in Act 3.[56] 'And so the spirit looks neither forward nor back' (*Nun schaut der Geist nichts vorwärts, nicht zurück*), Faust says to Helena, 'The present alone' (*Die Gegenwart allein*) – and she completes the line – 'is our joy' (*ist unser Glück*).[57] In other works, Goethe also celebrates this transformation of the moment through the aesthetic. In his public response to the archaeologist Friedrich Karl Ludwig Sickler, who had discovered an ancient grave illustrated with bas-reliefs at Cumae, 'A Grave Near Cumae' (1812), Goethe noted of one relief that 'the beautiful fluidity of movement that we admire in such artists is here fixed for the moment, so that we simultaneously see previous, present and subsequent movements, and are already transported into a different world'.[58] Then again, the poem entitled 'The Godlike' (1783) says of Humankind:

'We can give lasting / Life to the moment'.[59] And the later poem 'Testament' (1829) concludes with the following lines: 'Then bygone time gives permanence, / The future lives, and in advance: Eternity the moment is' (*Dann ist Vergangenheit beständig, / Das Künftige voraus lebendig, / Der Augenblick ist Ewigkeit*).[60] For Goethe, the 'permanence in change' (*Dauer im Wechsel*) is vouchsafed by experience of the aesthetic illusion. Or, as Friedrich Nietzsche put it in *The Birth of Traegdy*, the world is justified, but only as an aesthetic phenomenon; and the concept of the aesthetic moment reaches back to the Platonic-Thomist conception of Eternity as the *nunc stans*, 'the now that stands still'.

In his letter to C.F. Zelter of 29 March 1827, Goethe wrote: 'we must believe in simplicity' (*il faut croire à la simplicité*), adding that 'we must believe in [. . .] what is primordially productive, if we are to find the right path'.[61] In this sense, Hadot argues, the philosophy of Plotinus, for whom life is 'primordially productive' (that is, a simple, immediate, and constantly formative process), is a source, not just of Goethe's, but also of later Vitalist thinking.[62] A non-metaphysical, non-religious sense of the Numinous Divine would seek to follow the injunction contained in the lines from Goethe's great, late poem, 'Trilogy of Passion':

> [. . .] Hour by kindly hour
> Life is offered to us;
> Our yesterdays have left little record behind,
> And we are forbidden to know our tomorrows;
> And if ever, at evening, my heart misgave me,
> The setting sun still shone on sights that made me glad.
>
> Do then as I do, and face the moment,
> With joy and understanding, and without procrastination!
> Meet it quickly, with a good and lively will,
> Whether in action or in pleasure.
> Beloved, be only where you are and be wholly there – be ever childlike,
> And you will then be all things, and be unconquerable.[63]

Thus the sense of the Numinous does not so much reveal the Divine as reside in a way of seeing things, seeing them with 'the eyes of the spirit', so that we realize the divine nature of all things. This, then, is the true sense of the Numinous in Goethe – and, by extension, in Jung as well. For him, the sets of 'feelings', 'ideas', and 'events' that Otto described as numinous, can be understood in terms of Goethe's 'eyes of the spirit' as aesthetic experiences, ones that 'shape' us, 'impress' us, and 'leave their mark' upon us: in other words, they are 'archetypal'.[64] The power of the Numinous, the transformative effect of the archetypal, resides, not in a breakthrough from some transcendent realm, but in a profound, even life-changing alteration in the way we view the present and our life in it. Such a de-metaphysicized, de-mystified conception of the Numinous would reveal the divine nature of life itself – divine, that is, not in terms of an external, transcendent force, but inherently, immanently, immediately. As Jung pointed out, the philological root of the Numinous lies in the notion of divinity and of respect for the religious, but can we have a conception of the divine without God? The ancient Epicurean and Stoic belief in the sanctity of the moment might provide such a model of the divine without the belief in transcendence. That at any moment, 'in the briefest atom' of his or life, the individual may encounter 'something holy [*etwas Heiliges*] that endlessly outweighs all struggles and all distress' represented, for Nietzsche, 'the sense for the tragic'. And for Nietzsche, there is only 'one hope and one guarantee for the future of humanity' – 'our *retention of the sense for the tragic*'.[65] Seen in this light, the sense of Numinous evinced by Goethe and Jung allows them to emerge as proponents of a tragic aesthetic.[66] Tragic, that is, in the sense that we have to die, but we want to live; aesthetic, in the sense that we bring to bear upon our experiences all our capacities, physical and mental, emotional and intellectual, and fashion a response to the moment that would render it eternal. After all, 'the world into which we are born', as we read in the final pages of *Memories, Dreams, Reflections*, is 'brutal and cruel, and at the same time of divine beauty' (*MDR*: 392).

Notes

1 J.W. von Goethe, *Faust II*, ll.6272–74 (J.W. von Goethe, *Faust: Part Two*, trans. D. Luke, Oxford and New York: Oxford University Press, 1994, pp. 52–3).

2 R. Otto, *Das Heilige*, Munich: C.H. Beck, 1987, pp. 54–5.

3 'Two things fill the mind with ever new and increasing admiration and reverence, the more often and the more steadily one reflects on them: *the starry heavens above me and the moral law within me*' (*Critique of Practical Reason*, Part 2, 'Doctrine of Method of Pure, Practical Reason', Conclusion, in I. Kant, *Practical Philosophy*, ed. and trans. M.J. Gregor, Cambridge: Cambridge University Press, 1996, p. 269).

4 J.W. von Goethe, *Conversations of German Refugees / Wilhelm Meister's Journeyman Years or The Renunciants*, ed. J.K. Brown, trans. J. van Heurck / K. Winston (Goethe's Collected Works, vol. 10), New York: Suhrkamp Publishers, 1989, p. 177. Referred to in the text as GE 10 with a page reference.

5 J.W. von Goethe, *The Sorrows of Young Werther / Elective Affinities / Novella*, ed. D.E. Wellbery, trans. V. Lange and J. Ryan (Goethe's Collected Works, vol. 11), New York: Suhrkamp Publishers, 1988, Part Two, chapter 15, p. 245. This motif is used elsewhere in this work: see Part Two, chapter 8 (p. 216); and Part Two, chapter 14 (p. 241).

6 J.W. von Goethe, *From My Life. Poetry and Truth: Part Four / Campaign in France 1792. Siege of Mainz*, ed. T.P. Saine and J.L. Sammons, trans. R.R. Heitner / T. Paine (Goethe's Collected Works, vol. 5), New York: Suhrkamp Publishers, 1987, p. 597. Referred to in the text as GE 5 with a page reference.

7 *Torquato Tasso*, Act 5, scene 5, ll.3281–3285 (J.W. von Goethe, *Verse Plays and Epic*, ed. C. Hamlin and F. Ryder, trans. M. Hamburger, H. Hannum, and D.

Luke (Goethe's Collected Works, vol. 8) (New York: Suhrkamp Publishers, 1987), p. 135).

8 For an example of the discussion surrounding the veracity of Goethe's autobiographical writings, in this case the *Italian Journey*, see N. Boyle, 'Goethe in Paestum: A Higher-Critical Look at the *Italienische Reise*', *Oxford German Studies*, 20/21 (1991–1992), 18–31; R. Cardinal, 'The Passionate Traveller: Goethe in Italy', *Publications of the English Goethe Society*, NS 67 (1997), 17–31; and (for discussion of Boyle's thesis regarding the dating of the visit to Paestum, and the most recent comprehensive study of the Italian journey to date) N. Miller, *Der Wanderer: Goethe in Italien*, Munich: Carl Hanser Verlag, 2002, esp. note 14, pp. 640–2.

9 J.W. von Goethe, *From My Life. Poetry and Truth: Parts One to Three*, ed. T.P. Saine and J. Sammons, trans. R.R. Heitner (Goethe's Collected Works, vol. 4), New York: Suhrkamp Publishers, 1987, p. 266. Referred to in the text as GE 4 with a page reference.

10 In his review of the translation of *Erinnerungen, Träume, Gedanken*, Donald Winnicott argued that a psychotic illness had probably set in by the time Jung was four ('[book review] *Memories, Dreams, Reflections. By C.G. Jung*', *International Journal of Psychoanalysis*, 45 (1964), 450–5 [p. 451]). But Winnicott concluded: 'Jung's life has shown, I believe, how psychotic illness may not only give a person a lot of trouble but may also push that person on to exceptional attainment' (p. 55).

11 C.G. Jung, *Memories, Dreams, Reflections: Recorded and Edited*, ed. A. Jaffé, trans. R. and C. Winston, London: Collins/Routledge & Kegan Paul, 1963; referred to in the text as *MDR* with a page reference. For the German original, see *Erinnerungen, Träume, Gedanken von C.G. Jung*, ed. A. Jaffé, Olten: Walter-Verlag, 1971. For critical discussion of the genesis of this text, see A.C. Elms, 'The Auntification of Jung', in *Uncovering Lives: The Uneasy Alliance of Biography and Psychology*, New York and Oxford: Oxford University Press, 1994, pp. 51–70; and S. Shamdasani, 'Memories, Dreams, Omissions', *Spring: A Journal of Archetype and Culture*, 57 (1995), 115–37; reprinted in P. Bishop (ed.), *Jung in Contexts: A Reader*, London and New York: Routledge, 1999, pp. 33–50.

12 Goethe brought the first book of *Dichtung und Wahrheit* to a close with an account of how, as a 7-year-old child, he built an altar to the God of Nature – 'the God who is in direct contact with nature, who acknowledges and loves it as His work' (GE 4: 44). Similarly, during the period of psychic turmoil following his break with Freud in 1912, Jung's memories of life as a child – kindling a fire in a stone-wall, sitting on a stone and playing with the notion of identity – came back to him in the form of an intensified memory (*MDR*: 36), and he tried to re-establish contact with that period of his life. Collecting stones from the shore of Lake Zurich by his house, Jung began constructing cottages, a castle, a church – and an altar. As Jung placed this altar inside the church, he recalled the vision of the subterranean phallus that he had experienced as a young child (*MDR*: 197–8).

13 For further discussion, see D.C. Noel, 'Veiled Kabir: C.G. Jung's Phallic Self-Image', *Spring* (1974), 224–42; and B. Feldman, 'Jung's Infancy and Childhood and its Influence upon the Development of Analytical Psychology', *Journal of Analytical Psychology*, 37 (1992), 255–74. Given the importance attached in *Memories, Dreams, Reflections* to Jung's childhood dream of a giant phallus on a throne, it is perhaps not without significance to note that both Goethe and Jung were extremely knowledgeable about priapic literature.

14 In the light of his research for *Symbols and Transformations of Libido*, Jung interpreted the mannikin as 'a little cloaked god of the ancient world', a Telesphorus, such as the one that stands on monuments of Asklepios and reads to him from a scroll, or as a *kabir*, the natural deities that formed part of the cult of Demeter (*MDR*: 38–9).

15 This vision may well have been inspired, in view of the Jung family's devotion to reading scripture, by the passage in the Book of Exodus where Moses is permitted to see the backside of God (see R. Hayman, *A Life of Jung*, London: Bloomsbury, 1999, p. 18; compare with Exodus 33: 18–23). According to one commentator, Yahweh's wish to be seen only from behind 'may suggest that he is concealing his genitalia from Moses', since the word *kabod*, usually translated as 'glory', is used to allude to the male genitalia in the Book of Job, 29: 20 (J. Miles, *God: A Biography*, London and New York: Simon and Schuster, 1995, p. 125).

16 For discussion of Jung's paintings, see K. Luchsinger, 'Ein unveröffentlichtes Bild von C.G. Jung: "Landschaft mit Nebelmeer"', *Analytische Psychologie*, 18 (1987), 298–302; and U. Baumgardt, 'Betrachtung eines Bildes von C.G. Jung', *Analytische Psychologie*, 18 (1987), 303–12.

17 The significance in developmental terms of Goethe's experiences of painting is still under-investigated, but see W.D. Robson-Scott, *The Younger Goethe and the Visual Arts*, Cambridge: Cambridge University Press, 1981; and for the broader context, including examples of works by Goethe, see S. Schulze (ed.), *Goethe und die Kunst*, Ostfildern: Verlag Gerd Hatje, 1994; and H. Sieveking, *Fuseli to Menzel*, Munich and New York: Prestel, 1998.

18 N. Boyle, *Goethe: The Poet and the Age*, vol. 1, *The Poetry of Desire (1749–1790)*, Oxford and New York: Oxford University Press, 1991, p. 286. Boyle comments that 'the symbol of perhaps more ambiguous than Goethe consciously intended: the moment of good fortune that brings the sphere to rest over the centre of the cube is frozen in permanence only by the sculptural form, and perhaps the good fortune that has brought this rolling stone to rest in Weimar is also a matter only of a moment' (p. 286).

19 N. Boyle, *The Poetry of Desire*, p. 496. See Schiller's letter to Körner of 29 August 1787; and Knebel's to his sister of 31 August 1787, in W. Bode (ed.), *Goethe in vertraulichen Briefen seiner Zeitgenossen*, 3 vols., Munich: C.H. Beck, 1982, vol. 1, nos. 561–2, pp. 339–40.

20 See Jung's letter to Keyserling of 2 January 1928 (*Letters*, ed. G. Adler and A. Jaffé, trans. R.F.C. Hull, London: Routledge and Kegan Paul, 1973–1975, vol. 1, p. 49).

21 For pictures of the commemorative stones and monuments set up by Jung in the grounds of the tower at Bollingen, see D. Rosin, *The Tao of Jung: The Way of Integrity*, New York: Viking Arkana, 1996. For a recent discussion of Jung's tower, see T. Ziolkowski, *The View from the Tower: Origins of an Antimodernist Image*, Princeton, NJ: Princeton University Press, 1999, pp. 131–48.

22 Although Philemon and Baucis, deriving ultimately from the mythic corpus, find their major literary representation in Ovid (*Metamorphoses*, Book 8, ll.628–720), Goethe claimed, in his conversation with Eckermann of 6 June 1831, to have distanced himself from his classical source.

23 Curiously, Jung also called one of the numinous fantasy figures whom he encountered during his 'confrontation with the unconscious', Philemon (*MDR*: 207–10). According to F.X. Charet, *Faust* was 'probably' the source from which Jung took this name, but his explanation is unconvincing (*Spiritualism and the*

Foundations of C.G. Jung's Psychology, Albany, NY: State University of New York Press, 1993, pp. 242, 250 and 255).

24 For discussion of the 'daimonic-mythological' world-view, particularly in relation to Goethe's conception of the daimonic, see K. Jaspers, *Psychologie der Weltanschauungen*, 5th edn, Berlin, Göttingen, Heidelberg: Springer-Verlag, 1960, pp. 191–203; see also H.B. Nisbet, '*Das Dämonische*: On the Logic of Goethe's Demonology', *Forum for Modern Language Studies*, 7 (1971), 259–81; and W.M. Zucker, 'The Demonic: From Aeschylus to Tillich', *Theology Today*, 26/1 (1969), 34–50.

25 For a discussion of the importance of dreams for Goethe's close asssociate, Eckermann, and of dreams involving Goethe for Freud, see A. Ronell, *Dictations: On Haunted Writing*, Bloomington, IN: Indiana University Press, 1986.

26 Goethe's review of *Contributions to the Study of Sight from a Subjective Standpoint* (1819) by the Czech physiologist Johannes Evangelista Purkinje (1787–1869) was published in *On Morphology* (*Zur Morphologie*) (vol. 2, part 2, 1824; Goethe, *Weimarer Ausgabe*, 4 parts, 133 vols in 143, Weimar: Hermann Böhlau, 1887–1919), section 2, vol. 11, p. 282. Cited below as WA with section and volume number followed by page reference). Jung cited this passage in his inaugural dissertation for his medical degree, 'On the Psychology and Pathology of So-called Occult Phenomena' (1902) (*CW* 1 §28).

27 See Jung's seminar on the *Spiritual Exercises* of St Ignatius Loyola held in 1939, which have been published in part (see C.G. Jung, '*Exercitia Spiritualia* of St. Ignatius of Loyola: Notes on Lectures', *Spring*, 1977, 183–200 and 1978, 28–36). For further discussion, see K. L. Becker, *Unlikely Companions: C.G. Jung on the Spiritual Exercises of Ignatius of Loyola: An Exposition and Critique Based on Jung's Letters and Writings*, Leominster: Gracewing, 2001.

28 R. Brooke, *Jung and Phenomenology*, London and New York: Routledge, 1991, pp. 52–62.

29 For further discussion, see A. Seele, *Frauen um Goethe*, Reinbek bei Hamburg: Rowohlt, 1997, pp. 15–23. For a psychoanalytic discussion, see T. Reik, 'Warum verließ Goethe Friederike?', *Imago*, 15 (1929), 400–537, republished as *Warum verließ Goethe Friederike? Eine psychoanalytische Monographie*, Vienna: Internationaler Psychoanlytischer Verlag, 1930.

30 'Eliade's Interview for "Combat"', in W. McGuire and R.F.C. Hull (eds.), *C.G. Jung Speaking: Interviews and Encounters*, Princeton, NJ: Princeton University Press, 1977, p. 230. For further discussion, see R. Main, *The Rupture of Time: Synchronicity and Jung's Critique of Modern Western Culture*, Hove and New York: Brunner-Routledge, 2004.

31 For further discussion of Jung's concept of synchronicity, and some of its attendant problems, see P. Bishop, *Synchronicity and Intellectual Intuition in Kant, Swedenborg, and Jung*, Lewiston, NY; Queenston, Ontario; and Lampeter, Wales: Edwin Mellen Press, 2000, esp. p. 286, note 57, for discussion of Goethe's intuition of the earthquake in Messina in 1783, which attracted the interest of Thomas Mann.

32 WA 2.8, 37. For further discussion, see E. Förster, 'Goethe and the "Auge des Geistes"', *Deutsche Vierteljahrsschrift für Literaturwissenschaft und Geistesgeschichte*, 75 (2001), 87–101.

33 E. Cassirer, *The Philosophy of Symbolic Forms*, vol. 3, *The Phenomenology of Knowledge*, trans. R. Manheim, New Haven and London: Yale University Press, 1957, pp. 134–5.

34 E. Cassirer, *The Philosophy of Symbolic Forms*, vol. 4, *The Metaphysics of Symbolic Forms*, ed. J.M. Krois and D.P. Verene, trans. J.M. Krois, New Haven

and London: Yale University Press, 1996, p. 81; compare E. Cassirer, *The Individual and the Cosmos in Renaissance Philosophy* [1927], trans. M. Domandi, New York and Evanston: Harper & Row, 1963, p. 158. In his speech accepting the Goethe-Preis, given in the Goethe-Haus in Frankfurt in 1930, Freud noted that 'Goethe can be compared in versatility to Leonardo da Vinci, the Renaissance master, who like him was both artist and scientific investigator' (*Standard Edition of the Complete Psychological Works of Sigmund Freud*, general ed. J. Strachey and A. Freud, 24 vols., London: Hogarth Press, 1963–1974, vol. 21, p. 208).

35 WA 2.5, 12.

36 Herder, *Sculpture* (1778; *Plastik*), in J.G. Herder, *Werke*, 10 vols. (Frankfurt am Main: Deutscher Klassiker Verlag, 1985 –), vol. 4, pp. 243–326 (p. 280). For further discussion, see E.M. Wilkinson and L.A. Willoughby, '"The Blind Man" and the Poet: An Early Stage in Goethe's Quest for Form', in *Models of Wholeness: Some Attitudes to Language, Art and Life in the Age of Goethe*, ed. J. Adler, M. Swales and A. Weaver, Oxford: Peter Lang, 2002, pp. 99–125 (esp. p. 104).

37 WA 2.7, 54.

38 WA 2.7, 85.

39 WA 2.3, 121; cf. Goethe's comments in 'Problem and Response' (*Problem und Erwiderung*) in *Zur Morphologie* (WA 2.7, 85–6).

40 *Maximen und Reflexionen*, ed. Hecker, §1150 (WA 2.11, 371); cf. Hecker, §744 and §1147.

41 'As if by inspiration Plotinus gave me especial pleasure, so that I borrowed his works and spent my days and evenings, much to the displeasure of my room-mate, poring over them. For his part, he kept on telling me that these writings were completely incomprehensible and it was precisely their incomprehensibility that made them so irresistibly attractive to young, impressionable [*schwärmer-ischen*] people. [. . .] For a while I was gripped by Plotinus: for this way of thinking was rooted in Christianity (in turn rooted in Judaism), to which I was indebted for the greater part of my education; but the difficulties kept on mounting up, and I lost patience with slogging through obscure passages, secretly admitting that perhaps my friend might have been right after all' (WA, 1.27, 382).

42 See Goethe's letter to F.A. Wolf of 30 August 1805.

43 'Were the eye not of the sun, / How could we behold the light? / If God's might and ours were not as one, / How could His work enchant our sight?' (J.W. von Goethe, *Scientific Studies*, ed. and trans. D. Miller [Goethe Edition, vol. 12], New York: Suhrkamp Publishers, 1988, p. 164); cf. 'To any vision must be brought an eye adapted to what is to be seen, and having some likeness to it. Never did an eye see the sun unless it had first become sunlike, and never can the Soul have a vision of the First Beauty unless it itself be beautiful' (Plotinus, *Enneads*, 1.6 [9]; Plotinus, *The Enneads*, trans. S. MacKenna, revised B.S. Page, London: Faber and Faber, 1956, p. 64). Compare Goethe's conversation with Eckermann of 26 February 1824.

44 Compare the title of Pierre Hadot's helpful introduction, *Plotin ou la simplicité du regard*, Paris: Gallimard, 1997; for a discussion of Plotinus and Goethe, see p. 58. For a discussion of the reception of Plotinus and the tradition of *Naturphilosophie*, see P. Hadot, 'L'Apport du néoplatonisme à la philosophie de la nature en Occident', *Eranos-Jahrbuch*, 37 (1968), 91–132.

45 Plotinus, *The Enneads*, 6.9 [11], p. 624.

46 See, for example, his *Doctrine of Colours*, and his conversations with Eckermann of 13 and 18 February 1829.

47 See Goethe's conversation with Eckermann of 18 April 1827. For further discussion, see M. Jolles, 'Goethes Anschauung des Schönen', *Deutsche Beiträge zur geistigen Überlieferung*, 3 (1957), 89–116.

48 J.W. von Goethe, *Essays on Art and Literature*, ed. J. Gearey, trans. E. von Nardroff and E.H. von Nardroff (Goethe's Collected Works, vol. 3), New York: Suhrkamp Publishers, 1986, p. 78.

49 'From Makarie's Archive', no. 27; translated in Wilkinson and Willoughby, '"The Blind Man" and the Poet', p. 116; cf. GE 10: 420: 'A spiritual form is by no means diminished by emerging into appearance, provided that its emergence is a true procreation, true propagation. What is begotten is not inferior to the begetter, and indeed, the advantage of live begetting is that what is begotten can be superior to that which begets it.'

50 F. Frhr. von Biedermann (ed.), *Goethes Gespräche: Gesamtausgabe*, 5 vols., Leipzig: Biedermann, 1909–1911, vol. 4, p. 469.

51 M. Gigante, *Ricerche Filodemee*, Naples: Gaetano Macchiaroli, 1983, pp. 181 and 215–16; cited in P. Hadot, '"The Present Alone is our Joy": The Meaning of the Present Instant in Goethe and in Ancient Philosophy', *Diogenes*, 133 (1986), 60–82 (p. 69).

52 M. Aurelius, *The Meditations*, trans. G.M.A. Grube, Indianapolis: Hackett, 1983, Book 6, no. 37, p. 56.

53 'Auguries of Innocence' (c. 1803); 'Eternity', in W. Blake, *The Poems and Prophecies*, ed. M. Plowman, London and Toronto: J.M. Dent; New York: E.P. Dutton, 1927, pp. 383 and 333.

54 Freud, *Standard Edition*, vol. 11, p. 75.

55 *Faust I*, l. 1686; J. W. von Goethe, *Faust: Part One*, trans. D. Luke, Oxford and New York: Oxford University Press, 1987, p. 51.

56 Elsewhere, Goethe is equally insistent on the transient nature of beauty. In one of his distichs written with Schiller, Beauty itself asks Zeus why she is transient, and the god replies that only what is transient is beautiful: '*Warum bin ich vergänglich, o Zeus?' so fragte die Schönheit. / 'Macht' ich doch', sagte der Gott, 'nur das Vergängliche schön'* . Indeed, for Goethe, beauty has to be transient, in order for beauty always to be something living and fruitful (cf. Jolles, p. 106); the 'immortality' of art is something we impart to it, not something inherent in it.

57 *Faust II*, ll.9381–82; for further discussion, see Hadot, '"The Present Alone is our Joy"', pp. 61–4.

58 Goethe, *Essays on Art and Literature*, pp. 29–35 (p. 30).

59 J. W. von Goethe, *Selected Poems*, ed. C. Middleton (Goethe Edition, vol. 1) (Boston: Suhrkamp/Insel Publishers, 1983), p. 81 (trans. V. Watkins).

60 Goethe, *Selected Poems*, p. 269 (trans. C. Middleton).

61 WA 4.42, 102: *man muß an die Einfalt, an das Einfache, an das urständig Productive glauben, wenn man den rechten Weg gewinnen will.*

62 Hadot, *Plotin ou la simplicité de le regard*, p. 58.

63 Goethe, 'Elegy', in 'Trilogy of Passion' (Goethe, *Selected Verse*, ed. and trans. D. Luke, Harmondsworth: Penguin, 1964, p. 314).

64 In his 'Introduction to the Religious and Psychological Problems of Alchemy', Jung writes that 'the word "type" is, as we know, derived from $\tau\nu\pi o\varsigma$, "blow" or "imprint"', concluding that 'thus an archetype presupposes an imprinter'. But Jung went on: 'Psychology as the science of the soul has to confine itself to its subject and guard against overstepping its proper boundaries by metaphysical assertions or other professions of faith. Should it set up a God, even as a

hypothetical cause, it would have implicitly claimed the possibility of proving God, thus exceeding its competence in an absolutely illegitimate way' (CW 12 §15).

65 'Richard Wagner in Bayreuth', §4, in F. Nietzsche, *Untimely Meditations*, trans. R.J. Hollingdale, Cambridge: Cambridge University Press, 1983, p. 213 (translation modified). For further discussion, see A. Caranfa, 'The Aesthetic Harmony of How Life Should Be Lived: Van Gogh, Socrates, Nietzsche', *Journal of Aesthetic Education*, 35 (2001), 1–13.

66 For Michel Onfray, such a vitalistic celebration of the moment lies at the heart of the project of philosophical hedonism; see 'À ceux qui ne veulent pas jouir: Comment peut-on ne pas être hédoniste?', in M. Onfray, *L'Archipel des comètes: Journal hédoniste III*, Paris: Grasset & Fasquelle, 2001, pp. 267–82 (pp. 278–82).

Chapter 9

Accessing the numinous: Apolline and Dionysian pathways

Giorgio Giaccardi

The psychological reflection on the experience of the numinous has often been conducted through dichotomies as an attempt to represent something unthinkable and inherently paradoxical. Nietzsche evokes this idea when he writes of a god 'who frees himself from the dire pressure of fullness and over-fullness, from suffering the oppositions packed within him' (Nietzsche 1886/1999: 8). It is for human consciousness, as mystics like Böhme have pointed out, to become 'acutely aware of the divine contradiction in the depths of humanity and nature' (quoted in Dourley 2004: 61). Here, in particular, I consider the relevance of a polarity known as 'Apolline versus Dionysian' in the experience of numinous aspects of the divine. As I will frequently refer to the ideas expounded by Nietzsche in *The Birth of Tragedy*, a few introductory remarks are necessary to clarify my approach to this very controversial early work of his.

Nietzsche has been criticized either for conducting the analysis of the Apolline and the Dionysian on a merely aesthetical level at the expense of the religious viewpoint or for having made up these categories altogether. An example of the former line of criticism is seen in the following passage by Jung, in reading which it should be noted that Jung makes use of the term Aesthetism instead of Aestheticism with reference to Nietzsche's specific doctrine of the aesthetic, i.e. art's mediating role between Apollo and Dionysus (Bishop 1999: 230–5):

> Aesthetism is a modern glass, through which the psychological mysteries of the cult of Dionysus are seen in a light in which they were certainly never seen or experienced by the ancients . . . With Nietzsche, as with Schiller, the religious point-of-view is entirely overlooked, and its place is taken by the aesthetics.
>
> (Jung 1921/1938: 176)

However, scholarly and comprehensive appraisals of *The Birth of Tragedy* have acknowledged that the importance of Nietzsche's book lies primarily in its insights into the religious outlook before Socrates, as well as in its elucidation of the spirit of Greek tragedy (Silk and Stern 1981). Also, a recent contribution to a psychological understanding of the opposites in Nietzsche and Jung recognizes the existence of overlaps between the aesthetic, psychological and metaphysical aspects of the Apolline and Dionysian impulses as well as clearly stating that art for Nietzsche is religious (Huskinson 2004: 16–17).

As for the second kind of criticism, it was clearly spelled out by Wilamowitz: 'Apolline and Dionysiac are aesthetic abstractions like naïve and sentimental poetry in Schiller, and the old gods only supplied sonorous names for the contrast' (quoted in Silk and Stern 1981: 130).

While not entirely accurate in philological terms as a description of the meaning that the two gods held for the Greeks, the psychological relevance of the dyad Apollo vs. Dionysus has often been recognized as germane (Hillman 1972: 266–7). Huskinson also argues that if we consider them as psychological impulses, the Apolline and the Dionysian can be defined as conscious feelings of being distinct from one's environment and being conjoined with the rest of reality respectively (Huskinson 2004: 27).

In sum, the two composite gods evoked by Nietzsche may also be seen as representing archetypal forces that play an important role in shaping one's experience of the numinous and in providing pathways to access it. In this chapter therefore, after trying to convey my reflections on the idea of the numinous, I shall gather together some archetypal representations referring to Apollo and Dionysus and show how they seem to be pointing at underlying psychic structures which are involved in the experience of that emotionally charged and consciousness-transforming *mysterium tremendum* which Otto named 'numinous' (Otto 1923/1958).

The material I have collected for this piece comes mainly from areas of my experience of the numinous where I felt that the Apolline and the Dionysian categories were meaningful, i.e. Greek mythology, analytical psychology and music. In these three areas I have undertaken, to different degrees, either curricular studies or training in institutions where I remember having initially projected feelings of a religious nature, as I realize in hindsight. A literary exemplification of this phenomenon is given by the imaginary community which Hermann Hesse named Castalia and described in his novel *The Glass Bead Game* (Hesse 1943/1972), consecrated to music and mathematics, on which I shall say more later. Whenever I have been able to recollect those projections from the institution with which they were initially merged, the subject of the training has taken on the numinous quality. Following the thread of the mysterious energy with which it was endowed, I eventually came to look at the psyche as the realm where such energy ultimately originates. Touching base with this source seems to me the defining moment in the experience of the numinous.

When I applied for my training in analytical psychology in London, I recall that I wrote that my life used to flow like a steady river, but from time to time I felt the need to agitate the water, as it was the case in making that decision. I ascribe to Dionysus the need of stirring, bearing in mind that Nietzsche defines the Dionysian impulse as 'a mixed drink which must be constantly stirred' (Nietzsche 1872/1995: 5). Stirring the water brings up part of what lies on the bottom and unleashes psychic energy by connecting to the inexhaustible reservoir of the collective unconscious. Jung often referred to the movements of the water as a symbol of the living psyche and of its potential for releasing energy: '[The archetype] is like a deeply graven river-bed in the psyche, in which the waters of life, instead of flowing along as before in a broad but shallow stream, suddenly swell into a mighty river' (Jung 1922/1966: 81).

THE NUMINOUS IN A DREAM

Shortly after I started working on this piece I had a dream. It was set in a hilly landscape with medieval remains around a lake town where I spent my teens and early twenties. Unexpectedly, a knight on a horse appeared out of nowhere riding towards me. I made a split-second decision to take with me only a floppy disk containing some of my writings and then I began to run downhill. As I entered a wood, the knight kept riding after me. It all felt dangerous and exciting at the same time.

I knew that through this dream I had experienced a numinous event, which is why I would like to use it to expand on some aspects of the idea of the numinous.

The emotional quality of the sudden appearance of the knight is marked by surprise and novelty. The manifestation of numinous psychic contents typically engenders this kind of reaction even if the same content has already been met. In this sense, the experience of the numinous relies on a capacity for innocence. Also, the numinous event comes from far away, both temporally and spatially, in the same way as Apollo and Dionysus came to Greece from afar, neither being of Hellenic origin. It is about alien forces getting nearer to us. Besides, in the dream the arrival of the knight is obviously an occurrence entirely independent of my will, which is a typical feature of the numinous experience according to Otto (1923/1958).

Another aspect of the numinous presence in my dream is its high and ambivalent emotional charge. As I run down the hill, into a wood, I am in a state of arousal for being part of an adventurous, unexpected and mysterious occurrence, animated by that peculiar kind of energy which Otto describes with words like urgency, vitality, passion, emotional temper, movement, excitement, activity, impetus (1923/1958: 23). The sense of *mysterium* springs from the encounter with a layer or an area of psychic experience whose meaning is still unknown, facing which emotions are bound to be ambivalent. For some of these psychic contents, like complexes, the meaning may be unravelled and integrated so that they would lose their overpowering quality (Jung 1947/1960: 186–7). However, the underlying ocean of energy, which crystallizes in the psychic forms experienced by individuals as complexes and by the collective as myths, is an inexhaustible source of meaning which can never be entirely resolved. Numinous experiences of an Apolline and Dionysian kind, due to their archetypal nature, spring from this depth and therefore feel gripping and unfathomable at the same time.

Back to the dream, where although I was feeling overpowered by the eruption of unconscious forces which set me on the run, I could still make the choice of bringing one single object with me, a floppy disk, perhaps an ego-object that I was not willing to leave behind. I wonder if this need of clinging on to something familiar while going through the experience of the numinous may be seen as functionally equivalent to the rituals which are just as necessary when dealing with overwhelming energies. In this respect, the files I brought with me may point at writing as a ritual aimed at containing the experience of the numinous (as well as perhaps having contributed to evoking it in the first place), thus providing an Apolline response to a Dionysian epiphany.

The manifestation of the numinous in this dream presents structural elements which include not only an event of an extra-ordinary nature, but also a certain kind of emotional response of the subject involved in a super-individual experience and the recourse to symbolically meaningful rituals. These elements need to be seen as a whole as they derive their meaning from the interrelations with one another within the psyche. As Dourley observes,

> Jung denies that divinity should be conceived as an 'absolute' somehow beyond the human. Rather the divine and the human should be imagined as 'functions' of each other dialectically related and wholly contained within the organic dynamic of the psyche.
>
> (Dourley 2004: 59)

Seen from this angle, the Apolline and Dionysian pathways represent two archetypal modalities of the intrapsychic morphology of the numinous, which I shall look at according to the three building elements outlined above, i.e. the nature of the event, the interplay between individual and universal, and the mediating ritual.

APOLLINE AND DIONYSIAN PATHWAYS

The event: meeting the gods

Dionysus is the god that unleashes collective instinctual energies and brings a state of unrestrained frenzy. It represents the moment when individual forms of existence break down and cause human beings to plummet into an experience of primordial unity among themselves through the medium of the body and rituals, such as dancing, singing and the dismemberment of living beings. Nietzsche sees the Dionysian experience as preceding the Apolline, both historically – with specific reference to the pre-Homeric origin of Greek tragedy – and psychologically, as Nietzsche points out when he describes Greek tragedy as 'the Dionysian chorus disburdening itself again and again in an Apolline image-world' (Nietzsche 1872/1995: 27), so that the horror of reality would be transfigured into and redeemed through Apolline soothing illusions. The level of existence which Dionysus reconnects to is both tragic and ecstatic. Countless forms of existence push one another in and out of life, so one can experience both the 'infinite primordial joy' of existence and the 'maddening sting' of the pains for the destruction of phenomena (Nietzsche 1872/1995: 60). This is why Dionysus is at the same time liberator (Lysios) and destroyer (Zagreus). Living beings seized by Dionysus are no longer individuals and can thus partake of a primordial energy – the will to power in later Nietzsche's language – which on account of its inherent inexhaustibility is ready to sacrifice even its highest types.

Such awe-striking characterization of the Dionysian mode is evocative of a highly numinous experience, which Nietzsche ultimately intuits as the most radical as it refers to the moment of creation, of things coming into being, intertwined with the experience of death and destruction in a cease-less transformative flow. Death is an essential attribute of the psychology of Dionysus, whose mythological variations depict him both as the son of Persephone and as the rescuer of Semele and Ariadne from the underworld, while the Orphic Mysteries remember the cycles of his death and rebirth. Jung assimilates the disintegrative aspect of Dionysus-Zagreus to a Wotan-like moment, where Wotan is 'an elemental Dionysus breaking into the Apolline order', or a windy storm which uproots anything that is not firmly grounded (Jung 1936/1964: 391–2). The dark side of the numinous, in its Wotan–Dionysus nature, may shatter and overturn the 'law and order' myth of the ego when the latter fails to acknowledge the psychic existence of Wotan and is only able to experience it through projection, as happens in the initial interaction between the cousins Pentheus and Dionysus (Euripides trans. 1997).

According to Nietzsche, the Apolline pathway provides a soothing out-come for the individuals shattered by a Dionysian disintegrative experience. Its grammar revolves around keywords like individuality, beauty, clarity and sight. The restoration of individuality from orgiastic self-annihilation allows us 'to delight in individuals' to which the Apolline 'attaches our sympathetic emotion [and] satisfies our sense of beauty which longs for great and sublime forms'. The influence of the Apolline is as powerful as it is deceitful in conjuring up 'detached pictures of the world', which both prevent and cure our dissolution anxiety (Nietzsche 1872/1995: 79). In other words, the underlying Dionysian energy is redeemed and condensed through the Apolline in discrete experiences of the world – persons, images, dreams, art – which may feel beautiful, sublime, clear, stable. Civilizations too, as Freud understood them, are attempts at creating areas of stability relatively shielded from the instinctual tumultuous energy. As Walter Otto puts it,

> [The Apolline] proclaims the presence of the divine not in the miracles of a supernatural power, not in the rigor of an absolute justice, not in the providence of an infinite love, but in the victorious splendour of clarity, in the intelligent sway of order and moderation . . . Clarity and form are the objective aspect, to which distance and freedom are the subjective pendant.
>
> (Otto 1954/1979: 79)

The accounts of Apollo's birth are quite revealing of the numinosity which emanates from illumination and revelation. On account of Hera's curse, Apollo could only be delivered by his mother Leto in a place that had not yet seen the light. Upon his birth on the island of Delos (literally 'the visible one'), which having just emerged from underwater had seen the sunlight for the first time, the whole island shone all day with a golden light, while Zeus put a stop to Hera's anger by taking away the feeling of indignation from her – all too human to cling to in the moment of Apollo's epiphany. In the same vein, Callimachus' 'Hymn to Apollo' proclaims: 'Neither does mother Thetis mournfully lament for her Achilles/ If she hears "Hie Paian, Hie Paian"' (Kerényi 1954/1983: 32).

Another aspect of Apolline numinosity is that it is experienced as coming from above, both in its awe-inspiring and in its dreadful aspects. Not only does Apolline creativity, with its fascination on humans, possess an Olympian and spiritual quality, but also its way of striking those who reject him comes from both afar and above. As Kerényi reminds us, Apolline is the trembling from above, from the spirit and its mightiness or its extreme and ethereal lightness, Dionysian from below, from the earth and its mysteries (Kerényi 1954/1983: 30). A patient of mine recently drew my attention to the fact that a war which is fought from the sky is somehow less human, a remark which I associated with Apolline death coming from afar and from above, preventing the involvement of the body and of the affects which are rooted in it. Apolline distant arrows, shooting from afar, may be seen as the mythological precursors of the just as mythological idea of 'smart bombs'.

Not only lack of acknowledgement, but also unilateral identification with Apollo can be fatal. Two famous instances in the twentieth-century literature of Apolline identifications, culminating in deadly Dionysian possessions by virtue of enantiodromia, are portrayed in the life and death of the protagonists of Thomas Mann's *Death in Venice* and Herman Hesse's *The Glass Bead Game*, respectively Aschenbach and Knecht. Aschenbach, whose life up to the point of the unfolding tragedy was consecrated to Apollo, rapidly precipitates into a spiralling state of Dionysian possession and death, heralded by an archetypal dream analyzed in depth by Astrachan (Astrachan 1990).

Knecht's death also comes at the end of a life consecrated to Apollo, in the form of his dedication to the superior manifestation of human spirit known as the Glass Bead Game – a synthesis of aesthetic and scientific arts practised in the imaginary elitist province of Castalia. It is anticipated by an inner stirring in Knecht's psyche, where disturbing feelings of disengagement from the outside world and of incipient creative sterility begin to surface. Knecht would eventually leave Castalia with a view to finding a role in society where he might heal this sense of one-sidedness and disconnection from a vital source of energy. However, his rushed-through endeavour to return into his body, symbolized by his diving into a cold lake for a swim with Tito, the boy he is mentoring, results in him drowning, suggesting a failure in his attempt at a Dionysian initiation. Nonetheless, unlike Aschenbach's, Knecht's death is a gentle occurence on which Hesse's narration does not dwell and spares the reader of any painful detail, rendering it a truly Apolline event, overseen from the distance since Apollo cannot be contaminated by nearness to death – or by nearness to anything too human.

Hesse's description of the multiple connections between scientific and artistic disciplines in the Glass Bead Game conveys a compelling sense of numinosity. Science and cognition imply distance and dominance of the form, so the numinous quality they may assume is inherently Apolline. The following passage from *The Glass Bead Game* encapsulates the spirit of this search for a clear and all-encompassing vision:

> Every active Glass Bead Game player naturally dreams of a constant expression of the fields of the Game until they include the entire universe. Or rather, he constantly performs such expansions in his imagination and his private Games . . . The true and ultimate finesse in the private Games of advanced players consists, of course, in their developing such mastery over the expressive, nomenclatural, and formative factors of the Game that they can inject individual and original ideas into any given Game played with objective historical materials.
>
> (Hesse 1943/1972: 132–3)

Such spiritual free-climbing may indeed feel ecstatic.

Emotions in the interplay individual – universal

Both the Dionysian and the Apolline exert their numinous power on individuals by reconnecting them to a super-personal source of energy. The emotional impact engendered by such experiences has to do with the feeling of being overwhelmed by a universal force and being part of a higher order respectively.

The Dionysian way entails the dissolution of individuals through boundary-breaking experiences that put them in touch with an underlying, universal and primordial energy. In this process, what Nietzsche referred to as the Primal Unity dismembers into sets of antinomies which are endowed with a life of their own. Individuals who are willing to painfully sacrifice ego-ruled structures may ecstatically partake of the mysteries of this level of existence. A similar situation is envisaged by Jung in that kind of creative process whereby the artist 'is overwhelmed by a flood of thoughts and images which he never intended to create and which his own will could never have brought into being' (Jung 1922/1966: 73).

The Apolline quest for the universal, on the other hand, is about the reduction of multiplicity in pursuit of a sublime form of purity, with a view to allowing an ordained and all-inclusive structure to emerge, where nothing should be felt as missing or else the completeness and self-sufficiency of the moment would be spoiled. The numinosity of this experience for the individual lies in the feeling of being part of a higher structure – either by playing a part in it or simply by being allowed into the contemplation of its beauty. The Apolline universe revolves around a centre, whereas Dionysian dismemberment implies the fragmentation into a multiplicity of centres of consciousness so that the generation of energy comes from the embodiment of opposites rather than from their reconciliation. In this sense, symbolic structures like Mandalas, where the freed-up psychic contents acquire new meaning by becoming part of a totality, are evocative of an Apolline newly formed order (Hillman 1980: 157–8). After all, Apollo is the God of architecture, and Mandalas are architectural creations of the psyche, assembled under Apollo's powerful promise that 'behind the seeming chaos there was knowledge and purpose' (Dodds 1951/1997: 75). This Father-like wisdom is the exact reverse of the Nietzschean Dionysian wisdom opening up the way to the 'Mothers of Being' where the *principium individuationis* is shattered (Nietzsche 1872/1995: 56).

An Apolline insight of a meaningful totality, endowed with numinous power, is described by Hesse as follows:

> I suddenly realized that in the language, or at any rate in the spirit of the Glass Bead Game, everything actually was all-meaningful, that every symbol and combination of symbols led not hither and yon, not to single examples, experiments, and proofs, but into the centre, the mystery and innermost heart of the world, into primal knowledge.
>
> (Hesse 1943/1972: 113)

If we were to look at the destiny of the ego in the Apolline and Dionysian experiences of the numinous, it would appear that in the Apolline pathways it remains intact, while the overall psychic landscape in which it is embedded acquires a new significance and confers to the ego a numinous sense of being part of a grand-scale and meaningful design. This gives rise to a particular kind of inflation based on the ego entering the orbit of a galaxy, fitting into it without friction and experiencing it as a whole universe. The individual and a universe come together and for some time can co-exist without eroding each other's psychic realities. A similar experience is described in the Emperor Hadrian's reflections in Yourcenar's *Memoirs of Hadrian*:

> I could see myself as seconding the deity in his effort to give form and order to a world, to develop and multiply its convolutions, extensions, and complexities. I was one of the segments of the wheel, an aspect of that unique force caught up in the multiplicity of things; I was eagle and bull, man and swan, phallus and brain all together, a Proteus who is also a Jupiter. And it was at about this time that I began to feel myself divine. Don't misunderstand me: I was still, and more than ever, the same man . . . What more can I say except that all that was lived as god-like experience? . . . I was god, to put it simply, because I was a man . . . If Jupiter is the brain to the world, then the man who organizes and presides over human affairs can logically consider himself as a part of that all-governing mind.
>
> (Yourcenar 1951/1986: 127–8)

Conversely, in the Dionysian pathway to the numinous the ego is swamped by and dissolved into a flood of multiform energy, which is what Nietzsche described as the mystical triumphant cry of Dionysus that breaks the spell of individuation. The universal is here experienced in opposition to and at the expense of the ego and its constructions. As Jung describes in his reading of *The Birth of Tragedy*:

> The Dionysian is therefore comparable to frenzy, which dissolves the individual into collective instincts and contents, a disruption of the secluded ego from the world . . . Every man feels himself 'one' with his neighbour ('not merely united, reconciled and merged'). His individuality must therefore be entirely suspended . . . The creative *dynamis*, the libido in instinctive form, takes possession of the individual as an object and uses him as a tool or expression of itself.
>
> (Jung 1921/1938: 173)

By temporarily releasing individuals from their ego, the Dionysian experience also satisfies the human impulse to reject responsibilities, which according to Dodds has an important psychological function, democratically available to anyone, at times when social pressure on assumption of individual responsibility feels increasingly hard to face (Dodds 1951/1997: 76–7). This explains why Dionysus appealed to the archaic age when the individual began to emerge for the first time from the old solidarity of the family, but also raises the question whether the post-modern, post-Fordist and globalization-driven contemporary Western society, with its increasing pressure on individuals to take on new kinds of responsibilities and handle a greater degree of uncertainty, is equipped to provide functionally equivalent Dionysian rituals.

The rituals and the music

The importance of the ritual lies in being both a form of protection for those who come to make experience of a *mysterium tremendum* and a way whereby the presence of a certain god may be evoked. Indeed, as Otto indicates, not only may the numen seize and possess us, but it also fascinates us to the point that it then 'begins to be sought for his own sake' (Otto 1923/1958: 33). This element of fascination is what turned religion into something more than just expiation and propitiation and made the dread object also the goal of desire and yearning, thus providing the basis for the practice of evoking the gods. In this sense the numinous experience is not entirely involuntary, since individuals may intentionally try to establish a form of connection with the gods. Such intentionality is declined differently according to the Apolline and Dionysian modalities.

The Apolline rituals emphasize the role of the subject in the construction of those forms of the spirit where the Delphic god can manifest itself, as well as the necessity of a long period of preparation, which is both ritual purification and spiritual distillation. Dodds' description of the Pythia's prophetic possession throws light both on the several preparatory steps she needs to undertake to give the oracular response and on the necessity of human intelligence to put her words into order and relate them to the enquiry (Dodds 1951/1997: 71–4). The experiencing subject who, while remaining aware that the sense of the numinous comes from somewhere other than the ego, manages to keep a steady focus on the process achieves that paradoxical co-existence of individual affirmation and divine intervention which I see as inherent to the feeling of Apolline numinosity. Analytical psychology too is a prolonged and focused exercise, shared by two individuals, aimed at gradually and ritualistically building a boundaried psychological space where numinous energy may return to flow. Episodes of possession within the analytical container, like Pythia's revelations, are made intelligible through verbalization and reflection.

The Dionysian pathway to the numinous requires a different kind of attitude by the individual, which is about destructuring rather than building, with a view to reaching into creative chaos and allowing oneself to be temporarily overwhelmed by it. In this sense Jung can say of Nietzsche's Zarathustra that 'it simply poured out of him' (Jung 1998: 11), pointing out how even writing, essentially an Apolline ritual, can become a Dionysian practice, as it happens with automatic writing. The preparation to the epiphany of Dionysus consists of an invocation which entails disidentification from the ego and a waiting time to allow the god to manifest itself. A telling example of the coming together of the intentional and involuntary aspects in a Dionysian way is given by Lopez-Pedraza when he describes *juerga*, a form of Spanish music:

> The *juerga* is the most Dionysiac expression of all. It consists of a group (*thiasos*) of flamenco singers and aficionados singing for days, waiting for the *duende* to appear, waiting for the emotion propitiated by the music. It happens when some mysterious quality in the song strikes the group simultaneously. One can say it is an emotion that arises out of the mystery of Dionysiac aesthetics.
>
> (Lopez-Pedraza 2000: 39)

Artistic expressions can be powerful pathways to numinous experience inasmuch as they allow access to the energy encapsulated in the psychic aspects excluded by one's individual experience and/or by the dominant culture. In this context I find Jung's idea of art as a process of self-regulation, whether on an individual or on a collective basis, more to the point than the Freudian idea of art as sublimation.

Among the human means of expressing the numinous, all of which cannot be but indirect as argued by Otto (1923/1958: 70), music is an experience whose paradoxical nature of being at once intelligible and untranslatable endows it with the unique power 'to act simultaneously on the mind and senses, stimulating both ideas and emotions and blending them in a common flow' (Lévi-Strauss 1964/1994: 17). In a sense it is wholly other, representing the realm where 'passions enjoy themselves' (Nietzsche 1885/2001, Aphorism 106), but on the other hand it resonates within the human psyche which can thus partake of this enjoyment. Suspended between silence and expression, otherness and familiarity, autonomy and intentionality, and moving in between without resolution, music keeps open the channel between the infinite possibilities of the psyche and their concretizations in human experiences. Augustine condensed this paradox in the metaphor of the jubilation (wordless song): 'If you cannot talk about him, and it is improper just to keep silence, why, what is there left for you to do but jubilate – with your heart rejoicing without words, and the immense breadth of your joy not rationed out in syllables?' (quoted in McGlashan 1987: 327). McGlashan also acknowledges music's 'unique power to convey feeling coupled with its cognitive opacity', where 'nothing is said, everything is said' (McGlashan 1987: 342).

Music holds a special place with regards to both Apolline and Dionysian ways to the numinous because it is an essential attribute of the rituals associated with both gods, although on an iconographical basis it would appear quintessentially Apolline. Historically, the kind of music associated with the Dionysian rituals in ancient Greece (especially before 600 BC) is thought to have had an ecstatic character achieved through wild dancing and the use of instruments like the flute and percussion (Silk and Stern 1981: 139), whereas the Apolline music was marked by moderation, restraint and beauty, as symbolized by the power of Orpheus' lyre in taming wild beasts. Quite apart from their historical basis in the Greek culture, evidence of which is unfortunately quite scant, the existence of Apolline and Dionysian approaches to music is a psychological reality which has informed musical experience throughout history.

For instance, the old philosophical distinction made by the Greeks between *musica mundana* and *musica humana* may be seen as one of the many possible representations of the Apolline–Dionysian archetypal polarity in the realm of music. The former indicates the abstract music of the celestial spheres whose harmony may be thought rather than heard, the latter signifies the embodied music produced by instruments and perceived through senses. The *musica humana*, consigned to an inferior status by Plato, may be seen as the repressed Dionysian music associated with body, immediacy, collectively shared and potentially subversive emotions. Its inferior status eventually resulted in oblivion, in that nothing remained of the *musica humana* of the Greeks (Fubini 1995: 35). A victory of dismemberment over remembering, of Apollo allied with the Titans over Dionysus-Zagreus.

A strong link with the body is indeed an essential aspect of the Dionysian experience of music. As the Greeks knew, hearing is the most emotive of all senses (Dodds 1951/1997: 78), so music connects us directly with our inner world of affects, which Nietzsche thought could only be met by listening to its vibrations (Safranski 2001: 31). Dionysus is in turn closely associated with the body, as Jung recognizes in linking the Dionysian experience with the sensation function (Jung 1921/1938). Unlike Apollo, Dionysus can make full use of the expressive range of the body: he sheds tears, grows older, plays with his appearance, sings and dances, allies himself with Aphrodite, knows the physical pain of the process of destruction, is acquainted with the realm of death, dies and is reborn, is physically close to his followers and his epiphany does not require mediation. A state of Dionysian possession is an experience of the embodied soul which encompasses ecstasy and pain, elation and depression as long as they are lived in the body.

Lopez-Pedraza also suggests that jazz is the Dionysian music of the twentieth century (Lopez-Pedraza 2000: 41), as opposed to the Apolline character of classical music. Keith Jarrett, a pianist who has successfully performed both kinds of music, points to the physiological basis of this distinction when he states the need to resort to different circuitry for either genre. He also confirms the Dionysian nature of jazz by stating that a jazz player needs to disappear into the music and to avoid thinking about the kind of details one has to consider in classical performance (Rosenthal 1996). Another way of looking at the distinction between Apolline and Dionysian music refers to their relation with structures. As we know, the tonal system has been providing an ordering structure to Western music since the eighteenth century. Apolline music would either celebrate the dominant structure or challenge it through the creation of a new structure, like, for example, serial music in the twentieth century. Dionysian music would instead work in the interstices of the existing structure (both tones and beats), unhinging it rather than strengthening it, evoking primordial chaos rather than trying to order it, swerving rather than confirming, delaying rather than seeking resolution. I cannot think of a better example than John Coltrane's *Ascension*, where although structure is perceptible in the balance of the totality of instruments and the quietness of its initial and final states, throughout the 45 minutes of its duration 'your nervous system has been dissected, overhauled, and reassembled' (Spellman 1965). Which is very much what the Dionysian experience is about.

In classical music, too, the interaction between the performer and the piece, i.e. between the individual and the structure, can take a Dionysian turn. I am thinking of Bach, whose music, in spite of its Apolline character as far as sublime structure, rhythmic regularity and measured expression are concerned, was interestingly seen by Nietzsche as the starting point for the rise of Dionysiac music in modern times which would then lead to Beethoven and Wagner. Perhaps what makes one experience Bach's music in a more or less Dionysian way is its interpretation, which is ultimately a creative act in its own right. For instance, two interpretations of his Chorale Prelude 'Allein Gott in der Höh sei Ehr' ('Gloria in Excelsis Deo' – 'Glory to God in the Highest'), performed by the Russian pianist Samuel Feinberg in 1952 and 1962 respectively, represent two very different takes on the same musical material. In what is merely my subjective hearing of it, the last take, recorded by Feinberg only a few days before dying, was touched by a Dionysian inspiration, as I was led to think by the physical character of the performance, signalled by pronounced and frequent breathing of the pianist in the recording, and by the expansion of the time of the execution through repetitions of sections and dilatation of resolutions. Every single note comes across as fully weighed and lived in no Promethean hurry, under the overarching experience of death.

Music provides ways into pools of psychic energy which may be otherwise quite hard to tap into, hence its special place in rituals for accessing the numinous – or rather its being a ritual in its own right. Augustine could not accept this idea since he feared that his intellect might be sinfully distracted by the sensorial pleasure that he gained from music and singing, especially when the latter felt to him more moving than the truth (Storr 1997: 22). Music itself is in fact a 'truth', i.e. the psychic reality of the god whose voice can fill one's soul, body or mind in that unique way. This is why, as contemporary psychology is increasingly aware of, a strong attraction to a kind of music may have a compensatory function and reveal an aspect of the psyche which is lying dormant (Skar 2002: 631). After all, Dodds reminds us that the Corybantic rituals resorted to different kinds of religious music for diagnostic purposes. People were encouraged to find out about their psychic diseases by identifying what kind of tune would affect them most, so that they could then appease through sacrifice the corresponding and hitherto unacknowledged god by which they were troubled (Dodds 1951/1997: 77–9).

ENCOUNTER

Nietzsche observed that civilizations need enough Apolline transfiguring power in order to be able to open themselves to – and to withstand – Dionysian impulses. At the same time, Apolline forms need enough vital energy and Dionysian moisture lest they dry up. Thus 'these two art-impulses are compelled to develop their powers in strictly mutual proportion, according to the law of eternal justice' (Nietzsche 1872/1995: 91). In this sense Nietzsche could famously proclaim 'Dionysus speaks the language of Apollo; Apollo, however, finally speaks the language of Dionysus' (Nietzsche 1872/1995: 81).

That the two gods' languages actually came closer is clearly visible in their sharing the Delphic festival, so that in the winter months the Dionysian dithyramb was sung and in the summer months the Apolline paean followed. The two gods, initially more radically distinct, interpenetrated each other by the fifth century BC, when Dionysian wild rituals, under the influence of Apolline restraint, were confined to a body specially elected for this cult (Silk and Stern 1981: 179). Dionysian frenzy was both acknowledged and regulated. Walter Otto sees in the development of this 'working alliance' a new arena where the inherent dialectics of existence, instead of being confined within the Dionysian sea of opposites, may be experienced in a more integrated way, encompassing both impulses and spirit:

> Apollo with Dionysus, the intoxicated leader of the choral dance of the terrestrial sphere – that would give the total world dimension. In this union the Dionysiac earthly duality would be elevated into a new and higher duality, the eternal contrast between a restless, whirling life and a still, far-seeing spirit.
>
> (Otto 1960/1965: 208)

This final configuration of the relationship between Apollo and Dionysus, before their demise as historical gods, seems apt at holding a balance between them, while allowing them to remain two distinct god-figures who preside over different ways of accessing the numinous. Their getting closer, but not too close to fade into each other, allows a non-mutually exclusive experience of both and therefore averts the danger of revenge by the hand of either god, an outcome which figures like Pentheus and Marsyas powerfully symbolize.

References

Astrachan, G. (1990) 'Dionysus in Thomas Mann's Novella, "Death in Venice"', *Journal of Analytical Psychology* 35: 59–77.

Bishop, P. (1999) 'C.G. Jung and Nietzsche: Dionysus and Analytical Psychology', in P. Bishop (ed.), *Jung in Contexts: A Reader*, London: Routledge.

Dodds, E.R. (1951/1997) *The Greeks and the Irrational*, Berkeley: University of California Press.

Dourley, J.P. (2004) 'Jung, Mysticism and the Double Quaternity: Jung and the Psychic Origin of Religious and Mystical Experience', *Harvest* 50(1): 47–74.

Euripides (trans. 1997) *Bacchae*, New York: Dover Thrift Editions.

Fubini, E. (1995) *Estetica della musica*, Bologna: Il Mulino.

Hesse, H. (1943/1972) *The Glass Bead Game*, London: Penguin Books.

Hillman, J. (1972) *The Myth of Analysis*, Evanston: Northwestern University Press.

Hillman, J. (1980) 'Dionysus in Jung's Writing', in *Facing the Gods*, Dallas: Spring Publications.

Huskinson, L. (2004) *Nietzsche and Jung: The Whole Self and the Union of Opposites*, London: Routledge.

Jung, C.G. (1921/1938) *Psychological Types*, *CW* 6.

Jung, C.G. (1922/1966) 'On the Relationship of Analytical Psychology to Poetry', *CW* 15.

Jung, C.G. (1936/1964) 'Wotan', *CW* 10.

Jung, C.G. (1947/1960) 'On the Nature of the Psyche', *CW* 8.

Jung, C.G. (1998) *Seminar on Nietzsche's 'Zarathustra'*, ed. J.L. Jarrett, Princeton, NJ: Princeton University Press.

Kerényi, K. (1954/1983) *Apollo: The Wind, The Spirit, and The God*, Dallas: Spring Publications.

Lévi-Strauss, C. (1964/1994) *The Raw and the Cooked: Introduction to a Science of Mythology*, London: Pimlico.

Lopez-Pedraza, R. (2000) *Dionysus in Exile – On the Repression of the Body and Emotion*, Illinois: Chiron.

McGlashan, A.R. (1987) 'Music as a Symbolic Process', *Journal of Analytical Psychology* 32: 327–44.

Nietzsche, F. (1872/1995) *The Birth of Tragedy*, New York: Dover Thrift Editions.

Nietzsche, F. (1885/2001) *Beyond Good and Evil*, Cambridge: Cambridge: Cambridge University Press.

Nietzsche, F. (1886/1999) *An Attempt at Self-Criticism*, Cambridge: Cambridge University Press.

Otto, R. (1923/1958) *The Idea of the Holy*, London: Oxford University Press.

Otto, W.F. (1954/1979) *The Homeric Gods: The Spiritual Significance of Greek Religion*, London: Thames & Hudson.

Otto, W.F. (1960/1965) *Dionysus: Myth and Cult*, Bloomington: Indiana University Press.

Rosenthal, T. (1996) 'The Insanity of Doing More than One (Musical) Thing: An Interview with Keith Jarrett', www.tedrosenthal.com.

Safranski, R. (2001) *Nietzsche*, Milano: Longanesi.

Silk, M.S. and Stern, J.P. (1981) *Nietzsche on Tragedy*, Cambridge: Cambridge University Press.

Skar, P. (2002) 'The Goal as Process: Music and the Search for the Self', *Journal of Analytical Psychology* 47: 629–38.

Spellman, A.B. (1965) Liner Notes to John Coltrane's *Ascension*, Impulse Records.

Storr, A. (1997) *Music and the Mind*, London: HarperCollins.

Yourcenar, M. (1951/1986) *Memoirs of Hadrian*, London: Penguin Books.

Chapter 10

Numinosity and terror: Jung's psychological revision of Otto as an aid to engaging religious fundamentalism[1]

Roderick Main

RELIGIOUS FUNDAMENTALISM AND DEPTH PSYCHOLOGY

Originally applied to certain groups of American Protestants in the 1920s,[2] the term 'fundamentalist' is now widely used, by journalists, government officials, scholars, and general publics, to refer to extremist and militant movements within any religion. Not only Protestant but Catholic and Orthodox movements, not only Christian but Jewish and Islamic movements, and not only Abrahamic but Hindu, Buddhist, Sikh, Confucian, Shinto, and other religious movements have attracted the label 'fundamentalist' or been considered candidates for it (see Marty and Appleby 1991; Ruthven 2004). While the validity and usefulness of such wide usage have often been questioned, many scholars have concluded that no better term is available to designate a cluster of characteristics shared, in various combinations and to varying degrees, by the diverse movements (Marty and Appleby 1991: viii–ix; Armstrong 2001: x–xi; Almond *et al.* 2003: 16–17; Ruthven 2004: 5–10).

In their book *Strong Religion: The Rise of Fundamentalisms around the World* (2003)[3] Gabriel Almond, R. Scott Appleby, and Emmanuel Sivan, attempting to distil an understanding of religious fundamentalism applicable to its numerous global varieties, identify five ideological and four organisational characteristics. The ideological characteristics are (1) reactivity to the marginalisation of religion: fighting back against the forces of secularisation; (2) selectivity: the choice of certain texts and traditions over others, or of some aspects of modernity to embrace (e.g., communications technology) and others to oppose (e.g., religious pluralism); (3) moral Manichaeanism: the stark division of reality into the good, the light, and the saved, on the one hand, and the evil, the dark, and the damned, on the other; (4) absolutism and inerrancy (not necessarily literalism): the belief that sources of authority, often textual, are of divine or inspired origin and are true and accurate in all particulars; and (5) millennialism and messianism: the belief among many, though not all, fundamentalists that history will have a miraculous culmination, ushered in by an all-powerful redeemer, in which the suffering and waiting of the faithful will end and a reign of eternal justice begin. The organisational characteristics of fundamentalism are (6) elect, chosen membership: the belief that the faithful are divinely called; (7) sharp boundaries: the attempt to separate the saved from the sinful, believers from infidels, through regulating their living space, their dress, their education, and their exposure to media; (8) authoritarian organisation: typically there is a charismatic leader–follower relationship; and (9) behavioural require-ments: members' time, space, and activity are considered to be group rather than individual resources (ibid.: 92–104).[4]

The above characteristics have been distilled from studies carried out primarily by political scientists, historians, anthropologists, sociologists, and scholars of religion working from historical and sociological perspectives (see Marty and Appleby 1991, 1993a, 1993b, 1994, 1995; Almond *et al.* 2003). Nevertheless, the characteristics also seem to cry out for depth psychological interpretation. For example, each characteristic evinces sharp splitting and polarisation – between the religious and the secular; the selected and the rejected; good and evil; divine truth and human error; redemption and perdition; believers and infidels; the righteously observant and the culpably negligent – and the major depth psychological theories offer profound and compelling accounts of just this sort of splitting and polarisation. The importance of the intrapsychic dimension of fundamentalism has been sig-nalled even by non-psychological commentators. Malise Ruthven, for example, points out with reference to the September 11th hijackers and other Islamists that 'The *jihad* (struggle) against *kufr* (disbelief) which [they] espouse is not so much a "war between civilisations" . . . as a struggle waged over contested identities within the individual self' (2002: 18). Recently, numerous depth psychological studies pertinent to an understanding of religious fundamentalism – though often focusing more immediately on terrorism, violence, and war – have indeed been forthcoming (see, for example, the books by Hillman 2004; Jones 2002; Stevens 2004; the collections edited by Beebe 2003; Covington *et al.* 2002; Zoja and Williams 2002; the articles and chapters by Britton 2002; Brooke 2000; Dourley 2003; Giegerich 2002; Guggenbühl-Craig 2002; Papadopoulos 2000, 2002; Ulanov 2002; Young 2004; and the papers by Figlio 2004; Samuels 2005; Wieland 2005).

This depth psychological work is especially needed since fundamentalist movements, for all their selective deployment of pragmatic rationality in promoting their causes (Marty and Appleby 1991: vii; 1995: 2), have an irrational core that is inaccessible to argument and that, in the political sphere (for example, in the Israel–Palestine conflict), can act as a wild card disrupting attempted solutions based on reasonable compromise (Ruthven 2004: 3). Depth psychology, as the discipline *par excellence* for exploring and theorising about the irrational, may be able to provide insights that enable this irrationality to be more effectively engaged.

Especially, depth psychology can illuminate the unconscious interdependence that has been noted between fundamentalist movements and the secular or liberal cultures they oppose (see Armstrong 2001: 178, 370–1). As certain secular values such as pluralism are intolerable to fundamentalists (see Ruthven 2004: 46), certain fundamentalist values such as exclusivism are intolerable to secularists (see ibid.: 47–9). Yet elements of – or potentials for – both outlooks exist within everyone, and the purity of a fundamentalist or secularist identity can only be sustained by denying the alien and contaminating elements or potentials through repression and projection. Fundamentalists project their unwanted secular inclinations onto – and, through projective identification, into – secularists, and secularists project their unwanted fundamentalist inclinations onto and into fundamentalists. Each reinforces the other in a demonised identity (see Main 2003: 198).

This dynamic is especially troubling since almost all of the academic disciplines by which fundamentalism is studied embed predominantly, if not exclusively, secular assumptions. There is therefore likely to be an in-built conflict between the disciplinary theories and their object of study, and this conflict will undoubtedly colour the understanding of fundamentalism emerging from these studies. Since almost all depth psychological theories, including the psychoanalytic traditions stemming from Freud, similarly embed secular assumptions, they too, for all their insight into the irrational and into the very dynamic we are discussing, are likely to be caught in this polarisation when they turn their attention to fundamentalism. It is true that some contemporary psychoanalysis, especially that influenced by Winnicott, takes a much more positive view of religion than did Freud and other earlier psychoanalysts (see Jones 2002: 82–105). However, these approaches that are positive about religion remain, at bottom, uncompromisingly naturalistic in orientation. Winnicott's intermediate area exists between an inner subjectivity that is conceived naturalistically and an outer objectivity that is also conceived naturalistically. The intersection or interaction of these two domains in a 'third area' cannot generate anything that is transcendent in a sense that would be acceptable to many religious adherents.[5] The question therefore remains of whether and how it might be possible to go beyond the conflict and polarisation and to open possibilities for richer understanding and even transformative interaction with fundamentalism. C. G. Jung's (1875–1961) analytical psychology may have something to offer at this point.

ANALYTICAL PSYCHOLOGY: SACRED AND SECULAR

Born of a long line of pastors, yet trained in science and medicine, Jung struggled throughout his life to resolve the tension he experienced, in himself and in his culture, between the conflicting claims of traditional religion and an increasingly secular modernity. Analytical psychology was forged out of this struggle and as a historical consequence embeds assumptions of both a secular and a religious nature (Main 2003: 191, 2004: 91–114; cf. Homans 1979/1995: 156–7). Like other depth psychologies, analytical psychology is a secular discipline in the sense that it is concerned with natural and human-centred principles and methods of explanation rather than supernatural ones. This is evident within Jung's writings in his concern for the actualities of lived human experience (Jung 1938/1940: para. 88), in his refusal to engage in theological speculation (ibid.: para. 2), and above all in his relentless concern to be seen as an empiricist or scientist rather than a philosopher (ibid., 1973: 227, 1976: 567).

At the same time, analytical psychology can fairly be characterised as religious. Many of Jung's explicit statements suggest this: 'man's vital energy or libido is the divine pneuma all right', he wrote to Fr Victor White (1973: 384); 'the soul possesses by nature a religious function', he writes in *Psychology and Alchemy* (1944: para. 14); 'I don't need to believe [in God]. I know', he stated in his *Face to Face* interview for the BBC in 1959 (McGuire and Hull 1978: 414). Again, Jung frequently equated his psychological concepts with traditional religious ones – for example, in his analyses of the doctrine of the Trinity (1942/1948), the symbolism of the Mass (1942/1954), and the problem of evil (1952a).[6] Above all, analytical psychology, alone among the major depth psychologies, genuinely keeps the door open to the possible reality of the transcendent objects of religion. This is a point that has been noted not only by Jungians (Tacey 1997: 315–16) but also by psychologists of religion (Wulff 1997: 637–8), including psychoanalytically oriented psychologists of religion (Jones 2002: 98–101). Usually this religiousness is treated as a liability for analytical psychology in academic contexts, and attempts are made to disguise it (Tacey 1997: 315–16). However, in the study of religious phenomena this apparent liability could prove to be a special strength (Main 2003).

The dual sacred and secular character of analytical psychology is especially clear in Jung's concept of archetypes, which he treats as having both a biological and a spiritual aspect (1947/1954: para. 414). But it is also evident in many of his other signature concepts, including the collective unconscious, individuation, the self, and synchronicity. For these on the one hand stem from empirical observation and biological and other scientific assumptions, yet on the other hand presuppose a dimension of reality that is intelligent, purposeful, and irreducible to material, social, or cultural terms. Here, however, I wish to focus on a further aspect of analytical psychology that exemplifies Jung's dual sacred and secular approach. This is his appropriation and psychological revision of the idea of the numinous.

THE NUMINOUS

Otto on the numinous

The details of Rudolf Otto's (1869–1937) characterisation of the numinous and of Jung's appropriation of the idea are presented elsewhere in this volume as well as in earlier publications (see, especially, Schlamm 1994). Here I shall present only the briefest summary, while highlighting those features that are especially pertinent to my subsequent discussion of religious fundamentalism.

For Otto, who introduced the term as a specifically religious concept (1958),[7] the numinous refers to the irreducible non-rational[8] and non-ethical aspect in the idea of God or 'the holy' (1958: xxi). He writes that 'the nature of the numinous can only be suggested by means of the special way in which it is reflected in the mind in terms of feeling' (ibid.: 12). It is a feeling of 'creature-consciousness' (ibid.: 10), which is not a natural feeling but can be evoked by association or analogy with natural feelings (ibid.: 9, 41–9). The numinous is not something merely subjective but is 'felt as objective and outside the self' (ibid.: 11).

Most famously, Otto stresses the uncanniness and ambiguity of numinous experience. In discussing the numinous, he writes, 'we are dealing with something for which there is only one appropriate expression, *mysterium tremendum* [tremendous mystery]' (ibid.: 12). He elucidates the idea of the numinous by analysing the component words in this expression. Implicit in *tremendum* he finds the qualities of 'awefulness', 'overpoweringness', and 'urgency' (ibid.: 13–24). Awefulness he glosses as 'daemonic dread' (ibid.: 16) and as 'the "wrath of God", prompting to a sense of "terror" that no "natural" anger can arouse' (ibid.: 19). Overpoweringness is 'a consciousness of the absolute superiority or supremacy of a power other than myself' (ibid.: 21). Urgency implies 'a force that knows not stint nor stay, which is urgent, active, compelling, and alive' (ibid.: 24). The term *mysterium* he considers to refer to a reality which is 'wholly other' (ibid.: 25–30), that is, 'quite beyond the sphere of the usual, the intelligible, and the familiar' (ibid.: 26).

In addition to the *tremendum*, Otto draws attention to the more attractive quality of 'fascination', *fascinans* (ibid.: 31–40). This quality denotes 'something that allures with a potent charm' (ibid.: 31), 'something that captivates and transports [the experiencer] with a strange ravishment, rising often enough to a pitch of dizzy intoxication; it is the Dionysiac element in the numen' (ibid.). Fascination, for Otto, encompasses 'a bliss which embraces all those blessings that are indicated or suggested in positive fashion by any "doctrine of salvation"' (ibid.: 33). Because of this additional quality of fascination, Otto's key expression is often expanded to *mysterium tremendum et fascinans* (tremendous and fascinating mystery).

'These two qualities', he remarks, 'the daunting and the fascinating, now combine in a strange harmony of contrasts' resulting in a 'dual character of the numinous consciousness' (ibid.: 31).

Jung on the numinous

References to the numinous begin to appear in Jung's work in the mid to late 1930s (e.g., 1934, 1934–9, 1938/1940).[9] By this time, Jung's own psychological model had reached a mature development, but he quickly appropriated Otto's term and used it to enrich his characterisation of the unconscious. Above all, he names the numinous as one of the defining characteristics of archetypes (1911–12/1952: paras. 225, 450; 1947/1954: para. 405; 1958: paras. 646, 731), and from this stems its pervasive role in his psychology of religion. He presents the numinous as the core of religious experience and for that reason as the basis of religious creeds (ibid.: paras. 9–10). The numinous gives religious symbols their power to convince (1911–12/1952: para. 344); it is what makes archetypal experience religious experience (1938/1940: para. 102); it is, Jung even asserts, the origin of the experience of God (1934–9: 258). More specifically, the numinous can cause a projection carrier, such as a religion or a religious leader, to have a highly suggestive effect, even giving it the quality of a saviour myth (1958: para. 784). The numinous is associated with illuminations, revelations, and saving ideas (1911–12/1952: para. 450); insightful and transformative experiences (1958: para. 720; 1942/1948: para. 274; 1952a: para. 584); religious statements and mythologems (1952b: paras. 450–1); metaphysical ideas (1955–6: paras. 781–2); and cultural symbols and prejudices (1961: para. 579). It can possess people and inspire them to believe they are prophets (1944: para. 41), and it can also give a religious and fanatical character to secular movements (1942/1948: para. 222).

For Jung, the psychological effects of numinous experience are ambiguous. He describes such experience as 'healing or destructive, but never indifferent' (1947/1954: para. 405). On the positive side, he notes that numinous images are vital forces in both mental make-up and human society (1961: para. 580). They give depth and fullness of meaning (1947/1954: para. 405) and thereby sate the soul's hunger (1958: para. 651). In psychotherapy, they are the factor that releases the patient from pathology (1973: 377; 1976: 56–7). On the negative side, the numinous is difficult to engage and therefore is usually feared or denied (1952a: para. 735). If denied and repressed, it finds alternative outlets, all the more dangerous for not being recognised as such (1942/1948: para. 274; 1944: para. 247). On the one hand, loss of the numinous – or rather loss of conscious relationship to numinous experience – leads to moral and spiritual collapse (1961: paras. 581–2, 584, 587). On the other hand, identification with numinous experience leads to inflation (1934–9: 258–60). The numinous affects what is uncontrolled in people and so can let loose dangerous psychic reactions in the public (1934: 216).

In sum, much of Jung's basic characterisation of the numinous straight-forwardly agrees with Otto's.[10] He retains from Otto an appreciation of the potent, compelling, and ambiguous nature of numinous experience (*tremendum et fascinans*) and, unlike other depth psychologists, remains genuinely open to the possible transcendent reality of the religious object (the *mysterium*).[11] However, in appropriating Otto's concept of the numinous, Jung modifies it in a number of ways that connect it more closely to the human and empirical. He diverges from Otto in presenting the numinous as an experience of the unconscious (see Schlamm 1994: 21–2). In this way he relates the numinous to the human psyche. He diverges, too, in stressing the need for consciousness to preserve its autonomy in face of the numinous (ibid.: 26–7). Thus he asserts the human as an independent source of value. Again, Jung diverges in his general psychological awareness of the risks of repressing numinous experience, being identified with and inflated by it, or psychotically splitting and projecting its components (ibid.: 26). Thereby he enriches understanding of the numinous with empirical psychological knowledge. Moreover, because of his particular association of the numinous with archetypes, Jung also shows awareness of the multiple ways in which the numinous can receive displaced expression in the form of both religious convictions and prejudices of a seemingly secular character (1942/1948: para. 222). In each of these various ways Jung's understanding of the numinous epitomises his dual sacred and secular approach.

ENGAGING RELIGIOUS FUNDAMENTALISM

We have seen that Jung's psychological model shares strengths found in the other depth psychological traditions but also has some distinctive features, including its dual sacred and secular nature and its appropriation and psychological revision of Otto's idea of the numinous. There follow some indications of how this combination of features might make analytical psychology an especially useful theoretical perspective from which to study and engage the difficult phenomena of religious fundamentalism.

Forestalling polarisation

'Fundamentalist movements', according to Almond and his colleagues, 'form in reaction to, and in defense against, the processes and consequences of secularization and modernization which have penetrated the larger religious community' (2003: 93), adding with italic emphasis that '*This defense of religion is the sine qua non of fundamentalism; without it, a movement may not properly be labeled fundamentalist*' (ibid.: 94). From the perspective of analytical psychology, reactivity to the marginalisation of religion is a natural phenomenon, fully to be expected in the light of the religious attitude in analytical psychology, articulated by Jung in the postulate that 'the soul possesses by nature a religious function' (1944: para. 14). As a natural psychic function, concern for religion – in the sense that Jung understands religion as 'the attitude of mind peculiar to a consciousness which has been changed by experience of the *numinosum*' (1938/1940: para. 9) – cannot be eliminated from the psyche. Furthermore, because, in Jung's understanding, the psyche is self-regulating (1928: para. 275), any one-sided neglect of its religious needs must sooner or later lead to a compensatory reaction. The implications of this for relating to religious fundamentalism are clear. Adherents of an outlook are likely to be much more accessible to those who regard their central concern as based on something real and inalienable than to those who regard it as illusory and regressive.

However, for fundamentalists not just any religiousness will do. Religion must be 'strong religion' (Almond *et al.* 2003). It must be a force capable of withstanding and even reversing the trends towards secularisation (ibid.: 2). For Jung, the awfulness, overpoweringness, urgency, and fascination of the numinous ensure that religion as he understands it is strong religion. Indeed, he specifically requires this when he presents religion, or its contemporary substitute, analytical psychology, as the only effective 'counterbalance to mass-mindedness' – 'mass-mindedness' being the pernicious manifestation in the social sphere of the rampant forces of modernisation and secularisation as Jung saw them (see Jung 1957; Main 2004: 117–43).

Because in its handling of the numinous Jung's model does not champion a secular point of view in opposition to a religious one, or vice versa, and moreover understands by 'religion' something no less potent than fundamentalists understand by it, attempts to engage fundamentalism from a Jungian perspective are less likely than other disciplinary approaches to prompt polarisation between the religious and secular. Since analytical psychology encompasses both the secular tendencies that marginalise religion and the religious tendencies that react to that marginalisation, both sides of the fundamentalist problem are contained. Each side should be able to forestall exclusive identification with the other, and so space for constructive dialogue between them can be maintained.

Addressing the non-rational

Analytical psychology takes seriously the non-rational element in religion. Academic studies of fundamentalist religious movements generally pay little attention to this. Even when the autonomous significance of religion is recognised (e.g., Almond *et al.* 2003: 4), the focus tends to be on the more rationally analysable organisational, social, political, historical, and ideological dimensions of religion rather than on its non-rational, emotional, experiential dimension. Aided by its assimilation of Otto's idea of the numinous, analytical psychology takes seriously the sheer overpowering intensity that can adhere to religious phenomena and recognises the futility of trying to address such powerfully motivated religion, institutionalised or not, by means of reason and reasonableness alone. Indeed, Otto's differentiated account of the numinous helps analytical psychology not only to acknowledge but also to analyse this non-rational dimension, identifying and tracing the vicissitudes of its component elements.

The dark side of God and religion

For example, the idea of the numinous, especially its *tremendum* element, helps to articulate Jung's controversial vision of the dark side of deity and religion. Jung shares with Otto the view that the terrifying, wrathful, and disturbing aspect of some religious manifestations is not a deviation from the true nature of religion but is inherent in human experience of the religious object and is an authentic expression of it. If this expression is primitive, its primitiveness is not something that can be casually left behind. It has to be constantly acknowledged and integrated with the more rational and ethical (Otto) or conscious (Jung) aspect of religion. 'Evil verily does not decrease', declares Jung, 'by being hushed up as a non-reality or as a mere negligence of man . . . God is the mystery of all mysteries, a real Tremendum' (1973: 541). Jung's clearest articulation of this dark aspect appears in his 'Answer to Job' (1952a), where he states that it is in the light of Job's realisation of 'God's inner antinomy' – His being evil as well as good – that Job's knowledge 'attains a divine numinosity' (ibid.: para. 584).

The particular benefit of this outlook for studying religious fundamentalism is that it enables the fear of annihilation, the militancy, and, in a small number of cases, the terrorism associated with fundamentalism to be viewed as a possible response to or action out of this dark side of deity. Dread, militancy, and terrorism may be not always deflections from religion but sometimes consequences of approaching too closely to the object of religion. Fundamentalist movements typically retreat into what has been called an 'enclave culture' within whose secure confines religion can be practised with maximum purity (Almond *et al.* 2003: 23–89). It is often only later that such movements launch their counter-offensives against the secular or compromised cultures surrounding them (Armstrong 2001: xi). The motivation for such counter-offensives may be not only the increasing threat to the survival of the enclave and its values from external sources but also the intolerability of the divine darkness and ambiguity that have been accessed by the religious intensity of the group itself, which exerts an overwhelming pressure to be discharged. Liberal religionists, almost as much as secularists, often have difficulty comprehending fundamentalist attitudes. Part of the reason for this, in a Jungian understanding, might be that liberal religion has historically neglected the darker side of God. The more deadly manifestations of religious extremism may be a kind of return of the repressed of this dark side of God, designated by Otto's *tremendum*.

The irrational attraction of religion

Assimilating the idea of the numinous, especially its *fascinans* element, also enables analytical psychology to acknowledge the intense attraction of religion – the fascination it can exert and the certainty it can instil in spite of its patent logical and historical fallacies and its terrifying and destructive potential. Because of its numinosity, writes Jung, experience of the archetype 'seizes and possesses the whole personality, and is naturally productive of faith' (1911–12/1952: para. 344). Numinous God-images 'not only give one the feeling of pointing to the *Ens realissimum* [realest Being], but make one convinced that they actually express it and establish it as a fact' (Jung 1952a: para. 558). As Otto stresses, this fascination can fill experiencers with a sense of blissful rapture and of having been saved (1958: 31, 33, 36). In certain circumstances, this can be so compelling that it leads experiencers to set their own and others' actual lives at nought.

Otherness and the readiness to project

Again, the element of mystery (the *mysterium*) in numinosity, characterised above all by the sense of being 'wholly other', helps account for the powerful sense that the source of religious terror and bliss is external to oneself. Whether their source actually is external is a complicated question for analytical psychology in view of Jung's late theorising about the psychoid unconscious and synchronicity, according to which there is an unknowable but inferable level of the psyche at which normal distinctions between inner and outer break down (Jung 1976: 22, 541). Nevertheless, religious terror and bliss are overwhelmingly *experienced* as responses to an objective, transpersonal reality, and this helps account for the readiness to project that is such a common feature of fundamentalist states of mind.

However, Jung explicitly locates the numinous as an experience of the unconscious, even if he remains open about the possible transpersonal nature of the unconscious (1942/1948: para. 222, 1955–6: para. 782), and this qualifies the sense that the numinous is, in Otto's phrase, 'wholly other'. As Jung writes, with implicit reference to Otto, 'It is . . . psychologically quite unthinkable for God to be simply the "wholly other," for a "wholly other" could never be one of the soul's deepest and closest intimacies – which is precisely what God is' (1944: para. 11, n. 6). If the numinous is an experience of the unconscious, it is, at least potentially, connected to the individual. Realisation of this makes it possible to recognise the dynamics of projection, albeit archetypal projection, in the attribution of numinosity.

The elements of the numinous, for instance in the split and projected terror and rapture of fundamentalism, can therefore be not just recognised but owned. The precondition then exists for attempting to dissolve these projections.

Splitting of the numinous

Where ambiguity and intensity are found together, as in the numinous as Otto characterises it, there is indeed a high risk that the elements of the ambiguous situation will be split and projected. Some version of this dynamic is articulated in all the major depth psychological theories. In Otto's own writings, however, this possibility is not explored. He writes about the 'strange harmony of contrasts' between the *tremendum* and the *fascinans*, without considering the possibility or the consequences of the harmony breaking down and the contrasting elements being sundered. Jung's psychological model, as we have seen, is particularly alert to this possibility (Jung 1952a; Papadopoulos 2000, 2002), yet articulates it without reducing the experience of the numinous to natural determinants, as would other psychoanalytic models (Capps 1997: 76–126; Jones 2002: 51–63). Understanding such splitting and projection is especially helpful for gaining insight into the moral Manichaeanism characteristic of religious fundamentalism, where one projects onto others the terrible and damned (the *tremendum*) and identifies with the blissful and saved (the *fascinans*), either directly or by subordinating oneself to a charismatic leader onto whom miraculous redemptive knowledge and powers have been projected.

Evocations of the numinous

Otto stresses that numinous experience is like no other kind of experience, being essentially uncanny or supernatural (Otto 1958: 16). However, he acknowledges that genuine numinous experience has close analogies with naturally occurring emotional experiences, and that the latter can sometimes evoke the former (ibid.: 41–9). This perspective, combined with Jung's psychological understanding of how numinous phenomena can receive indirect expression (1942/1948: para. 274, 1944: para. 247, 1958: para. 646), provides insight into an important potential link between religious and other discourses. For example, it often seems that the militancy characteristic of fundamentalist groups is more a political than a religious response – the response of marginalised ethno-cultural groups to the overwhelming military and economic might of other neighbouring or globally dominating groups. However, even if these situations are primarily political, their nature is such that they would be likely to activate religious emotions as well. For the very helplessness of the marginalised groups resembles and may evoke the 'creature-consciousness', the sense of 'nothingness before an overpowering, absolute might of some kind' (Otto 1958: 10), that for Otto and Jung is such an important element of the numinous experience. The political may thus hook up with the numinous and draw on its intoxicating and daemonic energy.

From militancy to terrorism

If we bear in mind the sheer intensity of what is entailed in numinous experience, the difficulty of containing and processing such experience in consciousness, and the consequent likelihood of the numinous being split and its components projected or identified with, then several psychody-namic accounts of religiously motivated terrorism become available. For example, if one identifies with the *fascinans* and believes oneself part of the saved remnant of humanity, while the *tremendum* is projected onto one's opponents who are therefore demonised, one can separate oneself from one's opponents, believe them to be different from oneself at the most fundamental eschatological level, and treat them as worthless and therefore as legitimate targets for hostile action. Alternatively, if, through repressing the *tremendum*, one loses consciousness of it and is unprepared for its unexpected return from the unconscious, one may become possessed by the *tremendum* oneself. A possessed person or group whose behaviour is characterised by awefulness, overpoweringness, and urgency could be swept along into overt terrorising activities.

The extreme act of suicidal terrorism can also be imagined in terms of experience of the numinous. For a person identified with a fusion of the terrifying power of the *tremendum* and the bliss of the *fascinans* but without adequate consciousness to ground these in mundane and humane realities could enter a condition of self-destructive ecstasy.[12] Ruthven, writing of the motives suggested by the Arabic document left behind by the September 11th attacker Mohammad Atta, appears to be describing just such a state of identification with the numinous, where reason, ethics, and consciousness are absent or insufficient:

> the actor who undertakes an apocalyptic mission *identifies his action with the will of God*; by so doing he *leaves to God the moral conse-quences of his act*. There is no hint of justification in the document. It is not a manifesto; nor is it an explanation. *The moral and intellectual arguments have been left entirely with God.*
>
> (Ruthven 2002: 35, emphasis added)

Jung discusses the condition of identification with the numinous in his seminars on Friedrich Nietzsche's (1844–1900) *Thus Spoke Zarathustra* (see Jung 1934–9). Referring to Nietzsche's identification with the numinous figure of Zarathustra and his consequent inflation, Jung comments: 'we have never before experienced how it feels when the *numinosum* is identical with ourselves, how it is when we are the *numinosa*. That is a new problem, and it puts us right in front of an entirely new task' (ibid.: 259). In Jung's analysis, Nietzsche's God (that is, God-image) had died, yet the psyche's inalienable religious function did not die with it. Nietzsche's psyche therefore continued to generate numinous imagery, with which, for want of any credible external referent onto which to project it, he identified.[13] The problem is new because it is a consequence of the unprecedented processes of secularisation and modernisation that have been undermining the credibility of traditional religious images. The new task it presents is, in Jung's view, to develop a consciousness strong enough to relate to and symbolise the numinous while avoiding identification with it.

Jung's analysis of Nietzsche provides an interesting further perspective on states of religious extremism, such as expressed in acts of suicidal terrorism. For it suggests that the self-destructive character of these states may stem not just from a sense of one's religiousness being helplessly beleaguered from without but also from the collapse of one's religiousness within, the inner death of the believer's God-image. In this condition both the dark side of deity and the intense attractiveness of religion, which I described in previous sections, would be lost to the consciousness of the person identified with them. Hostility towards the godlessness of secular societies could be a horrified defence against and projection of the inability of the fundamentalists themselves to maintain a credible God-image. Religious fundamentalism at its most militant could thus, ironically, be a supreme expression of ascendant secularity. It would then be bizarrely logical that when fundamentalists enact their hostility towards the processes and consequences of secularisation, they should also enact it, suicidally, against themselves. From Jung's point of view, this would be especially tragic, since the very place where the inalienable but lost religiousness might be recovered is in the dual sacred and secular selves that are cancelling themselves out along with others.

Notes

1 Some of the material in this chapter was previously presented in the Open Seminar Series at the Centre for Psychoanalytic Studies, University of Essex, 23 February 2005; at the XIXth World Congress of the International Association for the History of Religions, Tokyo, 24–30 March 2005; and at the 2nd International Academic Conference of Analytical Psychology and Jungian Studies, Texas A & M University, 7–10 July 2005. I am grateful to participants at those presentations for their helpful comments. I would like to thank the British Academy for an Overseas Conference Grant towards the expense of travelling to the conference in Texas.
2 For an account of the historical roots and precursors of twentieth-century fundamentalist groups in Christianity, Judaism, and Islam, see Armstrong (2001).

3 This is a re-issue, slightly revised and updated in the light of the terrorist attacks of 11 September 2001, of their contributed chapters to Marty and Appleby (1995), the fifth and final volume of The Fundamentalism Project sponsored by the American Academy of Arts and Sciences. These chapters draw upon 'more than seventy-five case studies and comparative essays' (Almond *et al.* 2003: 9) published in the five volumes of the project and are presented as a 'capstone statement' by the core members of the project, though by no means as the unanimous view of all the contributors (Marty and Appleby 1995: 3–7).

4 Other writers characterise fundamentalism with different emphases. For example, Malise Ruthven (2004) highlights the patriarchal character of fundamentalist movements, their close but complex relationship to nationalism, and their opposition to religious pluralism; while Tariq Ali's more rhetorical use of the term encompasses 'American imperialism', which indeed he dubs 'the mother of all fundamentalisms' (2003: 307).

5 For this reason, Rachel Blass (2004) has recently suggested that the passionate concern for truth that Freudian psychoanalysis shares with religion, even though adopting an opposing position on the nature of this truth, might provide a better ground for dialogue between psychoanalysis and religion than does the positive, reconciliatory attitude of the Winnicottian approaches.

6 This does not constitute a straightforward psychologising of religion, for it could equally be said that Jung's psychology has been 'religionised'. In other words, out of the tension between religion and science, Jung forged a psychology that partakes of both religion and science yet is fully identifiable with neither (see Main 2004: 91–114).

7 Otto, or his translator, did not coin the term 'numinous'. In English, it had been used adjectively since the seventeenth century (see *Oxford English Dictionary* 1989, s.v. 'numinous').

8 The term 'non-rational' was introduced by John Harvey, Otto's English translator, in an attempt to forestall misunderstandings arising from the pejorative connotations of 'irrational' (see Otto 1958: xvii–xviii), a move seemingly endorsed by Otto (ibid.: xxi).

9 Otto was the originator of the idea of the Eranos Conferences that began in 1933 (even though he never actually attended any of them), and Jung may have become aware of, or interested in, Otto's work through this connection (see Bair 2004: 413).

10 However, Jung is mistaken when he states that Otto used the term '*numinosum*' (1938/1940: para. 6; cf. 1934: para. 216, 1973: 468). Not Otto but Jung seems to have been the first to use this modern Latin term (see *Oxford English Dictionary* 1989, s.v. '*numinosum*'). Otto himself referred to his concept as 'the numinous' (in German, '*Numinose*'), in spite of his use of Latin terms for the elements of the numinous. Furthermore, probably because Otto uses the word *fascinans* so rarely – only once in his chapter on 'The Element of Fascination' (1958: 35) – Jung makes the mistake of referring to this element as the *fascinosum* (1959: para. 864). The mistake is unfortunate, though perhaps not insignificant from a psychoanalytic point of view, since the Latin *fascinosum* means 'having a large phallus', this meaning deriving from the ancient custom of hanging a *fascinum*, an image of a phallus, round the necks of children as a preventive against witchcraft (see entries under 'fascinosus' and 'fascinum' in Lewis and Short 1890).

11 Jung's appreciation of the numinous, with its full acknowledgement of the terrors and dangers of numinous experience, can be contrasted with Paul Pruyser's Winnicottian interpretation of it, which emphasises the more positive

fascinans aspect of the numinous (see Capps 1997: 111–16). Jung's openness to the possible transcendent origin of numinous experience can also be contrasted with Donald Capps's interpretation that links the *mysterium tremendum* to child abuse and childhood trauma (ibid.: 93–111).

12 Adolf Guggenbühl-Craig suggests that 'the motives for terrorism are a fusion between Eros and Thanatos' (2002: 84). Ali writes of the 'lethal exaltation' of suicidal terrorists (2003: 3). Wolfgang Giegerich also notes that a 'numinous quality might . . . help to explain the willingness of so many terrorists to serve as suicide bombers' and in the case of the 'jihad against America' specifically relates this 'religious-numinous quality' to anti-Semitism (2002: 73).

13 For more on Jung's intellectual and psychological relationship to Nietzsche, see Bishop (1995) and Huskinson (2004).

References

Ali, T. (2003) *The Clash of Fundamentalisms: Crusades, Jihads and Modernity*, London and New York: Verso.

Almond, G., Appleby, R. and Sivan, E. (2003) *Strong Religion: The Rise of Fundamentalisms around the World*, Chicago and London: University of Chicago Press.

Armstrong, K. (2001) *The Battle for God: Fundamentalism in Judaism, Christianity and Islam*, London: HarperCollins.

Bair, D. (2004) *Jung: A Biography*, New York: Little, Brown.

Beebe, J. (ed.) (2003) *Terror, Violence and the Impulse to Destroy: Perspectives from Analytical Psychology*, Einsiedeln: Daimon Verlag.

Bishop, P. (1995) *The Dionysian Self: C.G. Jung's Reception of Friedrich Nietzsche*, Berlin and New York: Walter de Gruyter.

Blass, R. (2004) 'Beyond Illusion: Psychoanalysis and the Question of Religious Truth', *International Journal of Psycho-Analysis* 85: 615–34.

Britton, R. (2002) 'Fundamentalism and Idolatry', in C. Covington *et al.* (eds.), *Terror and War: Unconscious Dynamics of Political Violence*, London and New York: Karnac.

Brooke, R. (2000) 'Emissaries from the Underworld: Psychotherapy's Challenge to Christian Fundamentalism', in P.-Y. Eisendrath and M.E. Miller (eds.), *The Psychology of Mature Spirituality: Integrity, Wisdom, Transcendence*, London and Philadelphia: Routledge.

Capps, D. (1997) *Men, Religion, and Melancholia: James, Otto, Jung, and Erikson*, New Haven, CN and London: Yale University Press.

Covington, C., Williams, P., Arundale, A., and Knox, J. (eds.) (2002) *Terror and War: Unconscious Dynamics of Political Violence*, London and New York: Karnac.

Dourley, J. (2003) 'Archetypal Hatred as Social Bond: Strategies for its Dissolution', in J. Beebe (ed.), *Terror, Violence and the Impulse to Destroy: Perspectives from Analytical Psychology*, Einsiedeln: Daimon Verlag.

Figlio, K. (2004) 'Social and Psychological Implications of Absolute States of Mind', paper presented in the Centre for Psychoanalytic Studies 2004–5 Open Seminar Series, University of Essex, 27 October.

Giegerich, W. (2002) 'Islamic Terrorism', in L. Zoja and D. Williams (eds.), *Jungian Reflections on September 11*, Einsiedeln: Daimon Verlag.

Guggenbühl-Craig, A. (2002) 'The Motivation of Terrorists', in L. Zoja and D. Williams (eds.), *Jungian Reflections on September 11*, Einsiedeln: Daimon Verlag.

Hillman, J. (2004) *A Terrible Love of War*, New York: The Penguin Press.

Homans, P. (1979/1995) *Jung in Context: Modernity and the Making of a Psychology*, 2nd ed., Chicago: University of Chicago Press.

Huskinson, L. (2004) *Nietzsche and Jung: The Whole Self in the Union of Opposites*, Hove and New York: Brunner-Routledge.

Jones, J. (2002) *Terror and Transformation: The Ambiguity of Religion in Psychoanalytic Perspective*, Hove and New York: Brunner-Routledge.

Jung, C.G. (1911–12/1952) *Collected Works*, vol. 5, *Symbols of Transformation*, 2nd ed., London: Routledge & Kegan Paul, 1967.

Jung, C.G. (1928) 'The Relations between the Ego and the Unconscious', in *Collected Works*, vol. 7, *Two Essays on Analytical Psychology*, 2nd ed., London: Routledge & Kegan Paul, 1966.

Jung, C.G. (1934) 'A Review of the Complex Theory', in *Collected Works*, vol. 8, *The Structure and Dynamics of the Psyche*, 2nd ed., London: Routledge & Kegan Paul, 1969.

Jung, C.G. (1934–9) *Jung's Seminar on Nietzsche's* Zarathustra, abridged edn, ed. J. L. Jarrett, Princeton, NJ: Princeton University Press, 1998.

Jung, C.G. (1938/1940) 'Psychology and Religion', in *Collected Works*, vol. 11, *Psychology and Religion: West and East*, 2nd ed., London: Routledge & Kegan Paul, 1969.

Jung, C.G. (1942/1948) 'A Psychological Approach to the Dogma of the Trinity', in *CW* 11.

Jung, C.G. (1942/1954) 'Transformation Symbolism in the Mass', in *CW* 11.

Jung, C.G. (1944) *Collected Works*, vol. 12, *Psychology and Alchemy*, 2nd ed., London: Routledge & Kegan Paul, 1968.

Jung, C.G. (1947/1954) 'On the Nature of the Psyche', in *CW* 8.

Jung, C.G. (1952a) 'Answer to Job', in *CW* 11.

Jung, C.G. (1952b) 'Foreword to White's "God and the Unconscious"', in *CW* 11.

Jung, C.G. (1955–6) *Collected Works*, vol. 14, *Mysterium Coniunctionis: An Inquiry into the Separation and Synthesis of Psychic Opposites in Alchemy*, London: Routledge & Kegan Paul, 1963.

Jung, C.G. (1957) 'The Undiscovered Self (Present and Future)', in *Collected Works*, vol. 10, *Civilization in Transition*, 2nd ed., London: Routledge & Kegan Paul, 1970.

Jung, C.G. (1958) 'Flying Saucers: A Modern Myth of Things Seen in the Skies', in *CW* 10.

Jung, C.G. (1959) 'Good and Evil in Analytical Psychology', in *CW* 10.

Jung, C.G. (1961) 'Symbols and the Interpretation of Dreams', in *Collected Works*, vol. 18, *The Symbolic Life*, London: Routledge & Kegan Paul, 1977.

Jung, C.G. (1973) *Letters 1: 1906–1950*, selected and ed. G. Adler with A. Jaffé, trans. R.F.C. Hull, London: Routledge & Kegan Paul.

Jung, C.G. (1976) *Letters 2: 1951–1961*, selected and ed. G. Adler with A. Jaffé, trans. R.F.C. Hull, London: Routledge & Kegan Paul.

Lewis, C. and Short, C. (eds.) (1890) *A Latin Dictionary*, Oxford: Clarendon Press.

McGuire, W. and Hull, R.F.C. (eds.) (1978) *C.G. Jung Speaking: Interviews and Encounters*, London: Thames & Hudson.

Main, R. (2003) 'Analytical Psychology, Religion, and the Academy', in R. Withers (ed.), *Controversies in Analytical Psychology*, Hove and New York: Brunner-Routledge.

Main, R. (2004) *The Rupture of Time: Synchronicity and Jung's Critique of Modern Western Culture*, Hove and New York: Brunner-Routledge.

Marty, M. and Appleby, R.S. (eds.) (1991) *Fundamentalisms Observed*, The Fundamentalism Project Volume 1, Chicago and London: University of Chicago Press.

Marty, M. and Appleby, R.S. (eds.) (1993a) *Fundamentalisms and Society*, The Fundamentalism Project Volume 2, Chicago and London: University of Chicago Press.

Marty, M. and Appleby, R.S. (eds.) (1993b) *Fundamentalisms and the State*, The Fundamentalism Project Volume 3, Chicago and London: University of Chicago Press.

Marty, M. and Appleby, R.S. (eds.) (1994) *Accounting for Fundamentalisms*, The Fundamentalism Project Volume 4, Chicago and London: University of Chicago Press.

Marty, M. and Appleby, R.S. (eds.) (1995) *Fundamentalisms Comprehended*, The Fundamentalism Project Volume 5, Chicago and London: University of Chicago Press.

Otto, R. (1958) *The Idea of the Holy: An Inquiry into the Non-rational Factor in the Idea of the Divine and its Relation to the Rational*, trans. J. Harvey, Oxford: Oxford University Press (original German edition 1917).

Oxford English Dictionary (1989) 2nd ed., prepared J.A. Simpson and E.S.C. Weiner, 20 vols., Oxford: Clarendon Press.

Papadopoulos, R. (2000) 'Factionalism and Interethnic Conflict: Narratives in Myth and Politics', in T. Singer (ed.), *The Vision Thing: Myth, Politics and Psyche in the World*, London and New York: Routledge.

Papadopoulos (2002) 'Terror and Panic', in P. Hall (ed.), *Negotiating Power*, London: The Champernowne Trust.

Ruthven, M. (2002) *A Fury for God: The Islamist Attack on America*, London and New York: Granta.

Ruthven, M. (2004) *Fundamentalism: The Search for Meaning*, Oxford: Oxford University Press.

Samuels, A. (2005) 'Fundamentalism', paper delivered at a conference on 'Intolerance', London School of Economics, 26 January 2005.

Schlamm, L. (1994) 'The Holy: A Meeting-Point between Analytical Psychology and Religion', in J. Ryce-Menuhin (ed.), *Jung and the Monotheisms: Judaism, Christianity and Islam*, London and New York: Routledge.

Stevens, A. (2004) *The Roots of War and Terror*, London and New York: Continuum.

Tacey, D. (1997) 'Reply to Responses', *Journal of Analytical Psychology* 42: 313–16.

Ulanov, A. (2002) 'Religion's Role in the Psychology of Terrorism', in L. Zoja and D. Williams (eds.), *Jungian Reflections on September 11*, Einsiedeln: Daimon Verlag.

Wieland, C. (2005) 'Masculinity, Fascism, Totalitarianism', paper presented in the Centre for Psychoanalytic Studies 2004–5 Open Seminar Series, University of Essex, 16 March 2005.

Wulff, D. (1997) *Psychology and Religion: Classic and Contemporary*, 2nd ed., New York: Wiley.

Young, R. (2004) 'Why?', *New Internationalist* 370 (August 2004): 20–1.

Zoja, L. and Williams, D. (eds.) (2002) *Jungian Reflections on September 11: A Global Nightmare*, Einsiedeln: Daimon Verlag.

Chapter 11

Rerooting in the mother: the numinosity of the night

John Dourley

THE NUMINOUS IN THEORY AND THERAPY

The most elemental force in Jung's psychology, theoretically and thera-peutically, is the experience of the numinous. Theoretically the unmediated experience of the numinous is the experience of God (Jung 1940: 8). Thera-peutically only the experience of the numinous is of healing value. In a most telling passage Jung identifies the experience of the numinous as the central concern of his work and as 'the real therapy' which releases from 'the curse of pathology' (1945: 377). All else is preliminary and so relatively ineffective. In his most explicit treatment of the relation of the psyche to religion Jung defines religion as 'the careful and scrupulous observation' of the numinous (1940: 7–8). This means that the individual's steadfast obser-vation of the numinous becomes a private religion and personal revelation. The dream book becomes the individual's personal bible different from more collective bibles only in the fact that its revelation is aimed exclusively at the dreamer.

Occasionally the inner dream or external hallucination will be so powerful as to leave an indelible imprint on the psyche of the individual addressed. St Paul's experience on the road to Damascus is a prime example (Jung 1940: 8). More frequently the more sustained scrupulous observation of the numinous works a progressive transformation of the total psyche as a more 'compendious' or 'supraordinate' personality comes consciously to the fore (1954a: 258). Jung understands the expressions of the unconscious in dream or external event to be scripted by the self. When the self depicts itself in its own dream drama it carries with it a numinous impact as the source of the individual's experience of divinity. The personality, thus informed by the progressive incarnation of the self, the only meaning of incarnation for Jung, is characterized by two distinctive traits: the personal integration of the many energies that make up the unique individual combined with an ever more extensive embrace of all that is.

Integration and extended relatedness become the hallmarks of the religious personality, the scrupulous observer, because the conversion

experience worked by the self builds the emerging personality on its reson-
ance with the psychic bedrock that is 'the eternal Ground of all empirical
being' (Jung 1963: 534). The term 'ground' in the German religious tradition, and in Jung's use of it here, is a synonym for God. In this sense Jung's
understanding of psychic maturity overcomes a false dualism between
individual development and social consequence. For Jung authentic psychic
maturation is simultaneously personal, religious and political. It is such
because at its heart is the individual's reconnection with the ground of the
totality, an experience which cannot be undergone without an extended
compassion as the basis of response to the surrounding political situation.

Jung's equation of therapy with the experience of the numinous and with
religious conversion has little or nothing to do with religion as commonly
understood. Where he speaks of therapy as religious transformation he is
explicit. 'This of course has nothing whatever to do with a particular creed
or membership of a church' (1933a: 334). In fact much of his therapeutic
effort was to reconnect a religious culture severed from the experience of
the numinous with the numinous and its healing power. Effectively much of
Jungian theory and therapy developed from the failure of institutionalized
religions to make available an experience of the numinous to their con-
stituencies. The failure of collective religion to fill this role is somewhat
ironic since the religious institution is a creation of the numinous and has as
its only legitimate function the mediation of the numinous which created it
for that purpose. In the societal wake of this failure Jung's psychology had
to turn to the natural roots and origin of the numinous in the psyche to
restore to his culture the sense of the sacred which had created the religious
institutions and their Gods now peculiarly unable to access the energies that
gave them birth. A bumper sticker displayed at a recent meeting of religionists in America could serve as a humorous reflection on the direction of
Jung's research. It read, 'Christianity has pagan DNA'.

His efforts to identify the psychological nature and dynamics of the
numinous in the interests of its personal and social revitalization led Jung
to the archetypal level of the psyche as the ultimate repository of the
numinous. When the powers of these depths impacted on human consciousness the impact left the victim convinced that he or she had been
addressed by a divinity beyond the psyche. Only in our time as the result of
a 'millennial process' did Jung think that the evolution of human consciousness was becoming fully aware that all divinities are projections of the
archetypal ground of the human psyche (1952: 402). He concluded that
humanity was currently entrusted with the recall of the Gods to their origin
in the psyche if humanity was to survive their escape from their psychic
origin (1940: 85). Jung hoped that once humanity came to acknowledge the
supernatural Gods as archetypal projections it could dialogue more safely
with them in the inner forum of the psyche from which they originated.
Contained within the psyche, the numinous powers that create the Gods

would be experienced as transcending the ego but on a purely intrapsychic basis. Their relation to the ego would then be revisioned as the mutual redemption of both the ego and the archetypal powers now no longer creating divinities beyond the human but working rather to divinize the human or to lead the human more fully into its natural divinity. The thrust of Jung's great work, 'Answer to Job', followed his mystic predecessor Jacob Boehme in describing a psychological cosmology in which God and the human, the archetypal and consciousness, were involved in mutual redemption as the base meaning of personal and collective history (Dourley 2004: 60–4).

THE RELIGIOUS AND SECULAR PERVERSION OF THE NUMINOUS

The perilous situation of unrecalled divinity is most obvious in the relationship between monotheistic communities bonded by three different One-and-Only Gods: Yaweh, the Christian Trinity, and Allah. Huntington in his *The Clash of Civilizations* documents the heightened body count along the 'fault lines' or borders where these religiously bonded communities intersect (Huntington 1996: 246–65). Unfortunately his deepest concern is limited to the maintenance of Western geopolitical power in the clash of these religious-based communities of which the West is one. Nevertheless his analysis of the role of collective religion stands as a helpful alert to the danger faith presents in bonding these mutually inimical communities and their national and political incorporations.

However, Huntington lacks Jung's depth in identifying the archetypal basis of these faiths and the numinous hold they exert over their collective victims. The most significant contribution Jung makes to the lessening of the universal danger of particular communities bonded by the numinosity of their religious conviction is to show the human source of this power and in so doing to contribute to its depotentiation. If all three One-and-Only Gods were traced to their psychic provenance and seen to be variants of one stage of the evolution of humanity, the ability to hate and take life in the name of any one of them would be greatly diminished (Dourley 2003). As long as their revelations are taken literally, as from a source extrinsic to the human, the loss of life attendant on such revelation is likely to continue.

Jung clearly identified the petrifaction of numinous processes of transformation into biblically based dogma. 'Belief in dogma is an equally unavoidable stop-gap which must sooner or later be replaced by adequate understanding if our civilization is to continue' (1912/52: 435). In the face of the threat to the species by religious literalism Jung appealed to the religious community to produce an apology not for this or that religion and its allegedly privileged position and God but for religious and symbolic discourse itself.

> Even intelligent people no longer understand the value and purpose of symbolical truth, and the spokesmen of religion have failed to deliver an apologetic suited to the spirit of the age . . . Exclusive appeals to faith are a hopeless *petitio principii*, for it is the manifest improbability of symbolical truth that prevents people from believing in it.
>
> (1912/52: 227)

Jung is here criticizing a literal faith as assent to the unbelievable revealed in biblical event and dogmatic amplification, misapprehensions he elsewhere describes as reducing dogmatic propositions to 'sacrosanct unintelligibility' and 'preposterous nonsense' (1948: 109–10).

What lies deeper in this criticism is the need to recover a societal sense of the archetypal from which numinous religious experience emerges. Jung concedes that in an earlier epoch the numinous still empowered the biblical and even the dogmatic before their degeneration into literal, historical accounts of divinities external to the human reacting with the human. The recovery of the archetypal psyche would coincide with the experiential discovery of the numinous as the source of religious experience whose power can initially only be expressed symbolically. Any other approach to the numinous basis of religious experience and expression would be akin to asking poets to write prose for the sake of clarity. The real question is why religion and its symbolic expression at all? Such a question would demand 'reflecting how it came about in the first place that humanity needed the improbability of religious statements and what it signifies when a totally different spiritual reality is superimposed on the sensuous and tangible actuality of this world' (1912/52: 227). Jung was confident that an appreciation of the genesis of the symbol would lead to a recovery of the numinous power of the archetypal unconscious as the source of symbol and so as the source of the sacred itself. Religion thus understood would no longer be a divine imposition on the human mind but a reconnection of the human mind with its own native depth. Thus a conscious reflection on the archetypal unconscious as the mother of the sense of the numinous expressed in symbol would remove from religion its appeal to 'people for whom thinking and understanding are too much bother', just as it would remove the latter from association with the truly religious (1912/52: 229).

Literal religion is not the only major contributor to the current loss of the sense of the numinous and so to the loss of an authentic religious life. In Jung's mind aspects of the so-called 'secular' world are equally involved in humanity's severance from a supportive profundity. The Enlightenment contributed mightily to freeing the human spirit from supernatural imposition in the areas of religion, philosophy and political power. It demanded that the religious and theological communities make themselves responsible to reason and that they disengage from the political manipulation of whatever constituency they allegedly served. In this the Enlightenment freed the mind from heteronomous invasion by extraneous religious authority, divine or human, and separated church from state. The victory was not without its own defect. In freeing the human spirit from ecclesial imposition on the mind and the body politic it also undermined whatever legitimate value religion might have in accessing the numinous, diminished as this capacity may have been in the religious situation the Enlightenment faced. The resultant societal and personal situation in our epoch is that of a prevailing consciousness unhinged from its depths. Official religion stands bereft of access to the powers that created it and which it was meant to serve. Indeed, its current spiritual bankruptcy is due in no small part to its taking on the Enlightenment on rational grounds and losing battle after battle because it could not distinguish the symbolic from the scientific (1954b: 477–8).

On the other hand a so-called 'secular' society has become almost a religion in itself, but a truncated religion equally removed from humanity's religious roots by its reduction of the human cognitive capacity and sensibility to a meaningless facticity evidenced in a science increasingly regressing to technological gadgetry. Though sworn enemies throughout much of the Enlightenment epoch, science and institutional religion join hands as common suppressors of the numinous experience. The former functions well within its own jurisdiction of the empirical and rational. In theory it ignores rather than attacks the source of the numinous. Yet, in fact, the relegation of the numinous to an area of mind other than the legitimate domain of science does tend to discredit the numinous and its expressions and to render the collective mind insensitive to those valuable dimensions of humanity from which the numinous derives. Religion severs itself from these same dimensions by externalizing its Gods and turning their revelations into revealed facts. A dead and implausible facticity becomes the object of a dehumanizing faith. In both the scientific secular and the religious institution the numinous perishes and with it the sense of the mind's connectedness with 'its primordial oneness with the universe' (1954b: 476).

While Jung appreciated the numinous as the basis of religion universally, he also feared its shadow as the power that could reduce entire communities to unconsciousness. He worked for both its restoration to society and to warn society of its possessive power. Religious and political faith were major concerns for Jung throughout his pages, no doubt, because of their devastating effects before and during World War II. As an antidote to group possession by the numinous, Jung understood the individual's experience of divinity to be rooted in some surpassing manner in the self. This was the power which sought incarnation in consciousness as the individual's ultimate resource and support. The experience of the self carried with it a numinosity of such intensity that Jung would liken it to the experience of being 'anchored in God' (1957: 371). Politically such anchoring serves as the ultimate source of freedom from the mass movements of ecclesial and political collective mindlessness. Jung writes, '*Resistance to the organized mass can be effected only by the man who is as well organized in his individuality as the mass itself*' (1958a: 278).

Functional religion would thus counter religious and political possession through rooting the individual in the numinosity of the self. But no one and no organization can do this when they are themselves uprooted from this human resource. In fact both secular and religious communities encourage such loss of consciousness on their behalf under the banners of faith, patriotism or commitment. 'Both [church and state] demand unqualified submission of faith and thus curtail man's freedom, the one his freedom before God and the other his freedom before the State, thereby digging the grave for the individual' (1958a: 266). The questioner of ecclesial systems is typically told that the articles of faith he or she might question are concrete historical facts and so not to be doubted. Jung's words here are again prophetic, this time of the contemporary situation of many churchgoers laboring under a theological authority which removes rather than fosters contact with the numinosity of their native divinity. In such an environment to grow up is to grow out and to leave the ecclesial communities to the surging numbers of fundamentalists fearful that their shallow but comforting and collectively reinforced certitudes would be corroded in the face of a human maturation which locates the divine at the basis of each individual life to be directly engaged there. Jung diagnosed this demeaning lust for certitude when he wrote that such faith 'is notoriously apt to disappear as soon as anyone starts thinking about it. Belief is no adequate substitute for inner experience, and even a strong faith which came miraculously as a gift of grace may depart equally miraculously' (1958a: 265). It is no wonder then that the temptation to forgo the pain of becoming conscious defeats the demands of engagement with the numinous present in the depth of every life.

An equally important cultural correlate of the removal of individual and society from the numinosity of their roots lies in Jung's early indictment of that social blight currently called 'patriarchy'. In the form of worship of the word Jung calls the patriarchal 'the congenital vice of our age' and traces it to '*the supremacy of the word*, of the Logos which stands for the central figure of the Christian faith' (1958a: 286). In Jung's view the Word is currently a pathologizing deity because religious literalism and historicism have severed the Word from the abyss which precedes it and so reduced it to an empty rationalism. Thus denuded the Logos becomes Blake's Urizen, a consciousness divested of its depths. Reduced to sterile reason and made the object of competing religious claims (who has the one true Logos?), a symbol that originally pointed to a divine reason in which humanity universally participates and which itself participates in a preceding and vitalizing abyss has 'become a source of suspicion and distrust of all against all' (1958a: 287).

The radical removal of the pathology of logocentrism in current religion and society would entail the rewriting of the Joannine prologue. In the beginning would no longer be the Word. In the beginning would be the silence of the nothing from which the Word and world proceed and in whom they continue to dwell. Getting behind or deeper than the patriarchal Logos would restore the sense of the Goddess or Great Mother, personal terms Jung uses as synonyms for the collective unconscious as the womb of both the mind and the numinous. Healthy regression beyond the Logos would mean the restoration of the Goddess as the mother of all definable forms of divinity. In the case of the monotheisms and their male divinities it would mean recovering the Goddess who has birthed all three and could give them a peace they cannot find in relation with each other or in themselves.

THE PRECEDENCE OF THE GODDESS

As Jung developed his psychology, the precedence of the Mother Goddess came ever more to the fore. Much of his psychology is devoted to the description of the base dynamic of individuation as repeated immersion in her restorative nothingness as the prelude to a life of enhanced compassionate activity in the world she also authors. This is the numinous maternal in the most extended sense. Jung used referents from a wide spectrum of human experiences to give some content to his conception of the unconscious as the mother of consciousness seeking ever greater incarnation in her child. Thus he relates the collective unconscious, the Goddess, to Plotinus' conception of the 'One', the 'world soul' and the 'unending All of life' whose nature it was to express itself in all that is real and so become real in her expression (1912/52: 138). Jung also understands the Great Mother as a sea (1912/52: 218), as the prime matter (1963: 18), the pleroma or fullness from whom all form was born (1965: 379), and as the 'Nothing out of which All may grow' (1933b: 75). These many designations collectively serve to point to her power and precedence as the ultimate source of the numinous. Renewed vitality through the experience of her numinosity is the goal of the quest of hero and mystic alike (1953: 169–70).

In so extending the conception of numinous energy or libido to every form of the 'creative force' Jung included in it much more than the sexual (1912/52: 137). This extension was at the heart of Jung's break with Freud (1912/52: 135–7). In Jung's eyes the reduction of energy in all its forms to sexual energy or its disguised variants constituted a form of literalism incapable of seeing the symbolic and so spiritual meaning of sexuality as more than a merely physiological reality (1912/52: 128–9). In challenging and transcending Freud's conception of libido as solely sexual, Jung redefined the numinous. Without denying the numinosity of physical sexuality, he increasingly understood the numinous as experienced in a variety of unities of psychologically significant opposites. The greatest was that of the ego with its maternal origin, the Goddess. For Jung intercourse with the Goddess becomes the deepest meaning of incest whose purpose is the renewal of conscious life. As this incest is sustained the great archetypal opposites in the womb of the Mother come into unity in consciousness, the male with the female, the instinctual with the spiritual, the evil with the good. In this specific context, and with an extended sense of the spiritual, Jung would argue that the deepest movement of psychic maturation was to 'a spiritual goal' (1954c: 212). This spiritual goal Jung understood as the unity in consciousness of all the archetypal opposites in life's matrix, among which instinct and spirit are but two of the greatest. Jung colored the 'spiritual goal' toward which the psyche moves in shades of violet to get at the idea that successful incest with the Goddess worked toward a unity of all opposites and, in particular, the red of passion with the blue of pure spirit (1954c: 211–13).

THE NUMINOSITY OF INCEST

When Jung equates the source of all energy with the Great Mother, he describes a process of incest which breaks the incest taboo, not in some physical and literal sense, but in a psychic and profoundly spiritual sense. 'It is not incestuous cohabitation that is desired but rebirth' (1912/52: 224). Violation of the incest taboo comes, then, to mean a variety of things all related to the suffering attached to the transformation of consciousness through incest with the Goddess. Such incest invariably means the sacrifice of an immature, though possibly comfortable consciousness, to the demands of self-loss in the interest of growth. It could come to the confrontation of the reigning patriarchal consciousness interested in maintaining the psychic status quo and so terrified of the new. Full incest means a kind of psychic death of the ego into the womb of the Great Mother with no guarantee of emergence or resurrection. Baptism and resurrection in the Jungian sense carry no sacramental guarantee of a happy return from the waters of dissolution or the grave. Nor are either once-upon-a-time realities. They describe cyclical processes which repeat in the psyche's effort to grow throughout a lifetime.

Though this incest has many faces, failure to enter it has as many dire consequences. One is the loss of energy which primordial wisdom describes as loss of soul. Such loss carries with it images not only of loss of personal energy but of a desiccation of all life, even the surrounding life of nature (1912/52: 250). Thus intercourse with the Great Mother describes for Jung a volatile process with a variety of outcomes. It is in birth from her that the original sin and gift of self-consciousness is committed and conferred. With this self-consciousness is born for the first time consciousness of death (1912/52: 271). For Jung, then, fear of death lies at the heart of the neurotic fear of life away from the Great Mother and leads to the devouring solace of that perennial unconsciousness she so readily provides to the living but unborn.

And yet those who have committed the original sin of attaining an initial conscious life can never escape the longing for reimmersion in the numinous eternity of her womb, 'the inner longing for the stillness and profound peace of all-knowing non-existence, for all-seeing sleep in the ocean of coming to be and passing away' (1912/52: 356). In this sense the initial birth from the Great Mother leads to a drive for a return to her which can become both 'the supreme goal' and 'frightful danger' of life's adventure (1912/52: 236). The danger is that of being consumed by the maternal source of renewal herself. 'It happens all too easily that there is no return from the realm of the mothers' (1912/52: 310). It is here that the wholly intrapsychic and numinous drama at the heart of Jung's psychology is most evident. An initial and ongoing othering from the mother is the price of the birth of an autonomous consciousness. But the othering itself is the basis of the equally legitimate drive to reunion, indeed momentary identification, with her. Only when both moments in this dialectic are honored and effected as integral to the total process of maturation is the full sweep of Jung's understanding of individuation understood.

Incestuous re-entrance into the mother, the ultimate form of numinous experience, is a necessary risk in all great tasks of life, or better, in the task of life itself. Without it the individual is impotent. But in it the individual risks annihilation. Jung describes the moment in these stirring lines,

> that is the dangerous moment when the issue hangs between annihilation and new life. For if the libido gets stuck in the wonderland of this inner world, then for the upper world man is nothing but a shadow, he is already moribund or at least seriously ill. But if the libido manages to tear itself loose and force its way up again something like a miracle happens: the journey to the underworld was a plunge into the fountain of youth, and the libido, apparently dead, wakes to renewed fruitfulness.
>
> (1912/52: 293)

In describing the joy and danger of incest with the Mother, Jung would seem to make this dialectic a fact of life universal. In the end his understanding of the psyche would challenge one to choose between the numinous though dangerous experience of re-entering the Great Mother and the psychic or even physical death of consciousness.

In these passages even Jung is not fully depicting all the forces at play in incest with the Great Mother. In the end not the ego but the self is the only agency that can work the initial birth from the mother, the return to dissolution in her, and the renewal of conscious life the moment of disso-lution affords. The completion of the cycle of birth, death and resurrection is the basis of the hero myth and so of the Messiah or Saviour complex. As a case in point, Christianity identifies its hero in the figure of Christ. However, Jung would strongly suggest that in turning the Christ myth into a personal, historical and literal event, the myth has lost its power and now cloaks rather than reveals the fact that it is a story of everyman (1912/52: 177–8). Restored to its mythical status, the story of Christ would be one among many religious stories serving to make explicit the processes of the renewal of the life of the spirit through the specifically Christian variant focusing on birth, death and resurrection as the ground movements in psychic maturation. At the heart of these stories is the universal 'longing to attain rebirth through the return to the womb and to become immortal like the sun' (1912/52: 212). The ultimate prohibition of the incest taboo is the prohibition to live out of one's own self-renewal by becoming 'the child or *oneself* in renewed and rejuvenated form' (1912/52: 258). Put simply, the goal of 'magical incest' is 'immortality' and the incest taboo forbids it (1912/52: 259). This is the taboo the hero must break to enjoy the numin-osity of identity with the mother and rebirth from her.

Because this process is endemic to the psyche as its deepest movement, it requires no intervention of a divine agency external to the psyche. This is what Jung means when he says that 'the reborn is his own begetter' (1912/52: 323). In doing this he identifies processes of spiritual self-renewal as native to the psyche itself. It is this wholly natural and intrapsychic dynamic of renewal which religious imagery projects above onto relationships with wholly other Gods or onto the past and unique historical events such as the life of Jesus. Jung removes the need for divine intervention from above or a relation to past definitive incursions of the divine into human history. He recasts all such sacred texts and events as documenting processes which are meaningful only if they occur in the experienced numinosity of the now of individual psychological life and its renewal.

FAR-REACHING CONSEQUENCES

Jung's deepest indictment of modern cultural consciousness is that it is uprooted from the source of the numinous which the symbolic sense carried and could restore. For Jung the loss of the symbolic sense threatens the very continuance of humanity for a number of reasons. Such a loss deprives the culture of its will to go on through depriving it of the numinous libido which the symbol mediates to consciousness as the basis of its will to live and thrive in the face of the challenge of the future. Writes Jung on this threat, 'Nevertheless, when a living organism is cut off from its roots, it loses the connections with the foundations of its existence and must necessarily perish.' The ultimate counter to such death is 'The anamnesis of the origins' as 'a matter of life and death' (1968a: 180). In these passages Jung is contending that an individual or culture forgetful of its roots in the unconscious will eventually lose the will to live. Effectively Jung is asking Teilhard de Chardin's repeated question and quest, 'from what source will humanity derive its will to survive and flourish in its task of completing God as the completion of human endeavour?' And Jung would remain open to Teilhard's conclusion: 'That religion will prevail which can provide such energy' (Teilhard de Chardin 1953: 272). Both are positing the question of accessing that numinous energy that makes life not only possible but passionate. Jung and Teilhard would thus eliminate all candidacy to religions or cultures uprooted from their origins in the psyche and infecting their environment with their own pathology. In this sense Jung saw his psychology as a religious endeavour insomuch as it could restore to those sickened by the uprooting powers of their literalistic, historicist religions the very 'foundations of religious experience' in the numinous depths of the individual (1912/52: 229).

Jung considered the Christ figure still to be the culture hero of his society (1968b: 36). Using Christianity to exemplify the religious dimension of his psychology, Jung would contend that the recovery of the numinous in full consciousness of its intrapsychic provenance is a necessary prelude to the modern's ability 'to participate in the substance of the Christian message', and, by extension, in any religious or archetypal message (1912/52: 230). Whether this ability to again participate immediately in the archetypal basis of the Christian or any religion is compatible with their current collective self-understanding is by no means clear at the moment. In not a few passages Jung strongly suggests that the Christian's appropriation of the sense of humanity's natural participation in the divine currently outstrips the Christian's imaginal capacity. He writes, 'The latter [the Christian] has far too little introspection to be able to realize what modifications in his present conception of God the homoousia of the self would involve' (1912/52: 393). In this passage, as he does elsewhere, Jung extends to every human being the status of two natures, consciousness and the unconscious, in one person which official Christianity reserved in its Christological councils to the unique figure of Christ. Effectively each individual is potentially, and is destined by the psyche itself to become, a Christ figure or equivalent in whatever religious symbolism this truth might be clothed. The psychological reality of Christ is the numinous experience of the self becoming incarnate in consciousness. Other religions and archetypal communities experience the same numinosity through the self figure in whatever variation it works in them. The question this citation poses is this, 'Could Christianity and, indeed, any of the monotheisms, proclaim the natural divinity of the human as the basis of humanity's potentially universal experience of the divine and remain faithful to their current self-understanding?' In the wake of the exclusion of gnosticism, and alchemy and the suspicion surrounding mysticism on the part of the great Western religions, it would appear that the recovery of their health would demand the integration of what they have made peripheral or excluded as heresy in the historical processes of their self-debilitation resulting in their current studied distance from the healing numinosity that created them.

The counter to such lethal consciousness is not a matter of reasoning but the recovery of 'spontaneous religious experience which brings the individual's faith into immediate relation with God' (1958a: 292). For Jung, in his more far-reaching statements, was convinced that the psyche taken in its totality participated in eternity. He will write of the self as having 'an incorruptible or eternal character on account of its being pre-existent to consciousness' (1954a: 401). Though he used many images to get at the concept of rerooting, in the final analysis, rerooting is a process of the intrapsychic reunion of the individual with eternity as the source of the finite in the here and now of time. Failure to connect with these roots is a personal disaster. 'It means the same thing as the conscious denial of the instincts – uprootedness, disorientation, meaninglessness, and whatever else these symptoms of inferiority may be called' (1954b: 415). Nor is this reunion of the individual with eternity a bloodless reunion with some unearthly immortality in a distant or post-temporal state. The consciousness it produces always 'retains its connection with the heart, with the depths of the psyche, with the tap-root' (1954b: 410). Out of such rootedness in the eternal the individual echoing the gnostic, alchemist and mystic of all ages, can say in the face of death itself, 'I am a vessel more precious than the feminine being who made you. Whereas your mother knew not her own roots, I know of myself, and I know whence I have come, and I call upon the imperishable wisdom which is in the Father and is the Mother of your mother, which has no mother, but also has no male companion' (Herakleon cited in Jung 1954d: 87). Such is the confidence that the fuller experience of the numinous generates.

IN THE END IT ALL COMES TO NOTHING

If the West is to recover its sense of the numinous and so of the humanizing divine, Jung's turn to the individual's inner life through the gnostics, alchemists and mystics is of crucial importance. Recently mystical scholarship has highlighted the apophatic experience, that moment of nothingness in which mystic and divinity become one without difference as the prelude to a more vital engagement with their world (Sells 1994). The thirteenth-century Beguines, Mechthilde of Magdeburg, Hadjewich and Marguerite Porete, belonged to this tradition (McGinn 1998: 199–265). Current scholarship reveals that this tradition was a significant influence on Meister Eckhart (d. *ca* 1328), (McGinn 2001: 9, 144, 148, 181). Mechthilde of Magdeburg is present in Jung's work (1912/52: 90, 1950: 176) and Meister Eckhart is a substantial figure throughout his pages (1971: 241–58).

Eckhart is explicit in identifying the Godhead as the fourth in God beyond the Trinity. He enjoyed a moment of identity with the nothingness of the Godhead, an experience of his native divinity which followed him back into the world (Eckhart 1978: 214–20). The only mystic Jung cites more frequently than Eckhart is Jacob Boehme. He too went to the point of identity with God beyond the Trinity but returned from it with the conviction that the unification of the divine opposites did not take place in eternity, as Trinitarian orthodoxy would have it (Boehme 1911: v). Rather the unity of the divine opposites is to take place in human consciousness which alone can perceive the divine conflict and undergo its resolution in processes at once redemptive of the divine and the human (Dourley 2004: 60–4). Boehme was a significant influence on Hegel and Jung's 'Answer to Job' completes Hegel's philosophy by elevating it to the level of psychology. There, in the footsteps of Boehme and Hegel, Jung describes the process in which a divine life torn between its unresolved absolutes is perceived as such by a superior and discriminating human ego. But this insight carries with it the intimation that only in the human can the reconciliation of the divine antinomy take place. Job is a forerunner of the Christ figure dying between archetypal opposites despairing of divine intervention (1952: 408). This despair becomes the prelude to a death and risen life in which the opposites come together as the thrust of both the psychological maturation of the individual and the eschatological direction of history (1952: 408). Such was Jung's final word on the numinosity of the cycle of death into the mother and resurrection from her as the ground movement of maturation in the individual soul and the base meaning of history.

When the experience of Eckhart and Boehme are united as foundational movements of the psyche the image of a double quaternity emerges whose key is humanity's dialectical engagement with the creative nothingness of its ground. Eckhart identifies with divinity as the nothing, the fourth, that precedes even Trinity, that is, Eckhart identifies with the mother, herself formless, from whom all form and the drive to form derive (Dourley 1990: 41–68). A moment of dissolution in the nothing frees Eckhart from the compulsion of form, of mind and the imposition of form on matter or others. It is at the heart of his doctrine of resignation or letting be. His dissolution in the mother is the height of the numinosity of the night.

Boehme also went into this night which he calls the *ungrund* or the One. But he realized that the nothing needs the ego to become self-conscious of its own latencies. In effect the return to the nothing demands and enables the reconciliation of its conflictual opposites in consequent consciousness. This reconciliation takes place simultaneously in both the divine and the human as their mutual harmony is achieved in humanity. In Jung's parlance both the divine and the human are mutually redeemed and enhanced when the antinomies in the archetypal ground of the unconscious embrace in consciousness. If Jung's myth could be reduced to a formula it would read: the deeper the ego's penetration into the unconscious, even into that nothingness beyond the archetypal, the greater the ability of the traveler to resolve divinely grounded conflict in oneself as the precondition to its resolution in society.

The gnostics, alchemists and mystics anticipated the experience of the numinous central to Jung's psychology and Jung's psychology proffers their numinous experience to the contemporary in psychologically theoretical and therapeutic form. The now-dawning spirituality in the West is built upon the recovery of the numinosity of one's natural divinity and upon intercourse with the nothing as the mother of the empirical, all to be embraced in its totality as the many and varied faces she shows to the world. To the revisioning of the numinous in the service of a functional spirituality Jung's psychology makes a substantial contribution.

At this point it should be obvious that the mystical values of the myth of the double quaternity move beyond idle psychological, sociological or religious speculation. The myth takes on survival value. If humanity cannot die into that fleeting point of rest in the nothing beyond the inner archetypal wars and their externalizations, then such wars will continue to threaten the species. Jung warned of the consequences. 'We are threatened with universal genocide if we cannot work out the way of salvation by a symbolic death' (1958b). Unless humanity does so, Jungians will have to continue writing their common paper in its many variants over the decades, '*Why the slaughter must continue*'. Hopefully a time approaches when this paper will no longer have to be written. Jung died during the Cold War when, then as now, archetypal absolutes pitted communities against each other in a potentially lethal interface. The divisions and carnage continue. Lives are daily sacrificed to the archetypal Gods in ever greater abundance. Yet a more optimistic Jung could write in the midst of it all, 'The afternoon of humanity, in a distant future, may yet evolve a different ideal. In time even conquest will cease to be the dream' (1954b: 493). Such an afternoon would draw ever closer if all were to come to nothing.

References

Boehme, J. (1911) *The Forty Questions of the Soul and the Clavis*, trans. J. Sparrow, London: John M. Watkins.

Dourley, J. (1990) *The Goddess Mother of the Trinity*, Lewiston: Edwin Mellen Press.

Dourley, J. (2003) 'Archetypal Hatred as Social Bond: Strategies for its Dissolution', in J. Beebe (ed.), *Terror, Violence and the Impulse to Destroy, Perspectives from Analytical Psychology*, pp. 135–59, Einsiedeln: Daimon Verlag.

Dourley, J. (2004) 'Jung, Mysticism and the Double Quaternity: Jung and the Psychic Origin of Religious and Mystical Experience', *Harvest*, 50(1): 47–74.

Eckhart, M. (1978) 'Blessed Are the Poor', trans. R. Schurmann, *Meister Eckhart, Mystic and Philosopher*, Bloomington: Indiana University Press.

Huntington, S.P. (1996) *The Clash of Civilizations*, New York: Simon and Schuster.

Jung, C.G. (1912/1952) *Symbols of Transformation, CW* 5.

Jung, C.G. (1933a) 'Psychotherapists or the Clergy', *CW* 11.

Jung, C.G. (1933b) 'The Spiritual Problem of Modern Man', *CW* 10.

Jung, C.G. (1940) 'Psychology and Religion', *CW* 11.

Jung, C.G. (1945) Letter to P. W. Martin, August 20, 1945, *C.G. Jung Letters*, 1: 1906–1950, ed., G. Adler and A. Jaffé, trans. R.F.C. Hull, Princeton, NJ: Princeton University Press, 1973.

Jung, C.G. (1948) 'A Psychological Approach to the Dogma of the Trinity', *CW* 11.

Jung, C.G. (1950) 'The Psychology of the Child Archetype', *CW* 9, 1.

Jung, C.G. (1952) 'Answer to Job', *CW* 11.

Jung, C.G. (1953) 'The Relations Between the Ego and the Unconscious', *CW* 7.

Jung, C.G. (1954a) 'Transformation Symbolism in the Mass', *CW* 11.

Jung, C.G. (1954b) 'Psychological Commentary on *The Tibetan Book of the Great Liberation*', *CW* 11.

Jung, C.G. (1954c) 'On the Nature of the Psyche', *CW* 8.

Jung, C.G. (1954d) 'The Visions of Zosimos', *CW* 13.

Jung, C.G. (1957) Letter to Bernard Lang, June 14, 1957, *C.G. Jung Letters*, 2: 1951–1961, ed., G. Adler and A. Jaffé, trans. R.F.C. Hull, Princeton, NJ: Princeton University Press, 1975.

Jung, C.G. (1958a) 'The Undiscovered Self', *CW* 10.

Jung, C.G. (1958b) 'Jung and Religious Belief', *CW* 18.

Jung, C.G. (1963) *Mysterium Coniunctionis, CW* 14.

Jung, C.G. (1965) 'Septem Sermones ad Mortuos', *Memories, Dreams, Reflections*, ed. A. Jaffé, New York: Vintage.

Jung, C.G. (1968a) 'Background to the Psychology of Christian Alchemical Symbolism', *CW* 9, 1.

Jung, C.G. (1968b) 'Christ, a Symbol of the Self', *CW* 9, 11.

Jung, C.G. (1971) *Psychological Types, CW* 6.

McGinn, B. (1998) *The Flowering of Mysticism*, New York: Crossroad Herder.

McGinn, B. (2001) *The Mystical Thought of Meister Eckhart*, New York: Crossroad Herder.

Sells, M. (1994) *Mystical Language of Unsaying*, Chicago: Chicago University Press, 1994.

Teilhard de Chardin, P. (1953) 'Contingence de l'univers et gout humaine de survivre', *Comment je crois* (1969), Paris: Editions du Seuil.

Chapter 12

The experience of the numinous today: from the novels of Haruki Murakami

Toshio Kawai

THE NUMINOUS AND THE MODERN SUBJECT

At the beginning of his book *Psychology and Religion*, Jung attempted to give a definition of religion.

> Religion, as the Latin word [*religio*] denotes, is a careful and scrupulous observation of what Rudolf Otto aptly termed the *numinosum*, that is, a dynamic agency or effect not caused by an arbitrary act of will. On the contrary, it seizes and controls the human subject, who is always rather its victim than its creator. The *numinosum* – whatever its cause may be – is an experience of the subject independent of his will.
>
> (1938/1940: 7)

In these words Jung follows the idea of the 'numinous' as first described and delineated by Rudolf Otto. In this understanding the numinous is beyond the conscious intention and control of the subject. In Jung's words 'it seizes and controls the human subject'. We could say that the numinous has to do with the experience of the collective unconscious. It is therefore no wonder that the word 'numinous' is keenly connected to the notion of archetype throughout Jung's writings. He says, for example, 'Wherever we find it, the archetype has a compelling force which it derives from the unconscious, and whenever its effect becomes conscious it has a distinctly numinous quality' (1942/1948: 223). If archetypes are to be understood as 'typical images and associations', the numinous quality of archetypes lays stress on compelling power and feeling-value. In this sense it is interesting to notice that the numinous is often connected with experiences of feeling and emotion in Jung's work. He writes:

> It would be an unpardonable sin of omission were one to overlook the feeling-value of the archetype . . . As a numinous factor, the archetype determines the nature of the configurational process and the course it will follow . . .
>
> (1947/1957: 209)

We might say that archetypes have static and objective aspects of typical patterns and dynamic and subjective aspects of feeling-value. And feeling-value is connected with the concept of the numinous.

Such use of the term 'numinous' might be criticized as subjectivist and psychologistic by philosophy and religion. The question now arises whether this understanding of the numinous corresponds to the original concept by Rudolf Otto. In his book *The Idea of the Holy* (1959) (*Das Heilige*, 1917) Otto tried to grasp the non-rational essence of the sacred in religion as is clearly noticed from the subtitle of the book ('An Inquiry into the non-rational factor in the idea of the divine and its relation to the rational'). In this context the term 'numinous' was coined. It means creature feeling (dependency) and *mysterium tremendum* (tremendous mystery) which includes awfulness and fascination. The *tremendum* component has three elements: awfulness, overpoweringness and energy. The *mysterium* component has two aspects: wholly other and fascination. We notice there are many descriptions of the numinous which suggest the importance of feeling experience. Creature feeling, awfulness and fascination are such examples.

Otto's approach to religion seems to have a remarkable characteristic. Religions might be studied in terms of their rituals, doctrines, beliefs and symbols. In this case the phenomenology of religion would focus, for instance, on God as love, Trinity, texts of prayers, nothingness, Ramadan, rite of initiation, etc. But the descriptions of the numinous give us the impression that subjective experiences are emphasized rather than the objective contents of religion. In this sense it is legitimate that Jung highlights the subjective aspect of the word 'numinous'. Religious philosophers or theologians might not agree with me and are of the opinion that the numinous is the essence of the holy and therefore not restricted to the subjective aspect in a narrow sense.

Jung's words underline clearly that the numinous is beyond the subject's control and not to be understood in a purely subjectivist sense. The numinous is experienced within the subject, but it is itself objective. There is a deep subjectivity which blends into the 'objective psyche'. In the quotation at the start of this chapter (1938/40: 7) Jung says, 'it seizes and controls the human subject'. The concept of archetype, which is often connected with the numinous, suggests that the numinous is beyond the personal. Nevertheless I would still say that the structure of this concept shows the tendency to lay stress on the subjective component, at least as the site in which this encounter occurs.

In this sense the visionary experience of Brother Klaus of Flüe in the fifteenth century is worth mentioning. Jung discussed it at length in his article 'Brother Klaus' (1933) and 'Archetypes of the Collective Unconscious' (1934/1954). Brother Klaus is famous for the so-called Trinity Vision which has a wheel with six spokes. But as Jung demonstrated, there was no mention of a wheel in the firsthand reports. Woelflin's biography narrates as follows:

> All who came to him were filled with terror at the first glance. As to the cause of this, he [Brother Klaus] himself used to say that he had seen a piercing light resembling a human face. At the sight of it he feared that his heart would burst into little pieces. Overcome with terror, he instantly turned his face away and fell to the ground. And that was the reason why his face was now terrible to others.
>
> (quoted in Jung 1934/1954: 13)

In another report of Karl Bovillus:

> I wish to tell you of a vision which appeared to him in the sky . . . He saw the head of a human figure with a terrifying face, full of wrath and threats.
>
> (quoted in Jung 1934/1954: 14)

We can see how God appeared as 'wholly other' to Brother Klaus and how terrifying this experience was for him. Brother Klaus tried to understand his experience as a rational one by reducing it to the idea of the Trinity. But the original experience was a wholly irrational one that seized him emotionally; it was not a typical form but a *mysterium tremendum*. In this sense it corresponds to the notion of the numinous very well.

We have tried to clarify the nuance of the 'numinous' in Jung's context which lays weight upon the subjective and feeling. But this understanding of the numinous is not, of course, entirely a construction of modern consciousness. It is characteristic in Jung that both modern and pre-modern aspects are discernible. On one hand, Jung emphasizes the experience and feeling aspect of the numinous. But, on the other hand, Jung shows how religion is or was in the pre-modern sense. In his memoirs (1963) he described his experience with the Elgonyi in Uganda. The indigenous people there praise the sun when it comes up, as described by an old man who said: 'In the morning, when the sun comes up, we go out of the huts, spit into our hands, and hold them up to the sun' (1963: 296).

Jung invited the old man to demonstrate the ceremony and to describe it exactly, and then he asked what this meant. The only answer he got was: 'We've always done it.' Then Jung noticed that it was impossible to obtain any explanation, and realized that they actually knew only that they did it, not what they were doing. Jung writes: 'They themselves saw no meaning in this action.' As Jung tried to know the meaning of the ritual, it is 'necessary' for modern people everywhere to know the symbolic meaning of ritual. In other words, reason must find a connection with the actions of faith. In the process of conscious knowing, the subjective feeling also plays an important role. But as the ritual of Elgonyi shows, the religious experience consists in the pure performance. Because the meaning is self-evident, no explanation, no deliberate knowing is needed. That is why Jung writes: 'They themselves saw no meaning in this action.' The numinous in the pre-modern sense is probably pure performance which, as such, is meaningful. Jung's work also recognizes this pre-modern aspect of the numinous.

THE NUMINOUS AND PATHOLOGY

In a remarkable statement, Jung reflected:

> We are as much possessed by autonomous psychic contents as if they were Olympians. Today they are called phobias, obsessions, and so forth; in a word neurotic symptoms. The gods have become diseases.
>
> (1929: 37)

This thesis can be understood in two ways. First, it suggests the decline of ordinary, traditional religions with their symbols and beliefs. Faithful experience of religion has become difficult today as religions have lost their symbolic, numinous power. In each of the religions more people are having difficulty experiencing the living meaning of religious symbols and rituals. The gap between faith and reason has widened so far that faith has broken apart. I have to add that I have no intention of denying that there are still many people who actively believe in and take part in a religion. But the logical meaning of religion was lost after the rise of modern science since Galileo and the Enlightenment. With knowledge of biology and physics, we can no longer believe, for example, in the literal idea of the Virgin Mary, or the Resurrection of Christ. In this sense, fundamentalism might be a counter-reaction and defense against the state of unbelief in the world and consciousness today.

Second, Jung's words mean that the numinous is experienced today in a personal and negative way as psychopathology. Irrational fear in case of phobia, for example, is similar to the awfulness in religious experience. A patient of mine had claustrophobia and was afraid of narrow places. She fell into a panic in an elevator. On the face of it, this seemed a meaningless symptom, and yet there was an underlying level of meaning. As in many religions, a hole or a spring in a narrow valley was a holy place which was regarded as a gateway to the other world. A narrow place was sensed by her as 'the numinous' which evoked not only anxiety but also a kind of uncon-scious fascination: it was for her *tremendum* and *fascinans*. It manifested as the ambivalent feeling of neurosis.

Or another patient of mine was afraid of cockroaches. In his case cockroaches appear, so to say, as the 'wholly other', as the numinous. His experience might be compared with that of devil in the Middle Ages. For non-Islamic people the hours spent in prayers and rituals in Islamic religious practice seem to be extremely long and a waste of time. But patients with compulsive disorder spend many hours on their compulsive rituals accompanied by feelings of anxiety and guilt. A patient of mine had a washing compulsion and had to wash his hands for at least half an hour every time he came home. The numinous seems to be experienced as a negative and ambivalent feeling by the modern individual. We do not give time to the gods voluntarily, in ritual, but involuntarily, in symptomatic behavior. In this sense the gods have become diseases.

Despite the similarity to religious experience, it must be said that the experience of the numinous as neurotic symptom has significant differences. The numinous is personal in the case of pathology and does not have any common symbolic meaning for the community as religious symbols once had. As the symptom has no objective validity and the subjective experience is important, we might conclude that the object of the symptom as such has no meaning and is arbitrary. It is of no importance if a patient is afraid of cockroaches or high places; what matters is the subjective experience as emotion. As was said before, Rudolf Otto's theories have a tendency to emphasize the subjective aspect and pay less attention to the content of religion. In the case of psychopathology, this tendency is much more remarkable. We might even say that the shift from objective content to subjective experience, especially to emotional experience, and the rise of psychology and psychopathology is simultaneous. Because the objective content is arbitrary, the object of emotion can be transferred to the other, that is to the therapist as transference neurosis.

Feeling has much to do with self-consciousness and is keenly connected with the rise of the human subject in the modern sense. Among feelings, anxiety is very important in the experience of the numinous. It is striking to notice that anxiety played a central role in the philosophy of the nineteenth and twentieth centuries. As examples we can mention Kierkegaard and Heidegger. Anxiety is felt because man is not anymore embraced by community, nature and God and stands alone as a single individual subject. In a state of anxiety one can feel oneself in contact with the object, but as it were without the protective devices of ritual or ceremony. So it is interesting to notice that Rudolf Otto stresses the moment of dependency in the experience of the numinous.

Along with feeling and emotion, meaning is important in psychotherapy. It was Freud who discovered the unconscious sexual meaning behind neurotic symptoms. Jung laid stress on the *telos* (purpose) of a neurotic symptom and tried to show its meaning and its goal. In this case, symbolism played an important role. In archetypal psychology, the image of god is seen through as a symptom. A symptom is traced back to a God (*epistrophé*). In all these approaches there is a tendency to find meaning in an irrational emotion. This linking between emotion and meaning is characteristic for the experience of the numinous in modern psychotherapy.

CHANGE OF PATHOLOGY

The focus on feeling has much to do with the rise of the modern subject and psychotherapeutic psychology. Emotion, especially negative emotion, appears in the conflict of the subject with the embracing power which might be embodied by or interpreted as parents, nature, or the divine. Then negative emotion appears, for example, as fear of night, guilty feelings about parents and God, resentment against parents, etc. Psychotherapy in its turn is concerned with coping with negative emotion. In this sense, negative emotion is important for health because it can be a tool to change the state of consciousness. Psychosomatic symptoms with so-called *alexithymic* character show clearly that lack of negative emotion brings a negative consequence. It is often reported that psychosomatic patients are over-adapted to reality, but are not capable of expressing conflicts and feelings.

In recent years, pathology seems to be shifting from feeling to action, from conflict to dissociation. As the increasing reports of dissociation and multiple personalities show, there are more and more cases without emotional conflicts. A patient with dissociation disorder does not have clear continuity of the personality. A very gentle person can be suddenly cruel and violent, or a rigid person can have many sexual relations when the personality changes. We might expect that there would be a conflict between different tendencies (tenderness and cruelty) or that this person would have a strong guilty feeling after having been violent to someone else. But such a person often does not feel any emotional conflict or guilty feeling. Another aspect of personality is simply acted out without conflict.

It is often reported that cases of wrist-cutting, violence and sexual acting-out are increasing. There are especially many young women and girls who cut their wrists but they are different from so-called borderline patients who try to commit suicide by cutting their wrists. Those dissociated women have no idea why they are cutting themselves and have no intention of dying. They simply cut their wrists to calm themselves or to feel a sense of reality.

It is probably symbolic that several shocking criminal deeds by children have been reported in Japan in recent years, for instance, children who killed other children for no apparent reason. There are also children who killed or hurt adults. In many cases no emotional reason – hatred, resentment, envy – nor pragmatic reason – to steal money or precious objects – may be recognized. It must be said that psychotherapy works with people who are aware of their problems and have conflicts about them. So it is very difficult to work psychotherapeutically with those who have no conflict and show no emotion, because everything is acted-out and cannot be psychologically contained and internalized.

From a historical point of view there was first a shift from a religious performance in the pre-modern sense to a psychological experience in the modern sense. While a religious performance had been as such meaningful and self-evident, symbolical comprehension and emotional experience on the part of the human subject became necessary in the latter case. Religious performance was not an end-in-itself any more, but needed subjective understanding and emotion. Then a new shift seems to be in process from psychological, emotional experience to action. The established modern subject seems to be cast away. I would like to call the dawning new consciousness postmodern consciousness, which is characterized by lack of conflict and loss of centricity of consciousness. But I will not go into postmodern consciousness in detail or at length. Instead, in this chapter I would like to restrict myself to the change in experiencing the numinous. Giegerich (2004) points out that the numinous as religious content has logically disappeared because the inner logic which was represented in religious ideas and symbols is already integrated into consciousness. He writes: 'only in the momentary acts of certain irrational, meaningless crimes . . . the numinous is an immediate reality as a tremendum'. The change of pathology corresponds to this transformation of the numinous.

THE NUMINOUS AS PURE ACTION AND HARUKI MURAKAMI

We may characterize the experience of the numinous in the present or postmodern context by analyzing various social phenomena mentioned in the last section. Or we may approach the experience of the numinous today by using case material which is characterized by dissociation and acting-out (Kawai 2006). In this chapter, I would like to illustrate features of the experience of the numinous in the present time by interpreting the novels of Haruki Murakami, who is one of the most famous Japanese novelists today, not only in Japan but also abroad.

Most of his works are translated into English and there are translations of his books in about twenty languages. The titles of his novels, to mention only the most known ones, are *Norwegian Woods*, *A Wild Sheep Chase*, *Dance, Dance, Dance*, *Hard-Boiled Wonderland and The End of the World*, *The Wind-up Bird Chronicle*, *Sputnik Sweetheart*, *Kafka on the Shore* and, most recently, *After Dark*. Although these stories are often enigmatic and difficult to understand, they are very popular and sell in their millions. Oe, a prize-winning novelist, complained that Murakami's writings fail to go beyond their influence on the lifestyle of youth (cited by Rubin 2005). But I find this criticism one-sided and am of the opinion that Murakami's work has a depth beneath its apparently superficial pop style.

The reason for these novels' popularity is that they can show a certain depth of general consciousness of which people are not clearly aware but have only a hunch or vague idea. In the last section, I mentioned that pathology is now shifting from neurotic symptoms and conflicts to dissociation and acting-out. In Murakami's novels, the tendency toward detachment and dissociation is remarkable and in this sense, they are pertinent material illustrating the present situation. By interpreting Haruki Murakami's work we will probably show a typical Japanese situation as well as a universal aspect of experiencing of the numinous today.

In his novels, the hero or heroine is often dissociated and remains detached. He or she seems to live in more than two worlds, more than two contexts. Because of this dissociation, human relationship is often complicated and lost. In many stories the wife or the girlfriend of the hero disappears suddenly in an enigmatic way and never shows up again. For example, in *The Wind-up Bird Chronicle* the wife of the narrator leaves their house suddenly; in *Sputnik Sweetheart* Sumire, who is longed for by the narrator, is lost all of a sudden on a Greek island. Very often two stories or two worlds even run parallel and independently in a novel. *Hard-Boiled Wonderland and The End of the World*, *Kafka on the Shore* and the most recent novel *After Dark* are constructed in this way. For example, *Hard-Boiled Wonderland and The End of the World*, as the title shows, has a story about 'Hard-Boiled Wonderland' in the odd-numbered chapters, and 'The End of The World' in the even-numbered chapters. Although the readers have some idea about the connection between two parallel stories, they are compelled to follow each story separately. In this way they are forced to experience their own dissociation.

In this discussion, I will not go into a full interpretation of the narratives of Murakami's novels, but focus on the theme of violence. In his novels there are often descriptions of sexuality and violence but with few exceptions, for example in *Dance, Dance, Dance*, the sexuality has often nothing to do with human relationship or sacred union, which indicates the lack of relation to reality and the dominance of dissociation. A typical novel in this sense is *Sputnik Sweetheart* which I discuss in another paper (Kawai 2004). More striking are the many scenes of violence and bizarre images in his novels. In *The Wind-up Bird Chronicle* many animals in a Chinese zoo are shot after the end of the Second World War. In *Sputnik Sweetheart* a Chinese ritual to build a gate is described. At the entrance of the city they construct a huge gate and seal in bones that have been gathered in old battlefields. 'When the gate was finished they'd bring several dogs over to it, slit their throats, and sprinkle their blood on the gate. Only by mixing fresh blood with the dried-out bones would the ancient souls of the dead magically revive.'

Much more striking and also disgusting is the torture of a Japanese soldier in *The Wind-up Bird Chronicle*. Lieutenant Mamiya told the hero of his experience during the Second World War. He was caught by Mongolian and Soviet soldiers and had to observe how his officer, Yamamoto, was skinned alive by a Mongolian soldier until he died. I would like to quote a few passages which, I should warn the reader, are quite shocking.

> The man started by slitting open Yamamoto's shoulder and proceeded to peel off the skin of his right arm from the top down – slowly, carefully, almost lovingly. As the Russian officer had said, it was something like a work of art. One would never have imagined there was any pain involved, if it weren't for the screams. But the screams told the horrendousness of the pain that accompanied the work.
>
> Before long, the entire skin of Yamamoto's right arm had come off in a single thin sheet. The skinner handed it to the man beside him, who held it open in his fingertips, circulating among the others to give them a good look. All the while, blood kept dripping from the skin. Then the officer turned to Yamamoto's left arm, repeating the procedure. After that he skinned both legs, cut off the penis and testicles, and removed the ears. Then he skinned the head and the face and everything else. Yamamoto lost consciousness, regained it, and lost again. The screams would stop whenever he passed out and continue when he came to consciousness again. But his voice gradually weakened and finally gave out altogether.

This certainly is a cruel and disgusting passage and readers will be disturbed by the detailed description. The cruelty contains something antihuman that was dominant during the Second World War. This culminated in the violence and massacres by the Nazis and the Japanese army. Japan's dark and violent past is an important background for Haruki Murakami (Rubin, 2005: 213). It is, however, important to see this scene not only in the context of war. The skinning and peeling is not only cruel, but once had a symbolic meaning. Just as a snake is regarded as a symbol of rebirth because it sheds its skin, skinning and peeling can be regarded as a symbol of rebirth and transformation.

Jung examines the symbolic meaning of skinning in several of his papers. In the discussion of the symbolism of the Mass, Jung quotes the vision of Zosimos, an alchemist of the third century, and sees there a parallel transformation to that of the Mass. In this vision the priest himself is sacrificed and goes through the transformation. The analogy to the Mass can be seen in an image of the priest tearing himself to pieces with his own teeth and eating himself. The vision of Zosimos gives us a strange and bizarre impression at first reading, but it contains in truth a symbolic meaning of transformation. Interestingly enough, there is a passage in the vision: 'And he drew off the scalp of my head with the sword.' Jung writes, 'There is, however, a scalping, which in our context is closely connected with the ancient rites of flaying and their magical significance' (1942/1954: 228). Jung refers to an old Attic fertility rite where 'an ox was flayed, stuffed and set up on its feet' (ibid.: 228). Jung mentions reports by Herodotus about a number of flaying ceremonies among the Scythians.

In Jung's interpretation, flaying signifies 'transformation from a worse state to a better, and hence renewal and rebirth' (ibid.: 228). Jung also sees the prototype of this renewal in the snake casting off its skin every year. So there is a symbolic meaning in skinning which has to do with transformation and renewal. The vision of Zosimos contains not only this image of skinning but also that of dismemberment. I would like to quote the following passage: 'For there came one in haste at early morning, who overpowered me and pierced me through with the sword and cut me in pieces, yet in such a way that the order of my limbs was preserved' (ibid.: 227). This description in the vision of Zosimos can be compared with the initiation of a shaman. In the case of shamanistic initiation, dismemberment and cutting off of the head are typical motives. In mythology, these motives can be seen in the figures of Osiris and Orpheus. So the vision of Zosimos has to do with shamanic initiation and transformation.

Although both skinning and dismemberment can be interpreted as symbols of renewal and rebirth, there is a significant difference in the ritual according to whether it is performed by dismemberment or skinning. The former is more penetrating, radical and instantaneous; the latter remains on the surface and takes more time, leaving the whole body intact. Thus skinning has a less penetrating, softer nuance than dismemberment. Because the skin has to do with the ego, as stated by Freud, it is closer to consciousness and more human. This human aspect appears in the pain, although the experience of pain seems to be inhuman. As skinning needs more time, pain and torture play an important role. But pain, like emotion and feeling, tends to pay focus on the experiencing human being. While the numinous in the pre-modern sense was pure performance, which was, as such, meaningful, pain tends to place the numinous in the experiencing subject. Therefore Jung says: 'The aspect of torture, then, is correlated with a detached and observing consciousness that has not yet understood the real meaning of dismemberment' (ibid.: 272). If the aspect of pain is emphasized, modern and human nuance is already discernible.

From the above discussion we can conclude that skinning is a symbolic, numinous ritual which is rooted in ancient traditions. In this ritual the content, the performance as such, is important and numinous, not the emotional experience, not the pain. As Jung says, 'The rite has no practical utility' and 'everything divine is an end-in-itself' (ibid.: 250). After the rise of the subject, in the case of the neurotic symptom and its psychotherapy, fear of skinning and felt pain would probably be central for the numinous.

Jung tried to get at the numinous in the pre-modern sense by interpreting the meaning of action and image.

Now that we have understood the symbolic meaning of skinning, let us come back to the novel of Haruki Murakami. Although a scene of skinning is depicted in his novel, there is no symbolic content, no overt symbolic meaning. Nor is there a subjective experience because the image is not internalized but simply acted out as violence in this case. There is only pure action, pure violence without meaning. There is neither rebirth for the poor officer Yamamoto, nor symbolic meaning for the observing Mamiya and participating Mongolian soldiers. Mongolians are hunting people and this skinning must be rooted in their ritualized shamanistic tradition of flaying. But the reader can not even sense the flavor of this traditional meaning. In the case of symbolic ritual, the identification between sacrificer and sacrificed is essential, as Jung tried to show in the symbolism of the Mass and the vision of Zosimos. This identification can appear as identification between God and human beings and between sacrificed and sacrificers. But in the case of Murakami, there is no such linking. God and humans have lost their connection, Yamamoto and Mongolians do not belong to the same community or worldview. They do not live in an age where war was also part of ritual. There is no interiority or inwardness. The Second World War was probably the last contribution to the destruction of interiority.

This pure action, pure violence without meaning should not, however, be devalued and rejected as ultimately meaningless and disgusting. Nor should we interpret this violence as loss of the numinous. On the contrary, this very pure violence seems to be the site of the numinous today, as Giegerich pointed out. The numinous today does not want to be categorized in the subjective feeling-experience and meaning-experience. The numinous has left its historical locus as feeling and meaning. It is moving toward pure action, pure negation. If violence has a meaning or context, for example because of hatred, resentment, or more pragmatic reasons, it is not uncanny and hence not numinous. It is numinous because there is no meaning, no reason. The 'overpoweringness' of the numinous today is partly expressed in the numbing lack of meaning, our inability to contain the *numen*.

PRE-MODERN PERFORMANCE AND POSTMODERN ACTION

Haruki Murakami's novels are indicating that the numinous in the present world is pure action, pure negation without meaning. But it is characteristic for Haruki Murakami's world and probably for Japanese consciousness that there remain traces of past religious meanings. This can be observed in the way that Murakami does not choose a purely meaningless violence, but a violence which reminds us of old sacrifices and rituals, as in the above mentioned scene of skinning which can be traced back to ancient rituals of flaying and shamanistic initiations. There are many other cases of violence in Murakami's novels which recall, in a certain sense, ancient rituals. I have already cited a story about the ancient Chinese ritual of building a gate depicted in *Sputnik Sweetheart*. In this case, dogs are sacrificed for the construction of a gate. In *Kafka on the Shore* the character Johnnie Walker who is the father of the protagonist, a boy named Kafka, must take out the heart of a cat and eat it, then cut off the head of the cat. This act is not only perverse and cruel, but evokes some ritualistic associations and meanings.

The Johnnie Walker character says that he kills cats to gather their souls from which he wants to construct a special flute. While playing this flute, he tries to gather a still bigger soul. So there is a quest for the soul and an almost religious devotion in this violence. If pure violence without meaning were intended, Murakami could have chosen scenes and acts which have nothing to do with images of ritual or sacrifice. But many scenes of violence in his novels have to do with killing animals and thus evoke an association with ancient sacrificial rituals. Or perhaps we could deduce the possibility that all violence is inherently ritualistic, that violence is indelibly linked to the *numen*.

Many images of the old worldview can be seen in this connection. In the novel *A Wild Sheep Chase* the hero has to search for a special, dangerous sheep which had a star-shaped mark. This sheep, which had special powers and could take possession of a person, may be regarded as a totem animal or guardian spirit in a totemistic culture. The image of the other world, or the other side, very often plays an important role in many novels of Murakami. In *Dance, Dance, Dance* the other world opens up when the elevator stops on the sixteenth floor of the Dolphin hotel or when the protagonist goes through the wall. I have said that dissociation is an important theme in Murakami's novels. This is, however, not an arbitrary dissociation of personality, but rather has to do with dissociation in the world and worldview. The characters in Murakami's novels live between the pre-modern world of rituals and souls on the one side, and the post-modern world of pure action without meaning on the other. In this connection, it is interesting to note that features of modern consciousness are lacking in Murakami's world: conflicts, feelings, meanings are difficult to find there. This further suggests that lack of religious ceremony relates directly to the absence of moral consciousness, that, as Nietzsche said, when God is dead, all morality disappears and all things become possible.

Description of ritualistic images and the other world should not be taken as a message that we can go back to the old worldview and meaning and that such ritualistic images still have a symbolic meaning. Murakami is not making a case for the existence and rebirth of the mythical world in the individual human psyche, as Jung sometimes gives the impression of doing. The word of a cat in the novel *Kafka on the Shore* makes that clear. She calls 'perverse' what the Johnnie Walker character might be doing. Such a killing is not at all symbolic, but only perverse and criminal in the present world. Nor is the guardian sheep in *A Wild Sheep Chase* integrated but is lost forever at the end of the story. So it would be important to notice that we cannot go back to the old world where rituals and symbols are self-evident. But we leave the old world in respectful memory.

However, descriptions of traces of ritual give us the impression that Murakami is still attached to the old worldview. First, the more the lost world is described as lost, the more it is present as concrete content. In *Kafka on the Shore* there is commitment, especially by an old man, Nakata, who can talk with cats, to close the door to the other world. After the death of Nakata, a young man, Hoshino, takes over the task. But this whole effort makes the other world beyond the door much more vivid and present. Or the other world exists logically only as lost. Second, Murakami tries to show the old world as lost and still leave a locus for it. It is as if an empty room whose inhabitants have gone were still rented. Semantically, the old worldview is already lost, but syntactically, as a logical structure, it is still secretly kept. In these two ways the old worldview is still present in a refined way.

Murakami is probably a best-selling novelist because his work can talk to both pre-modern and postmodern sides of the psyche and corresponds to the state of psyche today, especially in Japan. The violence can be both meaningful performance and totally meaningless action. But seen from a psychological and historical point of view, his somewhat ambivalent position still leaves some problems open. And as he is a novelist who is still producing new novels and is 'in process', there are several possible directions already shown in his novels prefiguring the violence as numinous. One possibility lies in a confrontation with the violence. Murakami tries to show that one does not remain detached in the face of meaningless violence as in his early novels, but commits to an action. Another possibility for commitment to reality and politics is looked for in *The Wind-up Bird Chronicle*. The entire novel can be understood not only as a search for the lost wife and for relationship, but as a confrontation with Japan's past violence during the Second World War. The hero, Toru, fought against Noboru, his brother-in-law and a politician, through enclosing himself inwardly in a well. But it is debatable whether this somewhat rational commitment and responsibility is convincing or not.

The other possibility may be seen in the newest novel *After Dark*. In this novel a Chinese prostitute was robbed of money and all her clothes by a mysterious man, which is a violent scene. In the even-numbered chapters, this man watches from above the sleeping young woman, Eri. There are more complicated human relationships and mysterious coincidences but I will not go into the details. I would only like to suggest that here the numinous is not a meaningless violence, but is internalized as a form of consciousness, seen from above. To conclude, I would like to stay with these suggestions from a very experimental novel and await further developments in Haruki Murakami's future novels as regards to the numinous as pure action without meaning.

References

Giegerich, W. (2004) 'The End of Meaning and the Birth of Man', *Journal of Jungian Theory and Practice* 6(1): 1–65.

Jung, C.G. (1929) 'Commentary on "The Secret of the Golden Flower"', *CW* 13.

Jung, C.G. (1933) 'Brother Klaus', *CW* 11.

Jung, C.G. (1934/1954) 'Archetypes of the Collective Unconscious', *CW* 9, 1.

Jung, C.G. (1938/1940) 'Psychology and religion', *CW* 11.

Jung, C.G. (1942/1948) 'A Psychological Approach to the Dogma of the Trinity', *CW* 11.

Jung, C.G. (1942/1954) 'Transformation Symbolism in the Mass', *CW* 11.

Jung, C.G. (1947/1957) 'On the Nature of the Psyche', *CW* 8.

Jung, C.G. (1963) *Memories, Dreams, Reflections*, ed. Aniela Jaffé, London: Fontana Press.

Kawai, T. (2004) 'Postmodern Consciousness in the Novels of Haruki Murakami', in T. Singer (ed.), *The Cultural Complex*, London: Routledge, pp. 90–101.

Kawai, T. (2006) 'Postmodern Consciousness in Psychotherapy', *Journal of Analytical Psychology* 51: 437–50.

Murakami, H. (1993a) *Dance, Dance, Dance*, New York: Vintage International.

Murakami, H. (1993b) *Hard-Boiled Wonderland and The End of the World*, New York: Vintage International.

Murakami, H. (1997) *The Wind-up Bird Chronicle*, New York: Vintage International.

Murakami, H. (2002) *Kafka on the Shore (Umibe no Kafka)*, Tokyo: Kodan-sha.

Murakami, H. (2004) *After Dark*, Tokyo: Shincho-sha.

Otto, R. (1959) *The Idea of the Holy*, Harmondsworth: Penguin Books.

Rubin, J. (2005) *Haruki Murakami and the Music of Words*, New York: Vintage.

Chapter 13

Holy, Holy, Holy: the misappropriation of the numinous in Jung

Lucy Huskinson

The 'numinous' is a difficult subject to explicate principally because it is non-rational. The numinous defies intellectualization, which means that its meaning cannot be encapsulated adequately within this chapter or even within the most lengthy and detailed book. Elsewhere I have discussed how all attempts at defining the numinous will not only fall short, but an intellectual pursuit of it will push it further away from ego-comprehension (Huskinson 2002). The numinous object cannot be forced or summoned into consciousness; it is not subject to the ego's control. Rather, the numinous object is discovered in its autonomous manifestation where it calls the ego into response. If the ego's response is through reason alone, then, according to Jung, the unheard numen will overwhelm it, forcing the ego to live and breath its non-rational energy in a devastating act of compensation.

The numinous is an affective, living experience that overflows the boundaries of the ego. Any claim to an explanation of the numinous is merely a claim to analogy and metaphor – a limited approximation of that which remains unconscious and beyond our grasp. However, this is not to say that we cannot know the numen, and that such analogies and metaphors cannot hold profound meaning for us. Indeed, although the numinous cannot be understood on an objective level, it can be known subjectively, in a personal relationship pregnant with meaning. Furthermore, one's relationship with the numen can be communicated effectively to another person, who is also in a living relationship with it. Communication of numinous experience is enabled through symbolic language – in poetry, art, music, and other media that utilize analogy and metaphor. It is through the symbol that the numen communicates its meaning, and we must be receptive to such language if we are to hear its message. The symbol is of both rational and non-rational composition, and, as such, it is able to mediate between the rational ego and the non-rational energies of the numen. If the ego does not harness the power of the symbol, it will not only perceive the non-rational communication of the numen at the level of reason alone (thereby reducing the symbol to a sign and forfeiting the possibility of a personal relationship with the numen), but it will also be at greater risk of assault from the unheard numen. A symbolic framework is required if the ego is to ground its numinous experience and respond to it adequately, for the symbol protects the ego from the destructive energy of the numen.

The term 'numinous' was coined by Rudolf Otto in *The Idea of the Holy* (1917). Taken from the Latin word 'numen', the numinous describes the ineffable quality of religious experience. Otto introduced this term in order to promote the non-rational side of religious experience, which had been suppressed by orthodox Christianity, or 'the mother of rationalism', as Otto called it. Otto therefore sought to rebalance its 'one-sided intellectualistic and rational interpretation[s]', which 'found in the construction of dogma and doctrine no way to do justice to the non-rational aspect of its subject' (3).[1] In particular, Otto sought to counter the tendency of orthodox Christianity to conflate experience of 'holiness' with that of morality, which ensured that the holy was reduced to a rational concept devoid of its uniquely religious aspects. The word 'holy' thus came to be identified with an absolute moral attribute, denoting 'complete goodness'.[2] However, according to Otto, holiness comprises more than this: it contains 'a clear overplus of meaning' (5), which the rational faculty cannot decipher, for the 'deeper essence [of religion] is not, nor indeed can be, comprehended . . . [It] requires comprehension of a quite different kind' (2). His name for this unique 'category of value' is the 'numinous'. The numinous

> is perfectly *sui generis* and irreducible to any other; and therefore, like every absolutely primary and elementary datum, while it admits of being discussed, it cannot be strictly defined [or] taught, it can only be evoked, awakened in the mind; as everything that comes 'of the spirit' must be awakened.
>
> (7)

Already, from this brief introduction to Otto's concept of the numinous, readers who are familiar with Jung's work will begin to recognize an affinity between the two. Both thinkers sought to ground religious experience within a context beyond intellectual understanding and in one that does not, in Otto's words, 'promote in any way the tendency of our time towards an extravagant and fantastic "irrationalism"' (1923), nor, in Jung's words, promote the 'rationalistic fear' of the modern man, who 'will deny or repress its numinosity [so that] it will then be evaluated as an inexplicable, irrational, and even pathological phenomenon' (Jung 1942/1948: 274).[3] In other words, Otto and Jung sought a balance where religious experience is granted both rational and non-rational expression. We know that Jung was familiar with *The Idea of the Holy*, and we might assume that his ideas were influenced by it, for Jung often refers to the numinous when he, like Otto, discusses the limitations of the intellect for religious understanding:

although our whole world of religious ideas consists of anthropomor-
phic images that could never stand up to rational criticism, we should
never forget that they are based on numinous archetypes, i.e., on an
emotional foundation which is unassailable by reason. We are dealing
with psychic facts which logic can overlook but not eliminate.

(1952a: 556)

An aspect of God, which I cannot judge logically and cannot conquer
because it is stronger than me – because, in other words, it has a
numinous quality . . . I cannot 'conquer' a *numinosum*, I can only open
myself to it, let myself be overpowered by it, trusting in its meaning.

(1959: 864)

Jung's allusions to the numinous are many, and most often concern the
emotional, affective experience of the unconscious (with particular reference to the archetypes, complexes, and psychopathology). He thus describes
the numinous as 'inexpressible, mysterious, terrifying' (1967: 416); 'holy
dread' (1942/1948: 222); 'overwhelming – an admission that goes against
not only our pride, but against our deep-rooted fear that consciousness may
perhaps lose its ascendancy' (ibid.: 275); as having 'thrilling power' (1945/
1954: 396) and 'deeply stirring emotional effect' (1952b: 454); 'spiritual and
magical' (1947/1954: 405); 'healing or destructive – never indifferent' (ibid.:
405); capable of 'fateful transformations . . . conversions, illuminations,
emotional shocks, blows of fate' (1942/1948: 274); 'wholly outside conscious
volition, for it transports the subject into the state of rapture, which is a
state of will-less surrender' (1947/1954: 383); 'an experience of the subject
independent of his will . . . it causes a peculiar alteration of consciousness'
(1938/1940: 6).

The purpose of this chapter is, however, not merely to explicate the
similarities and differences in the thought of Otto and Jung, rather it is to
argue that Jung's use of Otto's term (and, consequently, the use of it by
commentators of Jung) is inaccurate. Jung is too quick to incorporate
Otto's term into his own theory. Indeed, one would be forgiven for thinking
that Jung was blinded by his enthusiasm for its appropriately mysterious
and fascinating connotations, for he fails to grasp its essential meaning, and
subsequently facilitates its mistranslation into his psychological theory.

In this chapter I shall argue that the 'numinous' is not, strictly speaking,
applicable to aspects of Jung's psychological theory, with particular
emphasis being placed on the individuation process. Rather, it is to Otto's
term 'the holy' that Jung, and we, should turn. Although I have insisted
that a pursuit of a definition or explanation of the 'numinous' will inevitably divest it of effective meaning, it is important that the rational categories that we adopt to make sense of non-rational experience remain
consistent.[4] Moreover, the difference in meaning of a 'numinous' experience

and one that is 'holy' is critical to the development and healing of the personality that is at the heart of Jungian theory. As I shall argue, a numinous experience cannot induce progressive change or enrichment of the ego, for, although an encounter with the numinous is overwhelming, it is without purpose; only in an experience of the holy can the ego be reborn into Selfhood.

THE DIFFERENCE BETWEEN THE NUMINOUS AND THE HOLY

In the introduction I raised the issue of the relationship between the numinous and the holy. We saw that the numinous is that which differentiates holiness from morality in religious experience, and that it is able to discriminate between the two because its non-rational nature comprehends the essence of religion, apart from its rational component. It, therefore, enables holiness to be experienced as a representation of something more than mere 'goodness'. It is in this sense that Otto refers to the numinous as '"the holy" *minus* its moral factor or "moment", and . . . minus its "rational" aspect altogether' (1917: 6). However, we must note that the numinous is not an isolated aspect of the holy; the numinous and the holy are not simultaneous manifestations of religious experience. Rather, the holy is a development of the numinous: it 'represents the gradual shaping and filling in with ethical meaning, or what we shall call the "schematization", of what was a unique original feeling-response, [*sc.* the numinous] which can be in itself ethically neutral' (ibid.). The numinous is not suppressed in the process of its development into the holy, rather the holy is 'the completion and charging of [the numinous] with a new content' (111), one that not only retains numinous elements of non-rational 'inconceivability', but intensifies them as the revelation proceeds (135). The holy is the numen 'rendered absolute' (110). The holy therefore represents the unification of the non-rational with the rational at their highest expression: neither aspect can either inhibit or overwhelm the other; rather an increased rational interaction with the non-rational reinforces its inconceivability.

Otto contends that the teleological process of attaining pure religious judgement and experience of the holy from the more crude, non-rational experiences of the numinous, underlies the historical development of all religious thought, and that it is, in part, the task of psychology to trace its course (110). At first sight, one may think that analytical psychology is insufficiently prepared for such a task because it has no concern for the objectively moral sphere of life. However, although Otto's argument focuses on the moral content of the holy, this is merely one facet of its rational basis. Otto alludes to others, including absoluteness, completion, necessity, substantiality (112), purpose, and personality (109), and it is these other facets that encourage a Jungian reading of Otto's idea of the holy, for analytical psychology is concerned predominantly with principles of completion, purpose, and personality. Thus, Jung tells us that penetration into the secret of the personality is the one idea and goal that has permeated his life and work, and from which everything can be explained (1967: 232). Although Jung is aware that this secret can never be unveiled for all to see, his work can be construed as an attempt to persuade us that something does lie behind the veil – that there is indeed a secret to discover; a personality to be found. In this sense, Jung attributes structure, order, and purpose to the personality. Jung tells us that 'all psychological phenomena have some sense of purpose inherent in them' (1916/1948: 456); the psyche 'has purposive orientation' and contains within it 'something like a preliminary exercise or sketch, or a plan roughed out in advance' (1916/1948: 493; cf. 456). This pre-designated teleological scheme, or *individuation process*, comprises many 'stages' and archetypal encounters before its goal or culmination is realized in the Self – 'the archetype of order par excellence' (1958: 805).[5]

If Jungian psychology were placed within Otto's account of the development of religious thought, it would appear once purpose has been established. In other words, we would place it in the realm of the holy, a developmental stage beyond the numinous and its rudimentary motivations of 'uneasy seeking and groping, yearning and longing' (Otto 1917: 115), which cannot induce progressive change or ego-enrichment. To consolidate this claim, I shall turn to Otto's account of the holy; but, before I do so, I think it is important to clarify the lack of purpose in Otto's account of the numinous. This is because Otto's account is often misleading, so that a brief examination of it occasionally suggests a view contrary to mine. For example, the basic idea that the holy, and the history of religious thought in general, is the culmination of a development that works itself out purely in the sphere of the non-rational numinous implies that the numinous is purposive. And the same is suggested by Otto's contention that the numinous can have positive or negative value (or, as Jung claims, can be 'healing or destructive'). However, this is not the case on both counts. The development of religious consciousness is an extremely gradual shaping initiated by man's capacities for reason and reflection, so that the value of the numinous is determined by the impression made by the numinous object on consciousness, and not by the numinous object itself, or the subject's disposition to it:

> It is important here to recognize the true account of the phenomenon. What passes over – undergoes transition – is not the feeling itself. It is not that the actual feeling gradually changes in quality or 'evolves', i.e. transmutes itself into a quite different one, but rather that *I* pass over

or make the transition from one feeling to another as my circumstances change, by the gradual decrease of the one and increase of the other.

(Otto 1917: 42–3)

Furthermore, at one point in *The Idea of the Holy* we read that the numinous 'appears as a strange and mighty propulsion towards an ideal good known only to religion and in its nature fundamentally non-rational' (36). The significant word here is 'ideal', which lends to the numinous a teleology that operates according to a moral code. However, this sentence is a poor translation of the original German, where the word 'ideal' does not feature. What Otto actually wrote is that the numinous 'appears as a strangely powerful drive towards a good that only religion knows and that is thoroughly irrational' (ein seltsam mächtiger Trieb nach einem Gut, das nur die Religion kennt und das irrational schlechthin ist). It should be noted that the good is non-rational, and, although the numinous is ascribed movement, it is movement without purpose. An examination of the five aspects of the numinous, as described by Otto, should confirm its non-purposiveness.

THE NUMINOUS AS NON-PURPOSIVE

Otto describes the object to which the numinous consciousness is directed as the *mysterium tremendum*. In his analysis of it he divides it into three aspects, the *mysterium*, the *tremendum*, and the *fascinosum*. Each may appear in isolation, in combination, or together as one. Otto places greatest emphasis on the *tremendum*, which he further divides into three elements. The first element is *awefulness* or *dreadfulness*, which is related to 'fear', but distinct from it, in that it is an *unnatural* fear: a 'terror fraught with an inward shuddering such as not even the most menacing and overpowering created thing can instil' (14). The second element is *overpoweringness* or *aweful majesty*, which describes the overpoweringness of 'an object over against the self'. This induces, 'as a sort of shadow or subjective reflection of it', *creature consciousness*, the feeling that we are impotent, 'of being but "dust and ashes"' in the face of that which is above all creatures (20). The third element is *urgency* or *energy*, which is expressed as 'vitality, passion, emotional temper, will, force, movement, excitement, activity, impetus' (23). This element of the numinous is particularly perceptible in wrath, and is central in the delineation of God as a 'living God' as opposed to a 'philosophic' God of mere rational speculation (ibid.). Otto notes that whilst philosophers have condemned expressions of the energy of the numen as 'sheer anthropomorphisms', he himself upholds their representation of 'a genuine aspect of the divine nature – its non-rational aspect', which serves 'to protect religion itself from being "rationalized" away' (ibid.).

In Otto's explanation of the three elements of the *tremendum* aspect of the numinous there is no claim to an underlying purposiveness. Although the element of overpoweringness implies purpose in its capacity to affect, Otto makes clear, in contrasting his idea with that of Schleiermacher, that overpoweringness is not concerned with notions of conditioning, causation, or creation, which would grant positive change or intention to its affectivity. It is, rather, a matter of 'creaturehood', where the focus is on the realization of limitation and impotency. Purpose is again implied with the element of urgency, where Otto ascribes to it a 'will'. However, Otto comes to identify this as 'Schopenhauer's daemonic "Will"' (24), which is, according to Schopenhauer, 'a blind incessant impulse' (Schopenhauer 1818 (I): 275).

The *mysterium* aspect of the numinous is an experience of the 'wholly other, that which is quite beyond the sphere of the usual, the intelligible, and the familiar' (26). 'Purpose', and notions of order in general, are orthogonal to the *mysterium*. Far from inciting positive change, confrontation with it arouses the response of stupor, a 'blank wonder . . . that strikes us dumb' (ibid.)

In contrast to the repellence of the *tremendum*, the *fascinosum* aspect of the numinous attracts. Otto refers to this strange harmony, of the daunting and the fascinating, as the most noteworthy phenomenon of religious consciousness. Even when we tremble before the numinous object, it allures us and becomes 'the object of search and desire and yearning' (32). This numinous aspect is experienced as entrancing, as it captivates and transports to a state of rapture and bliss. Otto describes it as the 'Dionysiac element in the numen' (31), a formless state in which the individual loses himself and the structure of individuation collapses in favour of a 'bizarre state of numinous possession'. Here, as with the *mysterium* aspect of the numinous, there is a distinct absence of purpose, and orderliness; there is only an intoxicating sense of appeasement, 'a value inexpressible, positive, and "fascinating". This is incommensurable with thoughts of rational human teleology and is not assimilated to them' (80).[6]

There is nothing in Otto's analyses of the different aspects of the numinous to suggest that it is purposive. Indeed, that Otto intended the numinous to be without purpose is best illustrated in his discussion of the 38th chapter of the Biblical book of Job, which is regarded by Otto as a depiction of the numinous moment 'in rare purity and completeness' (77). Job has been reasoning with his friends against God. God then appears in order to defend Himself, and he does so in such a way that Job proclaims that he is overpowered by superior strength. Job subsequently confesses his 'creaturehood': 'Therefore I abhor myself and *repent* in dust and ashes.' Otto asks what this 'strange "moment"' of experience is that here operates at once as a vindication of God to Job and a reconciliation of Job to God?' He concludes that the answer is found not in rational concepts, teleological reflections, or solutions, but in 'the sheer absolute wondrousness that transcends thought' (79). What is of particular interest to us is Otto's discussion that follows from this, where he refers to specific animals that feature in the 38th chapter of Job to support his conclusion. Otto intends to demonstrate that these animals symbolize 'the negation of purposiveness':

> The eagle, that 'dwelleth and abideth on the rock, upon the crag of the rock, and the strong place', whose 'eyes behold afar off' her prey, and whose 'young ones also suck up blood, and where the slain are, there is she' – this eagle is in truth no evidence for the *teleological* wisdom that 'prepares all cunningly and well', but is rather the creature of *strangeness and marvel* . . . And the same is true of the ostrich (xxxix. 13–18) with its *inexplicable* instincts [which] affords singularly little help if we are seeking *purpose* in nature: 'which leaveth her eggs in the earth, and warmeth them in the dust, and forgetteth that the foot may crush them or that the wild beast may break them' . . . It is the same with the 'wild ass' (verse 5) and the unicorn (verse 9). These are the beasts whose complete 'dysteleology' or negation of purposiveness is truly magnificently depicted . . . It is conjectured that the descriptions of the hippopotamus (behemoth) and crocodile (leviathan) in xl. 15ff. are a later interpolation. This may well be the fact; but, if so, it must be admitted that the interpolator has felt the point of the entire section extraordinarily well . . . Assuredly these beasts would be the most unfortunate examples that one could hit upon if searching for evidence of the purposefulness of divine 'wisdom'.
>
> (79–80)

Thus, Otto interprets Job's encounter with God as an experience of the numinous, and that, as 'all the glorious [animal] examples from nature speak very plainly', its underlying proclamation is the absence of purpose in the encounter. The message of the numinous experience is inconsistent with that of the Jungian psyche and its 'purposive orientation'. Jung's message is grounded within the meaning of the holy, and it is to the holy that I now turn.

JUNG AND THE PURPOSIVE CONTENT OF THE HOLY

The holy is the schematization of the numinous; that is, it charges the numinous with rational content, rendering it purposive, absolute, substantive, moral, necessary, personal, and complete. In the category of the holy, rationality schematizes the non-rational aspects of the numinous not only in 'the relation of the rational aspect of "the holy", taken as a whole, to its non-rational, taken as a whole, but also in detail of the several constituent elements of the two aspects', so that the *tremendum* is schematized by means of the rational ideas of justice and moral will, becoming *holy wrath of God*; the *fascinosum* by means of ideas of goodness, mercy and love, becoming *grace*; and the *mysterium* by means of the *absoluteness* of all the rational attributes applied to God (140). Schematization is the process by which the holy unites the rational and the non-rational, and in both aspects the holy is designated as an *a priori* category, referring back to an original capacity of the human mind that is not derivable from perception. The rational aspect is traced back to pure reason, and the non-rational is traced even further down, to the *fundus animae*, the 'ground of the soul' (112). Otto further contends that the *connection* between the rational and non-rational is also *a priori*; they naturally fuse and necessarily go together (136).

The holy mediation or connection between the rational and non-rational is that which comprises the 'symbol'. At the beginning of this chapter I mentioned that the symbol enables the effective communication of the numen because it is of both rational and non-rational composition, and that we must be receptive to its healing capacity if we are to be protected from the overwhelming and destructive energies of the numen. In other words, the holy is that which instils meaning and content in the *tremendum*, enabling it to be understood (as the wrath of God), which, in turn, enables us to have a conception of how we might find relief from it (as redemption). Without such mediation, we are unable to make sense of, and thus utilize, the creative energies unleashed in the numinous experience. Otto, in his discussion of atonement, seems to be describing the symbol, when he writes of the

> need of a covering or shield against the ὀργή [wrath] of the numen. Such a 'covering' is then a 'consecration', i.e. a procedure that renders the approacher himself 'numinous' . . . and fits him for intercourse with the numen. The means of 'consecration' . . . are derived from, or conferred and appointed by the numen itself, which bestows something of its own quality to make man capable of communicating with it.
>
> (54)

The symbol, as pertaining to both the object of perception and the subject's perception of it, is the incarnation of otherness that opens up a dialogue between the two. The holy comprises two different states (of reason and non-reason) and is that which actively binds them together. An experience of the holy is thus both an experience of completeness and of liminality (a threshold state in between two states). In Jungian terms, we might say that the transition from one state to another in the individuation process is holy.[7] We might also wish to call this holy mediation the *transcendent function* – a process where the spontaneous emergence of a unifying symbol unites opposing aspects of the psyche, and thereby establishes a new conscious attitude, which is more integrated and enriched with those elements that were hitherto unconscious (1917/1926/1943: 121; 1921: 827). According to Jung, ego-consciousness tends to focus exclusively on adaptation to circumstances in its immediate environment, and fails to integrate the unconscious material that is not relevant to its adaptation. The ego can thus easily develop a one-sidedness that does not correspond to the overall instinctive wholeness of the personality – that is, in accordance with its purposive function and unconscious plan. The transcendent function enables the personality to move from a one-sided attitude to a new, more complete, one. Without such mediation, the ego would remain entrenched in its prejudices and could initiate the compensatory forces of the unconscious in a devastating enantiodromia. In other words, the *tremendum* would awaken (schematized as psychopathology or the wrath of the Self). The symbol therefore restores the balance between ego and unconsciousness, and enables the ego to maintain a sense of its boundaries, thereby preventing its dissolution: 'You see, by means of a symbol, such dangers can be accepted: one can submit to them, digest them. Otherwise . . . it is a very dangerous situation: one is exposed without protection to the onslaught of the unconscious' (Jung 1934–1939: 1249).

Otto adopts the term 'sign', rather than 'symbol', but its meaning is closer to that of 'symbol' than 'sign' as Jung understands the terms. Otto maintains that 'From the time of the most primitive religions everything has counted as a sign that was able to arouse in man the sense of the holy, to excite the feeling of apprehended sanctity, and stimulate it into open activity' (1917: 143). Numinous experiences that blindly affect, such as 'the thing terrible, sublime, overpowering, or astounding, and in an especial degree the uncomprehended, mysterious thing, which become the "portent" and "miracle" . . . were not "signs" in the true sense, but opportunities, circumstances, prompting the religious feeling to awake of itself' (143). The numinous is neither a 'sign' in Otto's terms, nor a Jungian 'symbol', because it comprises non-rationality without a rational grounding. That is, it cannot act as an intermediary between God and man. It remains other. Otto describes the mental faculty of *divination* as that which enables only those individuals who are gifted with such a faculty to discriminate between the signs of the holy and mere circumstances that prompt religious feeling (144, 150). We could say that the faculty of divination enables the ego to be more aware of how consistent its adaptation is with the intentions of the whole personality, for it enables the ego to recognize the symbol (or Otto's 'sign'), and be receptive to its transformative power. To be in possession of this faculty suggests that one may be less susceptible to the destructiveness of the *tremendum*, for one's ego is not blinded by a one-sided prejudice, but enlightened and working in accordance with the intentions of the whole

Self. We must remember that the prejudiced ego is not able to summon the *tremendum*. This is not a matter of conscious *willing*; it is rather a matter of conscious *neglect*. The wrath of the Self manifests itself in response to the Self having been unheard by the ego, which is preoccupied in its establishment of an attitude that is inconsistent with the whole personality. Furthermore, we must note that holiness itself is not destructive. As mentioned earlier, its positive or negative quality is determined by man's rational and reflective capacities. To perceive the holy as destructive is equivalent to there being a flaw in the ego's reasoning, which is expressed in its prejudicial attitude.

If the Jungian personality is to develop towards wholeness and completeness it must harness the creative energies of the symbol and build a dialogue between rationality and the non-rational. The individuation process cannot be realized on the basis of numinous experience. Strictly speaking, the numinous cannot heal or create. The lack of a mediating symbol would mean there is no development, merely stagnation of the personality, where the unconscious is unheard, and consequently inflicts suffering upon the deaf ego. The conscious personality requires compensation from the unconscious if it is to flourish: 'Unconscious compensation is only effective when it cooperates with an integral consciousness; assimilation is never a question of "this *or* that", but always of "this *and* that"' (Jung 1934: 338). Reason and non-reason must be integrally connected and move on parallel lines if the personality is to be mentally stable; if they split apart or become dissociated, the personality will suffer from psychological disturbance, and an exaggeration of one or other will lead to a pathological state (Jung 1964: 52).

The healing, salvation, and enrichment of the personality is found in the meaning of the holy and not the merely numinous. The numinous is incapable of inciting 'fateful transformations' and 'conversions' as Jung suggests; and is never 'never indifferent'.

Notes

1 All such references are to the page number of Otto's *The Idea of the Holy* (1917).
2 This is clearly seen in Kantian morality, where Kant designates the perfectly moral will a 'holy will': 'A will whose maxims necessarily coincide with the laws of autonomy is a *holy* will, good absolutely' (Kant 1785: 78; cf. Otto 1917: 5).
3 All such references to Jung's works are to the paragraph number and not page number, with the exception of Jung 1964, and Jung 1967, which are to the page number.
4 And this means that, as commentators of Jungian theory, we should be aware of the inaccuracies in Jung's use of specific terminology and should not make similar mistakes. It is a mistake to understand the terms 'numinous' and 'the holy' to be synonymous as Jung does, and as Jungian commentators continue to do. A notable example of error, where the term 'numinous' is defined in terms of 'the

holy', is found in the acclaimed book, *A Critical Dictionary of Jungian Analysis* (Samuels, Shorter and Plaut 1986: 100.)

5 However, Jung is clear that he does not want to define each stage in terms of an objective, teleological formulation that applies to every individual: 'How the harmonizing of conscious and unconscious data is to be undertaken cannot be indicated in the form of a recipe' (Jung 1939: 524).

6 At one point Otto does imply that the *fascinosum* aspect is purposive. Otto cites St Catherine of Genoa, describing her experience of the over-abounding *fascinosum*: 'O that I could tell you what the heart feels, how it burns and is consumed inwardly! Only I find no words to express it. I can but say: Might but one little drop of what I feel fall into Hell, Hell would be transformed into a Paradise' (38). St Catherine's words imply that numinous experience has the capacity to incite positive change. However, Otto is using this passage to illustrate the numinous aspect of the holy (i.e. the numinous in its developed, schematized form). It is thus, not the numinous *per se*, but the holy that is purposive.

7 For instance, marriage, pregnancy, and birth exemplify the threshold of single person to union of two; and midlife is the threshold of youth to old age.

References

Huskinson, L. (2002) 'The Self as Violent Other: The Problem of Defining the Self', *The Journal of Analytical Psychology* (2002) (47): 439–60.

Jung, C.G. (1916/1948) 'General Aspects of Dream Psychology', *CW* 8: 443–529.

Jung, C.G. (1917/1926/1943) 'On the Psychology of the Unconscious', *CW* 7, 1953: 1–201.

Jung, C.G. (1921) *Psychological Types*, *CW* 6, 1971: 1–987.

Jung, C.G. (1934) 'The Practical Use of Dream-Analysis', *CW* 16, 1954: 294–352.

Jung, C.G. (1934–1939) *Seminars on Nietzsche's 'Zarathustra'*, ed. J. Jarrett, 2 vols., London: Routledge, 1989.

Jung, C.G. (1938/1940) 'Psychology and Religion' (The Terry Lectures), *CW* 11, 1958: 1–168.

Jung, C.G. (1939) 'Conscious, Unconscious, and Individuation', *CW* 9i: 489–524.

Jung, C.G. (1942/1948) 'A Psychological Approach to the Dogma of the Trinity', *CW* 11, 1958: 169–295.

Jung, C.G. (1945/1954) 'The Philosophical Tree', *CW* 13, 1967: 304–482.

Jung, C.G. (1947/1954) 'On the Nature of the Psyche', *CW* 8, 1960: 343–442.

Jung, C.G. (1952a) 'Answer to Job', *CW* 11, 1958: 553–758.

Jung, C.G. (1952b) 'Foreword to White's "God and the Unconscious"', *CW* 11, 1958: 449–67.

Jung, C.G. (1958) 'Flying Saucers: A Modern Myth, *CW* 10, 1970: 589–824.

Jung, C.G. (1959) 'Good and Evil in Analytical Psychology', *CW* 10, 1970: 858–86.

Jung, C.G. (1964) *Man and His Symbols*, London: Arkana, Penguin.

Jung, C.G. (1967) *Memories, Dreams, Reflection*, trans. R. and C. Winston, London: Fontana Press.

Kant, I. (1785) *Groundwork for the Metaphysics of Morals* (1964), trans. H.G. Paton, New York: Harper and Row.

Otto, R. (1917) *The Idea of the Holy: An Inquiry into the Non-rational Factor in the Idea of the Divine and its Relation to the Rational* (1971), trans. J.W. Harvey, Oxford: Oxford University Press.

Otto, R. (1923) 'Foreword by the author to the first edition of *The Idea of the Holy*'.
Samuels, A., Shorter, B. and Plaut, F. (1986) *A Critical Dictionary of Jungian Analysis*, London: Routledge & Kegan Paul.
Schopenhauer, A. (1818) *The World as Will and Representation* (1969), trans. E.F.J. Payne, 2 vols., New York: Dover Publications.

Chapter 14

The role of the numinous in the reception of Jung

David Tacey

> In spirit, something that we had thought irrevocably forgotten is made present again, a dormant trace is reawakened, a wound re-opened, the repressed returns and what we took to be an overcoming is no more than a long convalescence.
>
> Gianni Vattimo (in Derrida and Vattimo 1998: 79)

JUNG'S REPUTATION IN INTELLECTUAL CULTURE

I am interested in exploring the role of nonrational and 'religious' factors in the reception of Jung. In particular, I want to recontextualise Jung's reputation in the light of cultural and spiritual factors that come to the fore today as we move from a modern to a postmodern paradigm (Caputo 2001). This is a not a detailed study of Jung's critics or antagonists, but I want to suggest that some hostile criticism of Jung can be deconstructed to reveal prejudices and assumptions that are no longer relevant in a post-modern world (Tracy 1999). I argue that a religious or spiritual complex is responsible for irrational responses to Jung, and that his reputation is burdened by an outdated negative legacy that it no longer needs to carry. There is not a lot of evidence to suggest that either Jungians or anti-Jungians are aware of this change of climate, in which everything 'Jungian' can be viewed in a different light.

Writing on what he calls the 'worldwide phenomenon of Jung's banish-ment from academic life', Andrew Samuels reports that 'many solid aca-demics and psychoanalysts will have nothing to do with the man, his works, and his followers' (1996: 469). Samuels argues that Jung's alleged anti-Semitism is the most potent and inhibiting factor that has led to the exclusion of Jung from academic institutions and intellectual debates. He admits that 'archetypes, mysticism, philosophy, religion' (469) have acted as barriers to the intellectual appreciation of Jung, but does not develop this theme. I do not wish to overlook the role that political and racial factors (or misunderstandings) have played in the negative construction of

Jung, but I do want to argue that we can read this phenomenon as a religious problem.

It could be, however, that a combination of factors is most likely responsible for Jung's negative reputation, and that numerous factors should be brought into the debate, which will no doubt continue for years to come. Because Jung's popular standing is increasing in the world, I expect hostile academic criticism to increase in proportion to the rise in public interest in this seminal thinker. The Scribes and Pharisees, to retell an old story, will feel obliged to attack this increasingly charismatic and authoritative figure.

A PSYCHOLOGY OF RELIGIOUS EXPERIENCE

> The constancy of God in my life is called by other names.
>
> (Derrida 1993: 155)

Jung's work evokes a sense of the sacred in his model of the psyche and in his understanding of personality structure and transformation. The archetypes are the 'gods' of the universal mind, and the individuation process Jung advocates involves a dialectical exchange between the ego's will and the will of superior forces or archetypes. This form of psychology is 'religious' insofar as greater forces are felt to exist, to be real and have effect, and to influence the structure of personality and the stages of life. Jung writes: 'Our bowing down before law and order is a commendable example of what our general attitude to the collective unconscious should be' (1928: 395).

To some extent, the big names of religion have been replaced by the new names of psychology: the polytheistic Gods of Greece and Rome have become the archetypes, the monotheistic God of the Christian tradition has become the collective unconscious, the figure of Christ is the archetype of the Self (semi-divine, semi-human), the Christian Trinity becomes the psychological quaternity or mandala, Original Sin is the state of unconsciousness and the burden of the shadow, the action of the Holy Spirit becomes the transcendent function, Grace is the overcoming of neurosis, and Salvation is the reconciliation of opposites in the Self.

Other elements in Jung's science are the same as in religion: big dreams bring important messages and prophecies to humanity, visions occur by day or by night, the folly of humans is corrected by a mysterious moral force, and securing a relationship with eternity gives meaning and purpose to life. Some Jungians would disagree with this reading of Jung's work, and I am aware that my sketch is controversial. The matching parts between religion and Jungian psychology are by no means precise, but significant parallels do occur. I seek to make a general point about the religiousness of Jung's psychological system, and that it is less 'science' in the narrow sense than a reinterpretation of age-old and perennial religious truths.

Those early scientists who charged Jung with 'mysticism' were partly right, I believe, but they completely underestimated the importance of the mystical in human experience and in the development of consciousness (Teilhard de Chardin 1969). As Shamdasani realises, the crippling factor for Jung's reception was the timing:

> Jung developed these [religious ideas] at a time when such subjects were dismissed out of hand by the positivist and behaviourist approach dominant in psychology, or were reduced by psychoanalysis to nothing but psychopathology.
>
> (1998: 3)

Fortunately, postmodern science is reversing its earlier opinions about mysticism, and unravelling its former prejudices about this aspect of human experience (Berger 1999). Even scientific psychology is reconsidering the role of the mystical in personality development (Emmons 1999; Jacobs 2003).

NEGATIVE RELIGIOUS RESPONSES TO JUNG

One can discern immediately why large groups of humanity would have been repelled by Jung's psychology. The traditionally religious would find the whole enterprise unnecessary (Rieff 1966). Why try to reinvent the wheel in this way when we already have a perfectly good religious system? Why give new names to old forces when the old names are better, more dignified, steeped in tradition, and more profound (Buber 1952)? Jung would most likely agree with these protests, and he would defer to those who prefer dogmatic religion to depth psychology. He would admit that religion is richer, more developed, and more aesthetically pleasing than psychology (1934/54: 11). Moreover, it is strengthened not only by centuries of tradition but also by a vast and resourceful worldwide community.

But Jung would add that for a great many people in the educated world, 'religion' no longer works, no longer appears credible, and no longer speaks a language we can understand (1932). As such, it can no longer suffice as our major guiding light, or not without the assistance of depth psychology, which can translate its truths into a new scientific language that people can comprehend. Religion often insists on the literal truth of its scriptures and doctrines, whereas psychology treats those truths symbolically, an approach which is more suitable to modern taste (Armstrong 2005).

In this sense Jung's psychology is only relevant to those who are post-religious, post-traditional, or to those with interests in the psychology of religion (Wulff 1990: 411). It is a system of psychology designed for those for whom the old ways have paled and are no longer appropriate (Jung 1928/31: 150). Non-Christians and Jews, however, whether religious or secular, would likely feel alienated by aspects of Jung's psychology. Not only is Jung's model a psychological transposition of Christian mystical theology, but toward the end of his life his work became more focused on Christianity, on possible developments within its spiritual tradition, and future scenarios for a post-traditional Christianity (1952). Followers of Jung had not only to be 'post-religious', but needed also to share his (post)Christian emphasis, as well as tolerate his endless fascination for Christian theology, dogma, and history.

SECULAR AND HUMANIST RESPONSES IN A TIME OF TRANSITION

But for the secular world, Jung's work would present different kinds of problems. Here the issue is not that his work is unorthodox, heretical, or gnostic, but that it is imbued with a profoundly religious spirit. The universities, in particular, are a product of a secularisation process that has moved counter to religious belief. They are the offspring of the Intellectual Enlightenment, and as such are devoted to the pursuit of knowledge, facts, information, and science (Trias 1998). They are not especially interested in a new psychological system that presents spiritual reality for post-traditional seekers. As far as the universities are concerned, any form of religiousness is bad and not to be trusted, whether this religiousness is traditional (mainstream theology), or revisionist and new (new religious movements, religious postmodernism, or Jung's psychology).

This situation is changing at the present time, as the 'modern' assumptions and values of the universities give way to a new set of assumptions based on a rising postmodern culture. The postmodern is to some extent post-secular, insofar as 'religion' is achieving a new credibility in a range of major discourses, including philosophy, physics, biology, history, psychiatry, and psychology (Ward 1997; Pearce 2002). But it will take some time before the new set of assumptions becomes established in the universities. We are in a transition period, where the 'modern' is still the dominant paradigm, despite several years of postmodern research which is friendly to and encouraging of the religious point of view. But the universities, as cultural institutions, as bastions of authority, are still very much the loyal heirs of the Enlightenment and many within them will cling to this heritage for as long as possible.

This is only to be expected, and to some extent I support the academic resistance to religiosity, especially if the alternative is an oppressive religious regime. The gains of secular thought and culture, and the achievements of civil rights and liberal humanism, have been hard won and are vitally important for the West. The West would be ill-advised to give away these gains or social freedoms. It can only accept a new spiritual point of view if it can be shown that it is conducive to science and compatible with the humanism that has been the hallmark of Western civilisation for the last four hundred years. Religion can only be integrated by the post-Enlightenment West if it is able to work with science and philosophy as a close friend and ally (Caputo and Scanlon 1999). Religion can only be re-embraced if certain basic freedoms and human rights can be guaranteed. A religion that asks for complete obeisance to inflexible moral laws and religious authorities will not be viable. The thinking West will not, and cannot, tolerate any form of fundamentalism.

The Western knowledge paradigm will continue to resist any religious content that moves counter to reason or that seems superstitious and metaphysical. It will only integrate religion insofar as it is 'deconstructed'. It will only be acceptable if religion can be shown to be capable of a creative alliance with reason and philosophy. When that occurs, the new civilisation will be dawning on the horizon of possibility. The next stage of civilisation seems to be the stage in which religion and science, long separated by the Enlightenment, come together in a post-Enlightenment embrace.

In this future civilisation, the work of Jung will be important, and will not be dismissed as eccentric or regressive. Jung's 'time' will come, but only when culture has moved further along its present course. As Thomas Kuhn suggested in his theory of paradigm change (1970), eventually the new paradigm becomes 'reasonable', acceptable to leading minds, and ultimately irresistible. At that stage, a 'turning point' is reached, and the new model replaces the old paradigm that has been hostile to it.

POPULAR FASCINATION FOR JUNG

I would argue that negative or suspicious views of Jung's archetypes, mysticism, religion, and philosophy are largely confined to academic high culture and are not found in the general community (Tacey 2001). Indeed, the reason why Jung's popularity often surpasses that of Freud in the community is precisely because Jung offers a framework for understanding and respecting the spiritual dimension of human experience (Capra 1982: 396). The jaundiced approach to his archetypes and 'mysticism' is found only in the intellectual world where such views are forbidden, because secular humanism and rationality have shaped the prevailing academic worldview.

This vigorous 'current of negativity' in academic high culture contrasts markedly with the mainly positive reputation that Jung enjoys among youth and popular cultures, students, therapists, artists, film-makers, poets, and musicians. It seems that the broader community and 'creative' minds respond positively to his work, but the intelligentsia has trouble digesting his ideas. Jung appeared to have anticipated this years ago, when he wrote:

> The general public seems to have taken cognisance of the existence of the unconscious psyche more than the so-called experts.
>
> (1955: 709)

It could be that those who are most removed from the unconscious and its 'mystical' dimensions look upon his work with incomprehension. But those who are forced to take the unconscious into account, owing to their creativity or personal disposition, are more likely to accept the mystical intimations that arise from his psychology of the unconscious. They are more likely to receive Jung's knowledge without prejudice and without ideological resistance.

THE SHOCK OF THE NUMINOUS: CROSS-CURRENTS AT THE TURNING POINT

Freud and Jung both presented shocks and challenges to intellectual culture, civilised morality, and modernity. At the root of Freud's concept of the unconscious was sexuality, and sexuality has always been easier for intellectuals and scientists to deal with than spirituality. Sexuality is expressed in the human body, is evident to the senses, to the intellect, and to common desire. It did not take long for high culture, and even puritanical America, to get over its initial resistance to Freud, and to embrace his theory of sexual repression almost as common sense.

Jung's 'dialogue' with educated society would be different from Freud's, and would operate on a broader time frame. To integrate Jung's knowledge, society would require not merely ethical adjustment and recovery from moral shock, as with Freud, but a deep-seated transformation from secular humanism to a post-secular consciousness. Arguably, this change began in 1968 with the advent of postmodernity (Lyotard 1984), which includes within itself a post-secular dimension (Caputo and Scanlon 1999). In particular, I would like to draw attention to Caputo's essay, 'How the Secular World became Post-secular' (2001: 37ff.), which is not 'on' Jung but has great relevance to the place of Jung in the postmodern context.

The cultural change that would allow educated society to incorporate Jung and understand him did not take place until after Jung's death in 1961. His 'relevance' to society would only be discovered posthumously. In his lifetime his work met (in his own words) with 'consistent misunderstanding'

(Bair 2003: 5), since he was working in opposition to modernity, and pre-figuring a postmodern moment that had not yet arrived.

Jung does not challenge us with sexuality, but with something equally primary and perhaps more terrifying: the reality of the *numinous*. Numinous derives from the Latin *numen*, to nod, command or will, but refers to the awesome character of the divine will. The numinous is that which takes 'command' and displaces our will with its own (Otto 1923: 13ff.). Obviously this experience is alarming to many of us, and disturbing to those humanists who want to believe that human integrity hinges upon our refusal to bow down to any commanding will, especially one that is invisible and not accessible to common sense or scientific enquiry.

Intellectual culture is now at odds with itself. The numinous is 'back', but naturally enough, many intellectuals want to fend it off. The rational mind is having to take up arms against an unruly sea of numinosity, which is threatening to inundate the barriers erected against it. Intellectual culture looks out at the postmodern and post-9/11 world, and sees, in newspapers and on television, in world events and on the streets, a growing passion for religion, spirituality, and mysticism. After the collapse of the Berlin Wall in 1991, the real winner was not the capitalist economy but the religious impulse, which sought to find expression for its repressed life.

In 1994 the philosopher Jacques Derrida announced the 'return of the religious' to the post-Enlightenment world, and he said that high culture should 'respond, without waiting too long' (Derrida and Vattimo 1998: 41). Earlier, Derrida had noted that spirit demands new attention, but he railed against the academic establishment for not having the courage to deal with it. 'No one', he said, 'wants anything to do with it [spirit]' (1989: 2). Intellectuals were happy with deconstructive postmodernism if it meant the increasing relativisation and weakening of the gods and master narratives, but they were not happy to hear from Derrida that there could be an absolute reality (what Derrida calls 'the impossible') beyond our cultural signs. This was bad news and has not been welcomed (Caputo 1997).

Derrida was beginning to sound like Jung, and many stopped reading him, or did not read him properly. His complaints were also parallel to Jung's: he protested that he had 'been read less and less well over almost twenty years, like my religion about which nobody understands anything'. His interest in mysticism, he says, 'is what my readers won't have known about me' (1993: 155). One obviously does not have to be a Jungian to feel misunderstood and under-appreciated. As soon as anyone touches on the numinous, a kind of spiritual complex is triggered in the culture, which immediately sets up a resistance. Jung said 'the gods have become diseases' (1929: 54), and they are treated by the modern ego like pathogens in the body. The ego's anxiety triggers an automatic defence reaction, activating forces of resistance. As with any unconscious complex, the spiritual complex is triggered automatically and is hard to detect.

We discover such reactions in the recent reviews of Deirdre Bair's biography *Jung* (2003). Several reviews in the international press seemed to take hostility to Jung to a new level. One case in point is Stephen Frosh, who wrote:

> As the cultural wheel turns again and spirituality is back on the agenda, Jung is attractive to many because of his intense spiritual fire. One has to wonder, however, whether what is really happening is a new form of mystification. Too many lost souls are prepared to 'turn to Jung' in search of truth and meaning.
>
> (Frosh 2004: 24)

Many intellectuals are astounded by the return of spirituality, and use every opportunity to ridicule anything that speaks to – or of – our new spiritual hunger. 'Mystification' is the key here, with links back to Marxist tradition, and its allergic reaction to religion (Kovel 1991). Mystery is undermined as 'mystification', and in the same discourse religion is often identified with 'fundamentalism', and 'spirituality' with vulgar New Age commercialism. In other words, all associations with the numinous are negatively constructed. At this time of cultural transition, those who were merely cold or indifferent to Jung in the past have become positively antagonistic, since he appears to threaten the rationality that is crumbling. Jung becomes a monster threatening the Enlightenment, encouraging diseases and pathogens to enter the body corporate.

In recent times, there have been numerous hysterical attacks on the integrity of Jung's work, and Richard Noll in particular has had a field day, claiming all manner of things for Jung's psychology and his Zurich circle (Noll 1994). The basis of Noll's attack is a distorted and crudely literalised reading of Jung's religious vision and symbolic language. More recently, Jung has been constructed as an advocate of unreason, and linked with malign and dark political forces that oppose democracy and undermine social progress (Wolin 2004). The fact that Jung's work generates irrational rage, and not just intellectual criticism, indicates that a complex has been triggered in his reception. Criticism of his work degenerates into *ad hominem* attacks on his person and character. Fantasies abound that he attempted to set up a new religion with himself as cult leader (Stern 1976; Noll 1997), and this indicates that reason has been cast overboard in some discussions of his work.

Some thinkers cannot think clearly when religious elements are raised in society, culture, or psychology. Their thought is derailed by irrational factors, and their thinking becomes morbidly reactive and embittered – usually in the name of defending 'science'. It is as if they are responding to trauma, defending against the numinous as if it were some lethal enemy to be opposed with the mind.

THE AWFUL NUMINOUS: THE DOUBLE EFFECT OF THE SPIRIT

A student of mine once said 'Jung is awful.' She corrected herself and said, 'No, I mean awesome.' But I suggested we should stay with the interpretive possibilities of 'awful'. I looked up various dictionaries, and found that 'awful' has a range of meanings. The first is colloquial: 'extremely bad, unpleasant, ugly'; the second is also colloquial: 'very, very great', as in 'awesome'. The formal meanings are: 'inspiring fear, dreadful, terrible; full of awe, reverential; inspiring reverential awe, or solemnly impressive'.

The word 'awful' cuts several ways, and in this word we seem to find something of the range of responses found in Jung's admirers and detractors alike. They may have more in common than they realise. Both may be responding to the presence of the numinous. The popular currents that find Jung so fascinating are responding to its attraction, and the academic currents that are repelled are responding to its dreadful, foreboding aspect (Tacey 1997). In relation to the word 'awful', Rudolf Otto remarks: 'Of all modern languages, English has the word "awful", which in its deeper and most special sense approximates closely to our meaning [with regard to the numinous]' (1923: 14).

Jung took hold of the idea of the unconscious, which in medical circles had an 'unpleasant or ugly' meaning, and made it something 'very, very great'. He expanded its horizons, making it not only the deposit of unacceptable wishes and desires, but also the seat of human creativity, art, religion, and culture. The unconscious contained the lowest and – he argued – the highest in our nature. He made the realm of the numinous part of his territory, and in a letter of 1945 he wrote: 'The main interest of my work is not concerned with the treatment of neuroses but rather with the approach to the numinous . . . But the fact is that the approach to the numinous is the real therapy' (1945: 377). By this he meant that the encounter with the mystery of the psyche is what produces healing.

In *The Idea of the Holy*, Otto argues that the numinous generates a paradoxical effect. It inspires fascination on the one hand, and fear and dread on the other. Otto speaks of the *mysterium tremendum et fascinans*, whose greatness generates feelings of smallness and impotence in mortals, and can lead to a deep-seated anxiety in the ego personality (1923: 36). However, this same mystery can also generate pleasant or elated feelings of wonder, excitement, adventure, magic, and rapt engagement with the ground of being. When I first read Otto's description of the numinous I could not help thinking of the reception of Jung, and of the contradictory effects he has upon people. Some are deeply inspired and enraptured, others are repelled and diminished. Sometimes, the same people can experience a love/hate relationship with Jung and his work. Like the numinous, his work gives rise to bipolar and complex responses.

The numinous, writes Jung, is 'overwhelming; an admission that goes against not only our pride, but against our deep-rooted fear that consciousness may perhaps lose its ascendancy' (1942/48: 275). If the numinous goes against our pride and demands humility, one can see why the numinous is not fashionable in a culture governed by the ego and an hubristic intellect. Anyone who speaks for the numinous is going to be a target for the insecurities, defences, and retaliations of the ego, which is engaged in a resistance against the mystery that relativises its power. In his championing of the numinous Jung elicits from us a sense of primitive panic, the ambivalence we feel toward what *exceeds* us.

To base his work on an experience of the numinous is to risk his reputation in many fields. Religious tradition will question his authority and accuse him of gnosticism. Science will question his sanity and accuse him of charlatanism. Journalists will suspect him of self-aggrandisement and cultism. Logical thinkers will suspect him of mystification and charge him with mysticism. Jung anticipated this hostility when he wrote:

> The visionary work has about it a fatal suggestion of vague metaphysics, so that we feel obliged to intervene in the name of well-intentioned reasonableness. We are driven to the conclusion that such things simply cannot be taken seriously, or else the world would sink back into benighted superstition.
>
> (1930/50: 147)

The attack on Jung is part of the same spirit of the Enlightenment that feels 'obliged to intervene' against mystery in the name of reason. On the other hand, the celebration of Jung at the popular level works in reverse: here the work of reason is doubted, since it has landed us in a spiritual and moral wasteland (Tacey 2004). The popular mind is desperate to re-embrace mystery, and for it the Enlightenment project is bankrupt. Archetypes seem like treasures buried in the field, and books urging us to find Gods and Goddesses within ourselves experience instant commercial success (Bolen 1984). If the numinous is perceived as an affront to reason, Jung will appear as dangerously irrational. If we acknowledge the numinous as a treasure hard to attain, Jung will be seen as a liberator of our spiritual life. For the first group, he is regressive, turning back to the premodern period with its 'superstitions'. For the second he is a visionary who strives to give new language to ageless wisdom.

THE OFFENCE OF THE ARCHETYPES

Over recent years, I have spoken with numerous academics about Jung, and I have found that the key word linked with Jung, and the main sticking point is 'archetype'. I asked five senior colleagues, including two professors, what their views were of Jung. All five were negative, some intensely so. But it wasn't the anti-Semitic issue that was raised, or his views about women. It was 'archetype' that bothered them. 'What do you associate with Jung?' I asked. '*Archetypes*', said one professor, with an expression of evident revulsion. 'Archetypes have no validity, no proof.'

One of my colleagues used a different term: 'the collective unconscious', he said, and it was as if he were uttering a profanity. The passion was such that I was caught up in it, and in that moment the idea of the 'collective unconscious' seemed embarrassing to me as well. I felt like Peter, ready to betray my beliefs for worldly reasons. Such are the powers of suggestion, especially when one's senior colleagues are denouncing something that has become part of one's intellectual life. The pressures are such in academia that serious students often give up the Jungian project, since it becomes patently clear that such interests become barriers to collegial respect, peer acceptance, and the reward system of grants, awards, and promotions (Tacey 1997).

I asked another colleague, an American feminist, what she thought of archetypes. She laughed and said the idea was ridiculous. 'Why?' I asked. 'Well,' she said, 'the notion that there are invisible forces that direct and control us is just ridiculous.' 'We end up like puppets on a string, with Jung himself as the master puppeteer.' As she spoke, this daughter of a Southern Baptist minister made it clear that she would no sooner embrace Jung than go back to church in Texas and listen to sermons. Jung's archetypes were symbols of oppression, and she wanted to kill them off.

Another colleague said to me that he found Jung's ideas to be implausible and *dehumanising*. 'The archetypes as powerful invisible forces that control and dominate us are both morally repugnant and logically implausible. It takes away our dignity as human beings and it compromises our free will – these are what Jung wants to take away from us.' He went on: 'Jung seeks to replace our self-belief and our human will with a belief in archetypes, and subordination to them.' At the end of the discussion he said, 'the idea of a collective unconscious is similarly repellent; the implication is that our human will has to give way to collectivist forces that seek to squash and oppress our individuality'.

In this kind of response, Jung becomes the hook for the ego's projection of its own fearful dislocation, its deflating and demoralising realisation that it is not the master of its own house. Jung becomes the carrier of the negative image of the non-ego for an ego that refuses to consider the reality of the psyche and the unconscious. This is not unlike the negative projections that secular people often foist upon clergy and the religious. Since the priest or nun 'stands for' God, and since God stands over and above me, reducing my freedom and curbing my wishes, I therefore hate the religious figure because he or she symbolises the defeat of my own ego.

THE IDEA OF THE HUMAN: A DIALECTICAL
RELATIONSHIP WITH POWER

These projections are so potent that they rarely concern themselves with the facts, with the actual psychology of Jung and what it really says. Why bother reading the long volumes of Jung, when prejudice provides a shortcut to a final assessment? Although Jung 'stands for' archetypes and invisible dominants, his psychology is concerned with becoming conscious of these forces precisely so that our human will and freedom is not radically compromised by them. Jung is not the anti-humanist that people find in him. This is a projection of activated and negativised contents of the secular mind. The secular mind represses the sacred, and thus the image of the sacred is darkly ambivalent. Anyone who speaks on behalf of the sacred forces is not a liberator of the soul, but a tyrant who seeks to oppress and diminish human life.

If intellectuals were actually to read Jung, rather than trading in empty clichés and stereotypes, they would be surprised to find that Jung says very different things to what they imagine:

> Possession by an archetype turns a man into a flat collective figure, a mask behind which he can no longer develop as a human being. If one naively falls into an archetype . . . one is forced to act a part at the expense of one's humanity.
>
> (1928: 390)

> I must preserve my human dignity, my specific gravity, which I need so much if I am not to become the unresisting shuttlecock of unconscious forces.
>
> (1928: 395)

Jung's psychology does not support the idea that we must remain subservient to the archetypes. Jung recognises these forces, and asks that we respect them, but he argues that the role of consciousness is to break the hegemony of the gods and to achieve, through the extension of consciousness, increased freedom of the human subject. This apparently is too complicated for many people to understand, even for educated people who should know better.

But the point is that some people do not want to know better. They feel comfortable in and with their prejudices because they protect the ego from the numinous by declaring the forces to be illusory or ridiculous. To 'know more' about the archetypes, or about individuation, is a risk they cannot afford, because the ego refuses to begin any dialogue with invisible forces that might mock the conscious mind or even send it crazy. Once again, Jung seemed to anticipate this emotional problem, when he wrote:

In the realm of consciousness we are our own masters . . . But if we step through the door of the shadow we discover with terror that we are the objects of unseen factors. To know this is decidedly unpleasant, for nothing is more disillusioning than the discovery of our own inadequacy. It can even give rise to primitive panic, because . . . the anxiously guarded supremacy of consciousness is questioned in the most dangerous way.

(1934/54: 49)

I never press my views upon academic colleagues or students if they display resistance to or revulsion for Jungian ideas. I suppose I recognised fairly early in my career that these views were not destined for immediate authority in the academy. I respect people's need for detachment and distance, their need for ironic control and mastery. After all, the other side of the posture of mastery could indeed be 'primitive panic', as Jung suggests.

Here is where the influence of the university teacher of depth psychology reaches its limits. I can put these ideas forward, but I cannot insist on them, or make them convincing to someone who is sure they are nonsensical. That, I take it, is the job of the psychotherapist, to gently lead people to an acceptance of psychic reality and its relative autonomy. This is a matter of emotional maturity and spiritual education, which is hard to achieve in the context of university life, where the 'mind' is engaged in strictly intellectual discourse.

Jung's sophisticated argument is that the way to strengthen human dignity is not to resist the superior forces in an attitude of defiance, but to admit the existence of the forces and maintain a dialectical relationship with them. True dignity is achieved through surrendering the postures of the immature ego and moving into dialogue with supreme powers: 'The individuated ego senses itself as the object of an unknown and supraordinate subject' (1928: 405). We acknowledge what is greater, and only then do we achieve true freedom by recognising how we were unconsciously bound and tied by complexes and archetypes.

Far from being a new form of determinism, Jung's thought, like feminism, like Marxism, like Freudian psychoanalysis, is a liberation discourse, and not a regression to the ancient idea of the divine puppeteer. The notion that Jung is promoting oppressive subservience is not just a misreading of his work but the 'hidden work' of a feeling-toned complex. It is part of the spiritual complex that operates in the secular mind, a mind that turns the spirit dark and malign because it is not being attended to or nurtured. The numinous in such situations is a *tremendum* without fascination; it is an intolerable burden, a humiliation to the ego, and a defilement of human dignity.

In the typical denunciation of Jung, I am reminded of Mircea Eliade's statement about the modern phobia toward divinity:

The non-religious man refuses transcendence and accepts the relativity of 'reality' . . . He *makes himself*, and he only makes himself completely in proportion as he desacralizes himself and the world. The sacred is the prime obstacle to his freedom. He will become himself only when he is totally demysticized. He will not be truly free until he has killed the last god.

(1959: 203)

Some intellectuals want to kill the gods, and they want to kill Jung as well, as a modern spokesperson for the gods in our time. But to murder the sacred is to see it reappear in a thousand new guises, in the arts, cinema, music, and popular culture; in a myriad academic disciplines, and at the core of the postmodern itself.

OVERPOWERINGNESS: RELIGIOUS MIGHT, POLITICAL OPPRESSION

Here, I believe, the religious and the political readings of Jung's negative reputation can potentially come together. It seems that the unsavoury elements in Jung's personal and professional history serve as suitable hooks for negative projections. The alleged anti-Semitism, the shadowy associations with Nazi Germany which still require more research (Kirsch 2004), the denunciation by Freud and his circle, the patriarchal image of women, early interest in 'widgie' boards and séances – each unsavoury element acts as an attractor for a larger, more complete sense of distaste arising from an activated and hidden spiritual complex.

I think the Nazi stain and the religious problem have something in common: the problem of overriding power. Otto interprets the majesty (*majestas*) of the numinous as 'overpoweringness' (1923: 19). The religious power of the *numen* is rebuked, often with force, because it relativises and diminishes our human authority in a way reminiscent of an authoritarian political regime. 'God' and 'Nazi' are similar kinds of words to the modern mind. God is spoken about as if he were Hitler writ large, and just as monstrous. The charge of 'Nazism' against Jung may be masking a more primordial hatred of terrible overweening authority. God and Hitler are fused in the same resentment against higher power. The demonic construction of God or gods is largely the result of an ego that refuses its spiritual destiny, that is, to 'bow down' before the supreme powers (Jung 1928: 395) and enter into dialogue with them.

It is clear that the postmodern intellect is confronted today by a *numen* which stands over and above it, which diminishes its autonomy and relativises its freedom. In this critical moment, Jung appears to stand on the side of that which diminishes us. However, he makes this stand to 'know' the other side, and not to capitulate to it. Nevertheless, any recognition of the *numen*, even one which seeks differentiation from it, becomes identified with it by virtue of the spiritual complex that operates autonomously in contemporary attitudes. This complex confuses our thinking, and blocks out Jung's creative and liberational aspect. It will continue to do so until such time as the complex is encountered. The superior forces do not seek to destroy us, but to challenge us to enter a greater mystery and to engage us in the creation and extension of consciousness.

References

Armstrong, Karen (2005) *A Short History of Myth*, Edinburgh: Canongate.

Bair, Deirdre (2003) *Jung: A Biography*, Boston: Little, Brown and Company.

Berger, Peter (1999) *The Desecularization of the World*, Grand Rapids: Eerdmans Publishing.

Bolen, Jean Shinoda (1984) *Goddesses in Everywoman*, San Francisco: Harper & Row.

Buber, Martin (1952) *Eclipse of God*, New York: Harper.

Capra, Fritjof (1982) *The Turning Point: Science, Society and the Rising Culture*, London: Flamingo.

Caputo, John (1997) *The Prayers and Tears of Jacques Derrida: Religion without Religion*, Bloomington: Indiana University Press.

Caputo, John (2001) *On Religion*, London: Routledge.

Caputo, John and Scanlon, Michael (eds.) (1999) *God, the Gift, and Postmodernism*, Bloomington: Indiana University Press.

Derrida, Jacques (1989) *Of Spirit: Heidegger and the Question*, Chicago: University of Chicago Press.

Derrida, Jacques (1993) *Circumfession: Fifty-Nine Periods and Periphrases*, in Geoffrey Bennington and Jacques Derrida, *Jacques Derrida*, Chicago: Chicago University Press.

Derrida, Jacques and Vattimo, Gianni (eds.) (1998) *Religion*, Stanford University Press.

Eliade, Mircea (1959) *The Sacred and the Profane*, New York: Harcourt, Brace.

Emmons, Robert A. (1999) *The Psychology of Ultimate Concerns*, New York: The Guilford Press.

Frosh, Stephen (2004) 'Review of Deirdre Bair's Biography of Jung', *Sunday Telegraph* (London), January 11.

Jacobs, Gregg (2003) *The Ancestral Mind*, New York: Viking.

Jung, C.G. (1928) 'The Relations between the Ego and the Unconscious', *CW* 7 (1953/1966).

Jung, C.G. (1928/1931) 'The Spiritual Problem of Modern Man', *CW* 10 (1964/1970).

Jung, C.G. (1929) 'Commentary on *The Secret of the Golden Flower*', *CW* 13 (1968).

Jung, C.G. (1930/1950) 'Psychology and Literature', *CW* 15 (1966).

Jung, C.G. (1932) 'Psychotherapists or the Clergy', *CW* 11 (1958/1969).

Jung, C.G. (1934/1954) 'Archetypes of the Collective Unconscious', *CW* 9, 1 (1959/68).

Jung, C.G. (1938/1940) 'Psychology and Religion', *CW* 11 (1958/1969).

Jung, C.G. (1942/1948) 'A Psychological Approach to the Dogma of the Trinity', *CW* 11 (1958/1969).

Jung, C.G. (1945) Letter to P.W. Martin, in *C.G. Jung Letters*, ed. Gerhard Adler, trans. R.F.C. Hull, vol 1., Princeton: Princeton University Press, 1973.

Jung, C.G. (1952) 'Answer to Job', *CW* 11 (1958/1969).

Jung, C.G. (1955) *Mysterium Coniunctionis*, *CW* 14 (1963/1970).

Kirsch, Thomas (2004) 'Cultural Complexes in the History of Jung, Freud and their Followers', in Thomas Singer and Samuel Kimbles (eds.), *The Cultural Complex*, London: Routledge.

Kovel, Joel (1991) *History and Spirit*, Boston, MA: Beacon Press.

Kuhn, Thomas (1970) *The Structure of Scientific Revolutions*, Chicago: University of Chicago Press.

Lyotard, Jean-François (1984) *The Postmodern Condition: A Report on Knowledge*, Minneapolis: University of Minnesota Press.

Noll, Richard (1994) *The Jung Cult: Origins of a Charismatic Movement*, Princeton, NJ: Princeton University Press.

Noll, Richard (1997) *The Aryan Christ: The Secret Life of Carl Jung*, New York: Random House.

Otto, Rudolf (1923) *The Idea of the Holy* (1958), trans. John W. Harvey, London: Oxford University Press.

Pearce, Joseph Chilton (2002) *The Biology of Transcendence*, Rochester: Park Street Press.

Rieff, Philip (1966) *The Triumph of the Therapeutic*, New York: Harper & Row.

Samuels, Andrew (1996) 'Jung's Return from Banishment', *The Psychoanalytic Review* 83(4).

Shamdasani, Sonu (1998) *Cult Fictions: C. G. Jung and the Founding of Analytical Psychology*, London: Routledge.

Stern, Paul (1976) *C. G. Jung: The Haunted Prophet*, New York: George Braziller.

Tacey, David (1997) 'Jung in the Academy: Devotions and Resistances', *Journal of Analytical Psychology* 42(2): 269–83.

Tacey, David (2001) *Jung and the New Age*, London and New York: Routledge.

Tacey, David (2004) *The Spirituality Revolution*, London and New York: Routledge.

Teilhard de Chardin, Pierre (1969) *Human Energy*, London: Collins.

Tracy, David (1999) 'The Spiritual Situation of Our Times', in John Caputo and Michael Scanlon (eds.), *God, the Gift, and Postmodernism*, Bloomington: Indiana University Press.

Trias, Eugenio (1998) 'Thinking Religion: The Symbol and the Sacred', in Jacques Derrida and Gianni Vattimo (eds.), *Religion*, Stanford University Press.

Ward, Graham (1997) *The Postmodern God*, Oxford: Basil Blackwell.

Wolin, Richard (2004) *The Seduction of Unreason: From Nietzsche to Postmodernism*, Princeton, NJ: Princeton University Press.

Wulff, Martin (1990) *Psychology of Religion*, New York: John Wiley.

Index